No More Dodging Bullets

A Memoir about Faith, Love, Lessons, and Growth

By Amy Herrig

Inspired Forever Book Publishing
Dallas, Texas

No More Dodging Bullets: A Memoir about Faith, Love, Lessons, and Growth

Inspired Forever Book Publishing™
"Words with Lasting Impact"
Dallas, Texas
888-403-2727
https://inspiredforeverbooks.com

Library of Congress Control Number: 2019940624

ISBN-13: 978-1-948903-17-2

Printed in the United States of America

Dedicated to my husband, my children,
and George, Jim, John, Marlo, Michael, and Steve.

Table of Contents

May 13, 2015

As I sat next to my father on the bench outside the US Marshals Office, I thought, "Wow, is this it? Is it finally happening now?"

I looked down at my sandaled feet, thinking how I had thought carefully that morning about what I would wear, just in case today would be the day, not really believing that it really would be the day or that this day would ever come. In a quick flash of memories, I found myself evaluating the entire course of my life and realizing every decision leads to another choice or set of circumstances, and I had somehow ended up here. I suddenly realized today could be the day, and I had probably chosen the wrong outfit and definitely the wrong footwear—my clothing should really have been the least of my worries, but maybe I was just trying to focus on something frivolous to avoid thinking about what was really happening.

A woman in shackles, wearing a canary-yellow prison uniform, came walking by us, escorted by a US marshal. She was crying, and I assumed—and would later find out that I was correct—that she had just received bad news regarding a prison sentence. My father observed her and said, "Oh look; maybe we will get a yellow outfit too." It was a poor attempt at humor on his part, and I responded, begrudgingly, that yellow was not in my color wheel—another poor attempt at humor, but the truth as well.

I immediately thought that we wouldn't be getting any sort of yellow prison uniform because we weren't criminals. This ordeal we were going through would come and go quickly, and we would move on with our lives. In my mind, I wasn't anything like the woman who had just walked by—she had already been found guilty, so of course she was in shackles and a prison uniform, but I hadn't broken a law. Even if I was indicted, I was innocent, so I wouldn't be treated like her. Then the US marshals came out of their office to talk with us, and for the second time in less than a year, my entire world as I knew it turned upside down.

Chapter One

"*The Gas Pipe case was considered the nation's largest synthetic marijuana prosecution.*" That was written in an article in the *Dallas Morning News* regarding the federal prosecution against my father and me. In all our businesses, we had always striven to be the best at whatever we did, but we had never intended to become so headline worthy nor the "nation's largest" of anything scandalous. We had never sold anything that we understood or believed to be illegal or that we marketed as synthetic marijuana. Other than having a somewhat unorthodox upbringing with liberal, hippie parents who ran a counterculture business, and having a privileged childhood with both attention and money, I had always considered myself kind of a regular person who stayed under the radar—certainly not someone who would ever make the front page of the local newspaper or be featured on the evening news. But with the events of June 4, 2014, my life took a whole new direction. It wasn't my first life-changing experience, but this time there was much more at stake—absolutely everything that mattered to me and life as I knew it.

I was born Amy Lynn Shults in August 1975, the product of two very loving people who were thrilled to be new parents. They chose the name *Amy* because it means "beloved," and I was beloved, although my father would rarely ever use the name; always, to this day, he has called me "punkin." I was the center of my parents' universe. My father wore a pink shirt to the hospital because he just knew I was going to be a girl. My mother had a very difficult labor that led to complications postbirth, so my father did many diaper changes and late-night feedings, and our bond developed from the start. That's not to say that my mother and I didn't have a strong bond as well. We certainly did, but my father had the opportunity to bond with me early on in a way that fathers often don't.

It was a few years past the Summer of Love, but the hippie movement was still in full swing. My parents, Jerry and Lori Shults, were in the center of it. We didn't live in a commune or anything extreme—we had a house with all the modern amenities, and we looked like a traditional family, but my parents' belief system and ideology were liberal and exemplified the characteristics of the hippie movement. We were vegetarians, marijuana smoking was embraced, nudity was perfectly acceptable, and "make love not war" was certainly the mind-set.

My father had been raised in a military family in San Antonio, Texas, the youngest of seven children, where abuse had been prevalent. He had later volunteered for service in the air force, and he had come back a decorated soldier, though scarred. After one tour, my father had been done with the war. Seeing how easily the government could dispose of people for financial gain had been eye opening. He had returned to San Antonio, Texas, but after realizing the city had a declining economy, he'd moved to Dallas, where there had been a bustling economy with plenty of opportunities.

Dallas offered a welcoming environment for those who were looking to try something new, escape, and expand their minds. My father quickly discovered the counterculture movement of the time and the theme of "sex, drugs, and rock and roll," and he made friends easily. He quickly became a regular fixture at Lee Park, where hippies and war protestors gathered regularly to explore their freedom. He began attending the local pop festivals, where he also started peddling goods—T-shirts, pipes, and anything fun or desirable from local artists and his friends. From that income and his savings from the war, he opened his first official business. It was a small retail store known as a head shop—a store that sold smoking accessories, paraphernalia, and hippie gear—called the Gas Pipe. The original store had exposed gas pipes in the ceiling, and his initials were GAS—Gerald (Jerry) Allan Shults—and both inspired the name.

Meanwhile, Lorelei Ann Kieley was living out her teenage years in Richardson, a suburb just north of Dallas. Lori, as she was called by just about everybody, was a free spirit, the third of four children in a middle-class suburban family. Unfortunately, tragedy hit my mother's family early on. Her father died from diabetes complications when she was fifteen, and she and her siblings were left with an alcoholic mother whose alcoholism and violent rages increased after the death of her husband.

The common denominator in my parents' childhoods was the alcoholism and abuse. They were two people who had a lot of love to give and wanted a lot of love in return, but they had both come from highly dysfunctional families. My father went to war to escape his, and my mother graduated high school early and then was kicked out of the house during one of my grandmother's violent alcohol-induced outbursts.

The night my parents met, my mother told my father she

had a cold, and he offered her apple juice, which she thought was so kind. He also made her laugh; my father has always been the life of the party, making continuous jokes and spurting out one-liners at every opportunity he gets. Within a year, they were married. My mother's conservative family wasn't confident in my mother's choice in a husband. He was a long-haired hippie who owned a head shop. Eventually, though, his charisma and jovial personality won them over, as they do most people. With the help of my mother and her administrative and bookkeeping skills that she'd learned after high school at the Executive Secretarial School, he built the Gas Pipe into a very successful business over the years.

When I was born in 1975, the Gas Pipe was a stable business. Financially, things were tight, but we had enough. My parents had a handful of employees, but they really ran the store themselves. In my younger years, I was at the store with them often, either playing behind the showcases or sleeping in the office. The Gas Pipe was my home away from home. The employees were our extended family. Being an only child, I went practically everywhere with my parents. I had friends, and I would spend almost every weekend with my cousins, but my parents always treated me like a "little adult."

I have memories from as early as two years old, and I've heard that having memories from a young age is a sign of a happy childhood, which I did have. Our house was always a place for festivities. It was where everyone came to have a good time, and it was always filled with love. I don't remember entire events of my early childhood, but I have different flashes of memories—playing on the swing set, helping my mother in the kitchen, watching *The Three Stooges* with my father. One of my earliest memories and a story my parents love to tell occurred when the house was being remodeled, and I woke up from a nap. I walked out to the living room and cried and said,

"Messy," repetitively. I never liked a mess, and I guess I was just born that way. Much later in life, God would bless me with me an amazing daughter who is perfect in every way except that she is the messiest person I have ever known. Isn't it great how God teaches us things?

My childhood was a great one. The worst that could be said about my upbringing is that my parents smoked pot regularly and openly, but they were very involved parents who were extremely attentive and hands on. I never could understand all the negative views about pot smoking. I knew my parents were amazing people who worked hard, provided well in all aspects, and weren't hurting anyone. I was their world. Their lives revolved around the Gas Pipe and me.

In concurrence with the hippie lifestyle my parents led, I attended a Montessori school—something common now but considered very progressive in the mid-seventies. I was an inquisitive child and was always asking, "Why?" My parents encouraged this type of thinking and were always willing to explain things to me in a meaningful manner. They certainly didn't come from parents who had done that, and they both always expressed that they wanted to be different than their parents and never say, "Because I told you so," and they never did. They always took the time to explain things—a privilege I did not appreciate or truly recognize until I got older and found out how other people had been raised.

There was stress in my parents' lives due to the nature of their business. When my own legal ordeal started as an adult, I was sickened over how it may affect my children. My mother asked me if I recalled being scared or sad when my parents were battling their legal troubles. I didn't. I remembered feeling loved, and although I had known about the legal troubles, I had been oblivious to the severity of them. I hoped my children would feel the same, and I will always hope when they look back on their youth they will remember love and happiness and not the stress and turmoil that I tried so hard to hide and to overcome while still providing them with the most stable upbringing I could.

The first real legal issues for the Gas Pipe began in 1980, prompted and then intensified by the Reagan presidency and the "Just Say No" campaign. The government and law enforcement were strictly enforcing drug laws and laws relating to "drug paraphernalia"—rolling papers, bongs, and things of that nature. They all have a legal purpose and can be used with tobacco and are sold only for tobacco use, but if they could be used for illegal drugs such as marijuana, the government tried to deem them illegal. Today every product that is sold at the Gas Pipe is also sold on Amazon. Times have certainly changed. But in the early eighties, the Gas Pipe was attacked numerous times and had to fight to stay in business. The police would come in, raid the store, take everything, and allege it to be illegal—no warning, no cease and desist. They would come in with guns drawn, then handcuff everyone and make them sit there while they cleaned out the store. My parents would have to go through all the legal channels to attempt to get their stuff back and fight for their freedom, and often they would prevail, but it was never an easy battle. The authorities were relentless and made ridiculous accusations. One time during a trial, an officer said that even the belt buckles that were sold at the Gas Pipe should be considered drug paraphernalia because someone could use one as a rolling tray to roll marijuana joints. Rather than getting beaten down by the government, my parents pushed back and "won" by surviving and growing their business. They had everything taken multiple times—all the inventory, the money, everything—but they would always keep going. What started as a small, simple business for my father was now becoming a lifelong mission for my parents to prove that they had rights and freedom to run a legitimate business. My parents and their employees weren't hurting anyone or committing violent acts. They were simply running a business, paying taxes, and trying to make a living, but they were being treated like criminals. The more the government tried to stop the Gas Pipe, the harder my parents fought back. It was during this time that the Gas Pipe really locked down its roots and became a booming success. The saying "what doesn't kill you makes you stronger" couldn't have been truer.

By the mid-eighties there were four Gas Pipe stores—three in the Dallas area and one in Austin. In the early eighties, my parents also tried their hand at opening and running a full-service salon called the Hair Revue in the Oak Lawn area—the "gayborhood" of Dallas. The salon ultimately was a bust, but what fun times. I loved being up at the salon on Saturdays with my mother. Everyone doted on me. My mother always looked fabulous—she had hairdressers at her disposal daily. She still had a very liberal outlook on life, but her bell-bottoms and tie-dye had been replaced with glamorous furs, beautiful clothing, perfect makeup and hair—she was the epitome of eighties glam! She was really in her element running the salon, but it was a difficult business to manage, and eventually the Hair Revue closed.

The Gas Pipe had become very successful, and my parents were able to have a social life that exemplified the booming eighties lifestyle. We moved into a bigger, brand-new house that had a swimming pool and all the newest amenities. Every year my parents would have incredible Halloween parties. The costumes were fabulous, and cash prizes were given to the best costumes. Guests would bob for apples in my parents' huge eighties-style round bathtub that was in the center of their carpeted, eighties-style, massive master bathroom. One year my mother and I dressed up as Joan and Christina Crawford from *Mommie Dearest*—we looked the part, 100 percent. It was a fun time in life.

My uncle Jeff, my mother's younger brother, died in 1981 in a tragic accident. That was the one sad time I remember from my early childhood. My mother had taken him under her wing at a very young age, and he and his wife were living with us. He was so young—nineteen. I adored him and loved him so much. The death was beyond painful for my mother, and because I was so close with Jeff, it was difficult for me too. I was barely six, and I don't think children really know how to process grief. Following his death, I would get up every night in the middle of the night and sit in the kitchen for long periods of time. I didn't tell my parents for a while, and when I did, they couldn't understand why I never went to get them to tell them I couldn't sleep. I don't understand either. I guess I was just processing things in my own way. I didn't want to ask for help, something I struggled with way into adulthood. Nobody ever told me it was wrong or not okay to ask for help, but it wasn't something I ever felt comfortable doing. It would take me nearly forty years to learn that it's okay to reach out and lean on people and ask for help, and I had to go through some terrible times to learn that, but that lesson would be one of the many gifts that came from my struggles.

In 1983 the Gas Pipe legal battles were intense. It was becoming a never-ending battle; I was also at a crossroads because the Montessori school I had been attending stopped at age eight. My parents had looked at other schools in the Dallas area, but the public schools weren't on par with the standards I was used to at the Montessori school. Other private schools in Dallas were expensive, and my parents were afraid we would be shunned since the Gas Pipe legal ordeal had been made public. They had already been asked to step down from the board at the Montessori school I had attended since I was two. A few years prior, my parents had bought a small house at Lake Whitney, about an hour and a half south of Dallas, and they decided to make Lake Whitney our permanent home. We downsized in Dallas, getting a small condo as a base for when my parents worked in Dallas. They would mostly commute between Dallas and Lake Whitney, and we bought a bigger house at Lake Whitney. By the summer of 1983, we had officially moved to Lake Whitney, and I was enrolled at Clifton Elementary.

Chapter Two

I initially didn't want to move to Lake Whitney and live in the country. I was going to have to ride a bus to school, play sports, and make new friends—worst of all, as I told my parents, "Everyone there will listen to country music." I loved Madonna, the Go-Gos, Prince, and any synthesized eighties music because my father was always into the newest music and shared it with me. I also knew every Beatles and Queen song by heart because my mother always played them in the car, and we would sing along.

My first day of third grade at Clifton Elementary was pretty much a disaster. I insisted on wearing a bright-orange traditional Mexican flower dress. I was expressing myself, and at my culturally diverse, progressive Montessori school, this would have been perfectly acceptable. My mother encouraged me to wear something else, but I was a very headstrong child. Clifton had a 2A school in the heart of central Texas, and the town was a farming and limestone-factory community with a population of about 2,500 at the time. There were only about seventy students in my grade. The next closest town was Waco, Texas, about forty-five minutes away, which I'm not sure even had a population of one hundred thousand at the time. Clifton was an isolated community where everybody knew everybody and everything about everybody. We were outsiders from the start, but I was oblivious to that and wanted to wear my orange Mexican flower dress.

I don't recall being made fun of because of my dress, but I found out later that it was the talk of the day. I had to learn to play kickball and dodgeball that day. I had never played any sort of competitive sports in the Montessori environment because that was against the philosophy, and I certainly hadn't played a sport where a ball was thrown at you aggressively by your opponent. I was scared and to this day think dodgeball is the most ridiculous game ever invented. I was called "ignorant" and "butthole" on my first day of playing sports because I didn't know what I was doing, and I had certainly never heard words like that from children in the peaceful, nurturing Montessori environment.

I was asked multiple times, "Who are you kin to here?" I didn't even know what that meant. (In the city we used the word *related*, but in the country it was *kin*.) The only "kin" I knew of was my uncle Ken, and he did not live in Clifton. I didn't know why people were so concerned with my "kin," but I quickly deduced, due to the lack of activity or change in the town, that one of the few reasons someone voluntarily moved to Clifton was because they had family there, though we did not. I now sat in a classroom where I could only get out of my seat when told to do so, I had to raise my hand to ask a question or speak, and I took tests using a pencil and paper to add numbers rather than using blocks, beads, or other materials to count and learn in a freer and hands-on manner as in the

Montessori environment. It was like stepping into an alternate universe.

The only good thing that happened on that first day was meeting my lifelong best friend, Amy. She asked me my name, and I was so grateful someone wanted to talk to me. I promptly said, "My name is Amy," and she said, "My name is Amy too." We were immediate friends, and we've been in each other's lives ever since. As any good friend would do, she told me at some point that prior to talking to me, she had gossiped with others about my orange Mexican flower dress—I don't blame her; it was inappropriate for the environment. But what I really learned from that was what an amazing person Amy was because she didn't mind talking to the new girl in the ridiculous dress. Even though she and everyone made fun of me, which is unfortunately what kids do, she still took a chance on me.

I survived third grade and made more friends. I joined Girl Scouts, learned to wear more appropriate clothing to school, and even learned to play kickball (but never learned to like dodgeball). I loved our house in the country. It was on seven acres of wooded land on a cliff overlooking the lake, with a beautiful fountain and plenty of places to run and play. It was isolated and far from everyone, but that wasn't too unusual for the area, and I often had friends over.

My parents spent every Tuesday night in Dallas, and I would either stay with Amy or Emma, my godmother, who had relocated to Lake Whitney from Houston with her daughter. It was a great opportunity for all. Emma was employed by my parents to help take care of me and the house and cook (she's a wonderful cook), and she was able to raise her daughter in a better environment than Houston. I was able to have a second mother, so to speak, and a wonderful soul to help enrich my childhood.

I gradually learned to assimilate to life in Clifton, even though I'd had a very different early childhood than my fellow students. At the beginning of my Clifton school years, I always brought my lunch because I was almost all vegetarian, and I thought the Clifton cafeteria food was weird. I was not the typical child who enjoyed typical "kid food." One day my mother decided that she would surprise me and pack a whole steamed artichoke in my lunch. I loved steamed artichokes, so she thought this would be a great treat. Well, I was in the rural environment of Clifton—"hickville USA"—and I don't think the grocery store in Clifton even sold artichokes. I'm sure she had bought it in Dallas, so my ultimate embarrassment when I pulled out the artichoke at lunch was over the top. I quickly put it back in my lunch box and ate it later after school and asked my mother to never pack me anything like that again. I asked to start eating more in the cafeteria like everyone else, but that didn't happen often because I didn't like much of the cafeteria food. The only animal product I ate regularly at that time was fish, so I lived for the fish-sticks and mac-and-cheese days. As the years progressed, I learned to embrace hot dogs and hamburgers, and by my twenties I did learn to appreciate a quality steak and most meat products, except for meat in a can. Meat simply does not belong in a can, something my husband and I debate frequently.

I left my Dallas roots behind and was slowly becoming a country girl. The bus ride to school that I had once dreaded turned into the highlight of my day. Amy and I rode the bus together. As we got older and got to move to the back of the bus with the "cool kids," we would do things that kids weren't supposed to do, though I think all do—tell dirty jokes we had heard (but probably didn't really understand) and practice saying our newly learned cusswords. Oh, we thought we were so cool, but in reality we were simply awkward preteens.

Middle school was a good time in my life. I was in band, often sitting first-chair clarinet. I had become somewhat athletic as a basketball player, and I ran track. I tried out for cheerleading in seventh grade and didn't make it, which was rather devastating at the time, but I did make the squad in eighth grade. I loved the performing, the attention, the cute outfits with the short skirts—it was all right up my alley. Academics were pretty much a breeze for me, and I had fully adjusted to the more traditional public school style of learning and had great grades. I was responsible and a good student and didn't really get into any sort of trouble.

I was a good kid, but I was the stereotypical loudmouthed, boisterous, flashy cheerleader. I drew attention to myself constantly, and I liked boys—excessively. My mouth had no filter, and I gave myself permission to say whatever was on my mind. I desperately wanted to be popular, which wasn't that difficult with only seventy people in the entire grade, and I wanted to be noticed. I was flirtatious and liked for everyone to pay attention to me, particularly boys. I went through puberty early, and at thirteen I was fully developed and had a fit but curvaceous figure that looked more like it belonged to an eighteen-year-old. Like many teenage girls, I always thought I needed to lose weight, but it was never excessive. I also loved to eat good food, and I was active, so it was balanced, but I do remember thinking I was fat at times. Now I look at pictures from middle school and high school and think that I had a pretty great body, but I wasn't fully comfortable in my own skin back then. I don't think most teenagers are. I did, however, get comments and whistles from boys, and I lapped up the attention and put way too much importance on it and did things to encourage it.

I don't know why I had the need for so much attention. I think most teenagers take on a "role" in school, and I was the flirtatious, loud cheerleader who always got noticed. It wasn't due to a lack of attention at home. My homelife was good. My parents argued, but not constantly. They were passionate people—whether the passion was happiness or arguing, there was always passion. My mother and I argued regularly, and some of those arguments were very inappropriate—more like two sisters than mother and daughter—but we were also very close, and I think most teenage girls argue with their mothers. My father and I were close as well, spending time together by playing basketball, watching movies, or him teaching me to drive. We were a very close family.

I had the same boyfriend off and on from eighth grade through the beginning of my junior year in high school. We went to the movies and school dances, and I would go to his house regularly. A couple of times I went to church with him and his family. While God was always discussed and part of my family's life, organized religion was not part of the hippie thought process, and even though my father didn't have long hair anymore and my parents didn't dress like hippies, much of the hippie philosophy was still there. God was spiritual, the creator of all things, and an important part of life and our reason for being, but religion was man made and not necessary. I would go to church occasionally with friends, and I even went to a Baptist summer camp with friends for a week one year. I went to church with my boyfriend's family, and it was Church of Christ—very conservative, and I felt very awkward, as I typically always did in church. I look back on that relationship now, and I can't remember one thing he and I had in common—other than an active physical attraction.

I was sexually active at way too young of an age, but I justified it because I was in a "long-term" relationship, and I was the last in my close circle of friends to have sex. I know now, of course, that sex at such a young age is simply a waste, on so many different levels. Teenagers aren't comfortable enough with their bodies to really know what they're doing and therefore don't fully enjoy it. It's a quick thrill. The emotional maturity simply doesn't exist to understand or appreciate true intimacy. And the risks of having long-term consequences—either pregnancy or a disease—are not things children (and teenagers are children) should be exposing themselves to. Our bodies are one of the few things that truly belong to us and nobody else. Teenagers don't understand what it is to truly love and to truly give themselves to someone. Their psyches are not developed enough.

I've had many open, positive conversations with my kids about sex, and I think it's very important for parents to do so. As parents we have an opportunity and responsibility to make sure our children have healthy and respectful mind-sets about sex. There are two things I have told them that seemed to make a lasting impression. First, don't have sex with anyone you can't see yourself having a baby with, because no matter how careful you are, it can happen. And second, when you have sex with someone, it is like sharing underwear with all the people either of you have had sex with. I don't know where I got that from. It just popped into my head during one of the many quality conversations I've been fortunate enough to have with my children. But the idea of sharing dirty underwear seemed to really get their attention, and they still reference it when we have talks. I've also told my children, though, that being in love—truly in love—and being able to be completely comfortable and intimate with someone is one of the most beautiful things in the world, and sex can be a wonderful thing. I would eventually learn real intimacy, and I would experience the ultimate true love, but it would be much later in life.

As an adult I played a word association game one time. Everyone sat in a circle, and one person said a word; then the next person had to say the first word that came to mind in reaction to the word, and so on. The person next to me said, "High school." I instinctively said, "Miserable." It's not that I was truly miserable in high school. I have plenty of good memories and lifelong friends, and I had an overall good time, but I didn't know who I was, and I had such misplaced priorities and inappropriate behavior. I was trying to be who I thought I was supposed to be. Life is so much better—and happier—when we're comfortable in our own skin.

Chapter Three

The end of my junior year in high school was dramatic and negative. Amy and I had a huge fight that played out very publicly, though we made up later. My prom date ditched me at prom, and when I tried out for cheerleader at the end of the year, I didn't make it, which meant I wouldn't be a cheerleader my senior year. My on-and-off boyfriend and I officially called it quits, and I went to an end-of-school party at my friend Ryan's house—my first house party without parents present—where I drank alcohol and had a very promiscuous and negative sexual experience that solidified my reputation as "that kind of girl." Teenagers shouldn't drink alcohol, and it's not just a legal issue. It's because the development and maturity simply aren't there to always make wise choices even when sober, and when alcohol or drugs get added to the mix, the potential for bad decisions becomes even worse. The combination of teenagers, sex, and alcohol equals a recipe for disaster. And once you start down that path, it's hard to stop.

I began a slow tailspin. I very much had a "screw it" attitude and decided that since I was a year away from graduating,

I didn't care about being accepted in the town of Clifton anymore. I was going to move back to the Dallas area after graduating and attend the University of North Texas, just north of Dallas. I had been sexual, outgoing, and bold, but I had basically followed the rules otherwise. I was ready to let loose. The highlight of the summer between my junior and senior year was a massive party I threw at my house while my parents were in Dallas for the weekend. It was pretty much total high school debauchery, and that is why my children will never be left home alone if I'm out of town. There is just too much temptation. It was an epic party, and it seemed like the entire high school was there. The party set the stage for my senior year and the activities to come. I was no longer just the energetic, boisterous, sexually charged cheerleader—I was ready to party and have fun. I wasn't a cheerleader anymore, I quit band, and I had stopped participating in athletics my sophomore year. Participation in something productive is so important for kids to stay focused and motivated. I had lost that. I was going to party my way through my senior year, and as fate would have it, I soon met someone who was more than happy to help me in that quest.

My senior year in high school began what I would later in life refer to as "the sketchy years." It was the first time that my world would come crumbling down around me, and life as I knew it would change. It was during my senior year that my parents divorced, but prior to that happening, I had already started down a path of self-destruction, which was only intensified by the divorce.

I had started smoking marijuana occasionally, although I wasn't too impressed with it initially. I smoked marijuana for years before I ever really got "high." I was expecting a major effect and not the subtle euphoria that is more realistic. One of the many lies told about marijuana is how "out of your mind" it makes people. While I do think the effects of marijuana are exaggerated, I also do not think young people need to be smoking marijuana, drinking, or doing any drugs. Their brains are so young and developing, and nothing should hamper that process.

There was a dance club in Waco, which was about forty-five minutes from Clifton, called Highway 101. I convinced my parents to let me go, so Amy and I went. I knew all about the Waco party scene from our other friends at school who had started living in the "fast lane" recently. My preppy cheerleader look with perfectly styled hair had changed to Doc Martens, perfectly ripped jeans, and leather jackets. I had long, straight blonde hair and wore black eyeliner and bright-red lipstick.

The club itself was nothing special. It was one room at the end of a strip center. It had a bar, but I didn't go there to drink. I knew I could never drink, particularly underage, and then drive home from Waco. I just loved being somewhere I could dance and feel like I was part of something different, away from Clifton. I could lose myself in the strobe lights and the music, particularly the hard, rhythmic beats of the techno music that was so popular at the time. Some of our friends who frequented the club with us had already discovered some mind-altering substances, but at the time I was just happy to dance.

A regular group of us from Clifton began to frequent the club—me, Amy, Adrienne, Ryan, Frank, Tommy, Tony, and often Kelly, who was the most popular girl in school but had an ex-boyfriend who had found himself in some very serious trouble that plagued her emotionally, so she was suddenly wanting to explore the alternative world with us. I don't know what exactly we were all going through at that time of our lives that bonded us. We discovered a different world our senior year and went down a path together of what we thought was growth and self-discovery. It was a path with some dangerous and stupid choices, but we made memories and did have some fun times, although we are very lucky to have made it through.

That first night at Highway 101 would set in motion a series of future events. Amy and I both met the next men of our lives, and both would impact our lives in major ways. It wasn't love at first sight for either of us, but the introductions were made. Amy met Chris, who was older and going to college in Waco, but he and I did not like each other from the start. He would become her husband years later. And I met Brandon that night, who had lived in Clifton during elementary school, but I didn't know him well. There weren't necessarily sparks the first night I saw Brandon at Highway 101, but there was enough of an attraction that I was excited to see him the following week when we went back.

I was physically attracted to Brandon, and beyond that I'm not sure what the attraction was. He was bad news from the start. I learned quickly that he had been in rehab for drug problems and had dropped out of high school. He was supposedly trying to get his life back on track, even though he wasn't in school nor did he have a steady job. I don't think I looked at him as a long-term relationship, but something about the bad-boy persona caught my attention. He was different than anyone from Clifton, and he seemed completely smitten with me. Everyone told me from the start that Brandon was probably using me for money and social status, and he probably was, but I didn't care. My parents went out of town in January 1993, halfway through my senior year, to celebrate their twentieth wedding anniversary. And because Brandon had no responsibilities in life, he came to stay with me for a few days. We made our relationship official with sex, although I don't think it would have lasted if things hadn't changed drastically in my life soon after that.

During one of our nights at Highway 101, some of us bought LSD. Frank, Kelly, and I went back to my house and took the LSD, and I had my first "trip." We laughed hysterically the whole night. We looked in mirrors for what seemed like hours, making faces, listening to music, noticing sensations and images we had never noticed before. Every part of my body felt like a separate extension of another body. I remember looking at my toes and feeling like I had never really seen my toes before. We discussed the meaning of life, why we were here, where we would go. Frank confirmed he was gay, which of course we already knew, and the evening was positive and enlightening. Looking back all these years later, I know now one doesn't have to take LSD to experience those things—the ability to see ourselves and the world a certain way is within us naturally if we look for it. But I remember being really happy and having fun; I had seen the world in a way I never had before. Part of it was the innocence of it all. There were no expectations or a need to escape reality. I realize that doing drugs, particularly something as strong and unpredictable as LSD, can be very dangerous, but my desire for doing LSD the first time was innocent and for fun—I wasn't trying to see how wasted or out of my mind I could get. That would come later.

I knew Brandon and his friends did a lot of drugs—things such as cocaine that I had never contemplated doing. I felt that smoking pot was okay. LSD seemed peaceful—something that even my parents had experimented with during the height of their hippie days. At the time I didn't see it as the worst thing in the world, and I didn't see it as addictive because taking a "trip" would only be fun under the right circumstances. I did realize it could be dangerous, but unfortunately, I didn't think about that at the time. Cocaine I knew was dangerous, and nothing about it was helpful in expanding the mind, finding yourself, broadening your horizons, or any of the other hype associated with psychedelics. I knew from my parents and the open conversations we always had that cocaine was a no-no—as open minded as my parents were, they would not be accepting of it.

In March of my senior year, just two months after my parents celebrated their twentieth wedding anniversary, my father told me he was divorcing my mother. It was a Friday afternoon, the beginning of my spring break. He was driving me to Dallas to meet my mother because she and I were leaving that weekend to go on a girls' trip to New York. I had always wanted to go. I had been so excited, and now this was how the trip would begin. He gave me reasons why he was divorcing her. I knew they argued, and I would get so mad at my mother sometimes, like teenagers always do since the mother is often the "bad guy," but I never thought this would happen. As my father talked, I processed what was actually happening—my mother didn't even know yet. I felt terrible. I began to disconnect within minutes of my father talking.

I had to face my mother and pretend that everything was okay and act like I didn't know her world was about to be ripped out from under her. What I didn't know at the time was that she was pretty unhappy in the marriage, too, but she thought she would just stick it out. It was really *my* entire world that was being ripped out from under me. No matter what I had to deal with in life or how much I was struggling— no matter how bad the problem—my parents had always been my backbone. I loved our little family. My parents were my stability and my strength. We had quality time together, family dinners, and vacations. Weekend family breakfasts where my father made homemade pancakes were part of our regular routine and were cherished. We talked and communicated and were very close. That was all going to go away.

I immediately felt lost and scared. I was sad and angry, but I didn't know how to process that or admit it. We met my mother in Dallas, and I could barely look at her. It was impossible to pretend everything was okay. Before we left for New York, my father told her. Neither my mother or I had ever been to New York, and while it's a fun place, it's an overwhelming city even under the best circumstances, and it was too stressful and difficult to stay. We cut our trip short and came home so my mother could get a handle on things and figure out how to move forward. My parents weren't just married—they worked together and had built the business together.

When we got back to Texas, we drove home to Lake Whitney to see my father. It was clear at this point that my father was having a mental breakdown and was dealing with a lot from his past. He sought counseling, and my mother was compassionate. I was confused and angry, but I'll always remember my mother telling me that if he were sick from cancer or a disease, I would still talk to him, so I needed to talk to him now. I respect her greatly for having that perspective. My father was not himself. Many of the issues from his childhood and the war had been buried, but now things were coming to the surface, and that, among other things, led to the divorce.

I pretty much checked out mentally and withdrew. My life was crumbling apart; the one constant in my life was going away. I was angry but didn't know I could say that, and I really didn't know how to properly identify the emotion. I was angry at them both because I felt like they both should have done something different to fix it, and I was too immature to understand that sometimes things just can't be fixed. Sometimes things just happen, and in the long run it's for the better. But I was nowhere ready to see that at the time.

I went to Waco the night we returned from New York, and I didn't come back until the next day. Nobody questioned it. I think my parents and I were all in a state of shock and had retreated to our own little worlds. I went to Brandon's, and we drove with a group to Dallas and went to the Arcadia Club because Brandon and his friends knew the owner. I did cocaine for the first time and stayed up all night. I'll never forget doing that first line of cocaine and deliberately thinking that I was somehow getting back at my parents because they would be angry if they knew what I was doing—such a juvenile, ridiculous thought, but I was acting out. Brandon was impressed with my new gumption for partying, and I was ready to cling to him and go down the path of reckless fun because somehow that seemed more real and better than anything else in my life.

My mother moved to Dallas but would come to our home at Lake Whitney and stay in the guesthouse to see me. I was around less and less, so she came less and less, understandably so. I really didn't want to be around either of my parents because they were just reminders of the sadness and anger I was feeling, and I was trying to ignore that feeling. My father had a new girlfriend named Cindy, the younger daughter of my parents' good friends. She was only ten years older than me, but I tried to accept it. Cindy started coming to our house more and more, and I started partying more and more with Brandon and his friends.

I was seventeen and pretty immature, so instead of dealing with my feelings, I used my parents' distraction to my advantage. I had my father's credit card, and I would use it to take Brandon and his friends to Austin for the weekend. We would go shopping, out to dinner, to clubs all night (I had managed to get a fake ID)—I had no boundaries. I also had an ATM card that accessed a very small bank account that my parents used for general expenses. I had been given it several months back to access cash for approved purchases I would make for the household when my parents asked me to run errands. In the midst of the separation and pending divorce, nobody remembered that bank account. And I was never asked to return the card, so I used that money for partying and any other expenses I deemed necessary. By that time I had taken LSD a few times, and I was doing cocaine occasionally because Brandon really liked it. I was into whatever he was, and I was spiraling out of control.

Amy and I were still close, but I didn't get along with her boyfriend, and I don't think anyone really cared for Brandon. We were both wrapped up in our new relationships, so we weren't spending as much time together. When she had turned eighteen, she had received an inheritance from her father's death. She bought a fancy sports car and decided that since she was about to graduate high school, she would move out of her grandmother's house and get an apartment in Waco and drive back and forth to Clifton for school. I thought that was so exciting and would spend time there when I could, but it was a one-bedroom apartment, and she had a boyfriend, as did I, so it got a little crowded. And not only was it crowded, but it turned out that her boyfriend also had an affinity for cocaine. Four people who really didn't get along hanging out in a little one-bedroom apartment doing cocaine was a recipe for disaster.

My father sat down with me one night in April and tried to have a serious talk with me. He had received his credit card bill, and it was out of control. I had never abused the card before, so he gave me a stern warning. I listened and nodded, and then I called Amy that night to ask her if I could move into her apartment. Like any good friend would do, she said yes, but I don't know what we were thinking because we knew tensions were already high. I went to school the next day, and after I knew my father had left for work in Dallas, I went back home, packed up my stuff, left him a note, and officially moved out at seventeen years old. I called my mother and told her, and I don't think she knew what to say. Everything was such a mess and so out of control in all our lives that nobody knew what to do. I only had a little over a month left of high school, and they assumed I would still go to college as planned, so nobody made a huge deal about it. Neither of them were aware yet just how much of a negative influence Brandon was or how out of control the partying was. Otherwise, I think they would have intervened much sooner. I think they thought Brandon was a phase; I would graduate and move to college, and he would be gone. Since my parents were no longer together, I was holding on to Brandon tighter and tighter, desperately wanting to feel like I had something permanent in my life.

I did graduate, but barely—not because of my grades but because I had missed too many days of school my senior year. The last two weeks of school we (our little group that had discovered the club scene and partying ways of Waco) were informed that we had been absent too many days, and we had to physically be on the school grounds for so many extra hours between then and graduation, or we wouldn't graduate. That meant we were up there early every morning and had to stay late every afternoon. We did it, and we graduated. I was officially done with Clifton.

My relationship with my father was strained but still present. My relationship with my mother was okay, but she was in Dallas full time at that point and trying to move on with her life, understandably. I was still technically living with Amy in her apartment in Waco, and I had gotten a job waiting tables at a little restaurant down the street. I wasn't completely sure what I was going to do about college because Brandon had become my "stability," and the ridiculousness of using that word in correlation with him is not lost on me. But that's where I was in life—either I could stay in Waco and attend community college, or he could move to Dallas with me. My parents were starting to see the negative influence he had on me, and neither of my new options were appealing to them.

Tensions finally blew one night at Amy's apartment, and it was time for Brandon and me to leave. His cousin's apartment became my new home. Amy and I did not speak for a long time after that—the one time in our lives when we lost touch with one another. I was lost mentally and emotionally and was basically homeless, but I didn't want to go back home or leave Brandon. I had decided that he was the best thing in my life and that being with him also meant plenty of partying and drugs, meaning I didn't really have to think about the reality of my life. But the reality of my life wasn't as awful as I made it out to be—yes, my parents were getting divorced, but they still loved me. I could still go to college and have it paid for, and my life could still progress quite nicely. But I just couldn't see it that way. I was bitter and angry and didn't want to deal with any of it.

Brandon and I took a trip to Cancún. We really didn't have any money. I was waiting tables, and Brandon did odd jobs and sold drugs on the side. The trip had been a graduation present from months ago. It was the one thing I'd wanted, and I could take whomever I chose. I had chosen Brandon. I don't remember a lot about the trip, except it was the first of many times he was physically abusive with me. We had a big argument one night, and I don't even remember what it was about, but it led to him hitting and pushing me. I dismissed it as an isolated incident. I had angered him—the excuse girls make when they're in an abusive relationship. That wasn't the last time it happened, and it continued over the course of our relationship.

My parents convinced me to move to Dallas over the summer. Even if I didn't want to live in Denton on campus at the University of North Texas (UNT) and do the traditional college route, they convinced me I should still go to school there. I was already enrolled, and there was no reason not to go. UNT was a big commuter school. Many students lived in Dallas and drove to Denton. I was adamant that I wanted to stay with Brandon. They knew for sure he was bad news at this point, but all they wanted was for me to still think about my future. So in order to get me to move up to Dallas and go to UNT, they said that both Brandon and I could live in one of the condos they owned. At this point they knew I was a mess. They didn't know how to get me away from Brandon and didn't want to lose me completely, so to keep me in their lives and hopefully on some path toward a future, they reluctantly accepted him as part of the package. My father even went so far as to hire him at the Gas Pipe. We moved to Dallas, and I made plans to begin school in the fall. It appeared that I was starting down a better path. But Dallas had more to offer than Waco, in both good and bad ways.

Chapter Four

We moved to Dallas for a supposed fresh start. The cocaine usage subsided for me. I didn't really like the physical effects of it and had never done that much of it, so I just stopped doing it. I don't remember what Brandon decided about his cocaine habits (and he probably wasn't honest with me about his habits anyway), but things seemed to settle down a little, at least initially.

My parents' divorce was final, and it was amicable for the most part. They were still great friends, and as time went on, we would all go to dinner together regularly and celebrate holidays together. My father was still with Cindy. My mother had begun dating a wonderful man named JB. What a saint JB was (and is). He swept my mother off her feet, and to meet me in the condition I was in at the time and accept me unconditionally like his own daughter says a lot about this man. They were instantly in love, and everyone who met JB could easily see why. The only roadblocks were that JB lived an hour away from Dallas and that he had a son who, like many ten-year-olds, preferred for his father not to date anyone. My mother embraced both factors, and their future began.

I began college at UNT, but I also found a whole new world of partying. Even though I didn't live on campus, Brandon and I still met new people. Ecstasy, which had been huge in the eighties, was making a comeback. The rave era was also beginning around this time—all-night parties with DJs in a random warehouse or outdoor location where people danced the night away in Ecstasy-induced trances, walking around with glow sticks, hugging everyone, and saying "I love you" and "you're beautiful" to anyone they met.

Everything and everyone was alluring at raves. They were peaceful, fun, and exciting. Raves were the hippest, newest thing, and I felt that I was totally accepted; but then, everyone is accepted and loved when you're all on Ecstasy. I would get lost inside myself, dancing with techno beats pulsating all around me, tingling sensations throughout my body from the Ecstasy, and I'd walk around meeting people and talking and feeling like we were the chosen, beautiful people of our generation. I felt like I was part of something unique and special. That's why you went to a rave. First, you had to know someone who knew someone to even find out about the rave that weekend, and that alone made it seem like something that only select people got to be part of. Then once you were there, everyone had nothing but love and acceptance. Looking back, the experience was nothing more than a bunch of people dancing the night away on Ecstasy, but there was this feeling of self-discovery during it all. That was the medical reason for the invention of Ecstasy: to help people feel more intimate and deal with sexual issues in a controlled therapeutic environment—controlled environment being the key part—which is different than a bunch of kids experimenting with a drug. You can only imagine what effect a drug like that might have on a bunch of scantily clothed dancing young adults at a rave. However, that was something really cool about the raves—they weren't about sex or hooking up. They were about togetherness, friendliness, dancing, being jovial, and even loving. Although the amount of drugs consumed at those events was staggering (and dangerous—not something I would recommend for that reason alone), it was always a peaceful experience.

Unsurprisingly, I did not excel in my first semester in college. Brandon and I temporarily broke up, and everyone was thrilled, but we quickly got back together. During the breakup, I enrolled at my mother's post–high school alma mater, the Executive Secretarial School of Dallas, which, by the time I enrolled in January 1994, had changed its name to the Executive Business School of Dallas because the term *secretary* was no longer PC. I needed direction in life, and their program allowed me to get an associate's degree within six months. The crux of the degree was learning computer, office, and organizational skills that would enable me to be a super executive assistant. I excelled at school and completed the degree with flying colors. None of the faculty at the school knew of my weekend alter ego as a common fixture at the weekend Dallas rave scene, so I seemed to be juggling it all well. I was hired for a job in the school administration office while I attended school, and when I graduated, I landed a decent job making twenty-one thousand dollars a year as an executive assistant at an engineering firm. For 1994 that was good money, especially considering that I had only gone to school for six months. It was more than enough for me to support myself, with Brandon as a roommate, and party on the weekends.

I was nineteen years old and feeling okay with my life. Yes, I had a terrible boyfriend who couldn't keep a steady job (Brandon had worked at the Gas Pipe but was fired when we broke up, though my father eventually hired him back out of pity and to help me), and I was doing nothing on the weekends except raving all night long and sleeping all day, but I had a decent job and was a good employee, had an apartment in Dallas, and had plenty of friends (or party buddies), and while it wasn't the greatest, most responsible life, I was having fun and providing for myself. My parents helped me a little (took me out to dinner and occasional trips to the grocery store), but there wasn't a monthly allowance or regular financial support. I was living independently.

Brandon and I made plans to get married. My parents must have just played along to appease me, hoping the desire would eventually fade away. I had a ring, and my mother took me to get a dress. It was rather inexpensive, and she was probably just hoping once again to not alienate me. We didn't have firm wedding plans, but we were going to go to a beach somewhere. Then I got unexpectedly pregnant during the summer of 1994. I didn't want to have the baby. I knew enough to know that I didn't need to have a baby with Brandon, but he wanted to keep the baby because he knew that he needed to do whatever he could to hang on to me, and a baby would ensure that. I didn't look at abortion lightly, and it wasn't a callous decision that didn't affect me, but at the time it seemed to be the only decision. As I got older and had more respect for myself and life in general, my personal views on pro-life versus pro-choice changed, but I was too unaware at the time.

When I went to my doctor, and she confirmed the news that I was a few weeks pregnant, I began to bawl profusely. She said, "I take it this isn't a good thing for you," left the room, and came back in with a brochure for the nearest abortion clinic. It was odd how matter of fact the doctor was about abortion. There wasn't much discussion, and I don't remember any other options being mentioned. It was almost like she was giving me information on a new car or appliance—not a life-changing decision. I made an appointment immediately. As it turned out, I didn't actually have to get an abortion because there was no heartbeat (not surprising considering the state of my body those days), but I still had to go through having everything removed, and it's my understanding the process is the same. It's definitely one of those situations where my conscience to this day struggles with what my intentions were versus the actual events that transpired.

Brandon was not happy with my decision. We broke up again, and that should have really been the final time, but it wasn't. We eventually, and unfortunately, got back together.

I had yet to deal with the emotions from my parents' divorce. I had been with Brandon and distracting myself with partying and continuing to ignore my negative feelings. My mother had remarried by that point and relocated to Weatherford, where JB lived. I was happy for her. My father was still with Cindy, and I, along with everyone else, had grown to believe they were meant for each other, despite the initial opinions people often have when a girl shacks up with a rich guy twice her age.

I had slowed down a little in the all-night rave scene because, like all good things, it was kind of coming to an end and wasn't quite as fun as it had been. The music wasn't as good, and the Ecstasy wasn't as good—or maybe I was just getting bored and needing some sort of different fulfillment. While it would have been the mature and responsible thing for me to find a healthy hobby—maybe go back to school and continue my education or find something stable and productive to do—that wasn't in my psyche at the time. I was now an executive assistant for a real estate development group in the new up-and-coming Uptown neighborhood of Dallas. It was a pay increase, so I felt I was at least moving up a little and making accomplishments. But I was definitely still lost.

One night Brandon divulged that while we had been broken up, he had dabbled in heroin. I should have known that nobody just "dabbles" in heroin—it's far too addictive. But nevertheless, I was intrigued. I didn't fully understand the seriousness of it. This was before I had seen *Pulp Fiction* with the infamous scene of Uma Thurman's character overdosing on heroin. It was before *Trainspotting*, and it was before the well-publicized string of heroin overdoses that happened a couple of years later in the Dallas area. So instead of thinking, "Run now, and get away while you can," or being afraid and saying, "No, that's terrible," like a rational person should have, I asked, "Do you have any right now?" True to form, Brandon was more than happy to oblige. I didn't shoot up that night—we just snorted it. It was December 1994, and I began an affair with the devil.

A few months into the heroin usage, my father learned of our new habit. We had a mutual friend who went to my father out of concern. My father scheduled a lunch with me and my mother under the pretense that we were going to discuss plans for this joke of a wedding Brandon and I still thought we were going to have. My father announced to my mother that Brandon and I had a heroin problem. It was traumatic and awful: a lot of tears, anger, fear—very emotional. My father had had some time to process the news, but my mother, having just heard it, was shocked. The only positive thing I could say was, "I'm not shooting up." In my mind, that meant I wasn't an addict and that I could stop any time and be fine. So I did. It was kind of hard to stop but not painfully difficult. My usage wasn't at its worst. Brandon did have a more serious problem and would go to rehab. I stayed in the apartment and continued to work and pay the bills, and I didn't do heroin. Brandon stayed away about two weeks. He came home and got a temporary job at UPS, and we were clean, but after a short while we were back to our old ways. Like many addicts, Brandon would often sell his substance of choice as a means to support his habit. So he knew exactly how to find the heroin again—it took just a simple phone call.

I don't remember exactly how long it was that I used before I finally shot up, but it was inevitable. Like any drug, you build up a tolerance, and the high just isn't the same—you need more. You need something stronger. I had been using heroin daily for at least a few months, and while I was still functioning, going to work every day, being fairly responsible, and paying the bills, I couldn't even go a day without heroin. As par for the course, Brandon had been shooting up behind my back, and when I found out, I was livid. That was the line I had said I would never cross. But once again, instead of having the voice of logic that said, "Run now! Go! Be very afraid," I got over my anger and said, "Okay, I'll try it too." Once again Brandon was more than happy to oblige.

Whatever anyone has said or heard about the feeling of shooting up heroin, all the talk of it being euphoric, the ultimate high—all of it is true. We went into the bathroom, and I sat down on the covered toilet. Brandon got the rig ready, found my vein, and boom—it was in. The warmth rushed through my body before he had even completed the injection. I was instantly comfortable and cozy all over, feeling like I was on a cloud.

I asked, "How long will it last?" I didn't want it to go away. It was like floating in the sky, looking down on the world from a state of complete peacefulness and numbness. Nothing hurt; there was no pain, grief, or sadness—there was nothing at all but a feeling of complete relaxation and calmness in a state where it felt like nothing could ever go wrong.

Everyone knows that as awesome and positive as those feelings may sound, there isn't anything good about heroin. I will never forget that feeling the first time I shot up heroin, but I never had that feeling again—not once. I tried and tried, but nothing in life is ever like the first time. I chased that feeling, and I wanted that feeling, but I never achieved it again. Instead I found myself barely holding on, having to shoot up regularly just to keep from going through withdrawals and hurting. I had only thought I'd been hurting and in some sort of pain before I shot up heroin the first time. I had only thought I'd needed to numb out and forget the world around me, but I really hadn't. After heroin got ahold of me, I *did* need to numb out and forget the world around me because I was addicted and depressed. Instead of getting that awesome feeling of euphoria, I was just trying to keep from going through instant withdrawals and feeling the negative emotions that now surrounded my life.

Here's the other thing about heroin: whatever anyone has said or whatever you've heard or seen in the movies about withdrawals—that is not an exaggeration. It is the absolute worst physical torture. It would be a few months before I would go through a complete cycle of heroin withdrawals, but for the few months following the first time I shot up, I would get up every morning for work and shoot up enough so I could make it through the day without major withdrawals. When Brandon would pick me up from work, he would have a rig waiting in the car so I could shoot up immediately before we had to drive home in traffic. It's a wonder I kept a job and did so well at it, but somehow I did. I would spend every day counting down the hours until I could have my fix. The weekends were spent practically in a coma with heroin being injected all day long. It's really even more of a wonder that I didn't die.

My relationship with my parents was more than strained. I barely spoke to my father, and my mother was just trying to keep me in her life to make sure I was alive. I knew things were beyond out of control, but I couldn't stop. Mentally, I was to a point that I wanted to stop. I knew it was wrong, I knew this was not the life to live, and I knew I was addicted. But I couldn't stop—I physically couldn't stop. The slightest pain I would feel every day toward the end of my workday was enough to tell me I couldn't stop. By three o'clock in the afternoon, withdrawal symptoms would set in. If I could just make it until five o'clock, the pain would go away. I wouldn't really get high, because that euphoric feeling had stopped long ago, but it would stop the withdrawals. I was barely surviving and only shooting the drug to control the addiction.

Somehow Brandon had gotten in touch with a guy named Matt who wanted to buy a large quantity of heroin. It was some friend-of-a-friend situation. He knew it was fishy—this guy, out of nowhere, wanted to buy massive quantities of heroin. After much hesitation, the addiction and need for money superseded any reasoning, and Brandon made the deal. I didn't know much about the situation, but I feared this guy could mean nothing but trouble. It ultimately ended up being one of the biggest blessings of my life.

It was February of 1996, and I was twenty years old. I pretty much hated myself at that point. I didn't know how to get my life back on track, I had an addiction that was out of my control, my relationship with my parents was strained, I was in a relationship that was abusive on every level, and I didn't have many friends at that point. I had run up a ton of credit card debt—I had really just quit checking the mail at a certain point and stopped paying bills except for the essential utilities. I wasn't even eating regularly. Fast food was the food of choice, and a high-calorie, fatty meal would often sustain me a day or two. The office I worked at had Nutri-Grain cereal bars that I would eat every morning for breakfast because they were there and free. To this day I still won't eat cereal bars because they remind me of a really dark time in my life. My life was Brandon and heroin. I remember sitting at my desk at work, day after day, thinking, "I just want to quit using, but I can't." I wanted to stop, but I was too ashamed to tell anyone that I needed help, and I didn't feel like I had anywhere to go because I had alienated everybody. Then I got the phone call that ultimately saved me.

Brandon called me at work and said, "It happened. I got busted." The DEA—Matt, in particular—was in our apartment. They were searching the entire apartment and had arrested Brandon. He told me they were taking him to jail, the apartment would be a mess when I got home because they were going through all my stuff, and I would need to get a ride home from work. I said something about going through withdrawals, and he said there was nothing that could be done about that. That's how bad the addiction and subsequent withdrawals were—my apartment was being raided by the DEA, and my boyfriend was going to jail, yet my main concern was how I was going to get my next fix. I called one of the few friends I had to come and get me from work. I didn't tell my coworkers anything and left.

I called my mother when I got home and told her what had happened. Without any judgment and only minimal questions, she said, "Will you be okay tonight and then able to drive tomorrow?" I told her yes, and she told me to come to her house first thing in the morning. I tossed and turned and cringed in pain that entire night, going through the beginning of severe withdrawals. I miraculously managed to get in my car the next morning and make the one-hour drive to Weatherford, thanking God that I was being given a second chance in life.

Chapter Five

When I was twenty, many people I knew in my age group were going to college, maybe drinking a little too much sometimes or having minor recreational drug experiences, figuring out their majors or getting close to graduating, and pledging a sorority or fraternity—meanwhile, in the last five years, I had lost my virginity, experienced my parents' divorce, lived with an abusive boyfriend, been pregnant (albeit briefly), and had a severe drug addiction. At a pretty young age, and with some serious baggage, I was trying to start over in life.

My father wanted me to get better, and he wanted to help, but our relationship was a bit strained after Brandon had worked for him and lied to him numerous times. My mother and JB stepped up to the plate and helped me get my life in order. I was physically and mentally in bad shape. My apartment had been raided by the DEA, which led to me getting evicted because nobody wanted to rent to me after the DEA got involved. I was going through heavy withdrawals. The day I moved into my mother's house in Weatherford, my mother held me as I cried and cried and then showed her the track marks on my arm. She held me and loved me and treated them that day and every day after with cocoa-butter lotion until they faded.

While my mother did remain very nurturing and loving, the "tough love" came quickly—and rightfully so. My apartment in Dallas had to be dealt with. It was a disgusting mess, and I had a short time period to vacate. We had to get what few possessions I had out of there so I wouldn't lose them. We also had to clean it, and it hadn't been cleaned properly in at least a year. I thought I was going to die. It took two days to properly deal with the apartment, and those two days were my third and fourth days of withdrawals. All I really wanted to do was curl up in a ball. Every muscle and fiber of my body ached extensively, but my mother kept me moving, and it was the best thing she could have done. I'll always remember JB telling me on the night I moved in with them, "People in life can either bring you up or bring you down, and you need to surround yourself with people who bring you up." Those were good words to live by.

Had it not been for my mother holding my hand while also pushing me forward to stay motivated, I don't know how I would have survived. Anyone overcoming a drug addiction needs to make the best personal choice for how to handle it. Rehabs are great and have helped many people, but for me, going through those withdrawals without any medication to ease the physical, mental, or emotional pain was the best initial therapy.

After the physical pain subsided, I was flooded with feelings and emotions that I had been suppressing. Now that I was sober, I could feel everything. I would actually have to deal with things. I began to see a counselor for therapy regarding personal issues I had buried the past three years. My counselor helped me label my emotions, and *anger* was at the top of the list. She helped me learn to deal with the anger and not stay angry forever. I had ideas of how my life should be and what my parents should have done and how I would have handled things differently if I were them, and I just went on and on like I was in my own private, miserable drama, when in reality my life was just fine. I still had parents who loved me very much. Yes, they had divorced, but so had 49 percent of other couples. I wasn't out on a limb alone, and I needed to process my feelings properly and get on with life and stop the "pity party for one." My counselor said I needed to decide if I wanted to have a relationship with my family or not. If I committed to having a relationship with my parents, then I needed to accept things as they were and stop blaming them for everything. They had given me a wonderful childhood filled with love and opportunity.

I had made such a mess out of my life. I'd convinced myself that being a heroin addict would define me forever. It was the lowest of lows—shooting up drugs on a daily basis. My counselor encouraged me to embrace my past. It was something I should never forget; it was a traumatic and volatile time in my life that had obviously had a huge effect on me. But it did not need to define me forever.

I had been with Brandon for the majority of three years, and that relationship was abusive on so many levels—verbally, with him always insulting me and telling me I was fat, and physically. I eventually had to work through my misconceptions and learn what a healthy relationship looked like, but it took many years. Ultimately, Brandon did a very small amount of time in jail and then a mandated state rehab program. I went to see him in jail a couple times. My family was concerned about allowing the visits, but my counselor insisted it was needed for closure, so I was permitted to go. The visits did provide closure, and he was out of my life for good.

Gaga, my maternal grandmother, had recently lost her third husband from a sudden heart attack. She was about twenty years sober and was very involved in Alcoholics Anonymous. I went to stay with her for a week to keep her company, and she was able to introduce me to the twelve-step program. She and I shared stories and laughed and cried. Even though Gaga was often not the easiest person to be around, we were close and had some very special times, and that week was one of them.

I also attended some twelve-step meetings with a group in Weatherford. I learned a lot in those meetings about faith, moving forward, making amends, and learning from mistakes. It was good to meet other people who had as much shame as I did and were working hard to turn their lives around, but I felt my situation was different. Many of them talked about every day being a struggle to not drink or use. I didn't have that feeling. Because of my counseling, where I'd learned to process my feelings, I didn't have a need or desire to numb out and see how out of my mind I could become. I wanted to live and enjoy life, and I wanted to do things that other twenty-year-olds were doing. I didn't want to sit in a room and talk about my addiction and how it was a struggle for me to overcome it daily because, truthfully, it wasn't. Don't get me wrong—I can't say enough wonderful things about AA and NA. AA saved Gaga's life, and I know it has saved the lives of millions around the world. It is a phenomenal program. I just wasn't sure how it applied to me.

After discussion with my counselor and my parents, I felt confident in saying that while I had endured a very serious addiction with heroin, I was not an addict—it may be a fine line, but there was a difference. I would never want to go down that path again because my life was good and positive, and I was going to move forward and make something out of myself. I decided through counseling that I would be able to have a drink for my upcoming twenty-first birthday and that my bout with heroin was more of a condition of my mental state and unhappiness at the time and not a lifelong addiction. To this day, even when I've gone through some of the most awful times, I've never even thought about going down that path again. The one thing from AA I still use in my daily life is the Serenity Prayer: "God, grant me the serenity to accept the things I cannot change, courage to change the things I can, and the wisdom to know the difference."

At twenty-one, I had no money, and I had lost touch with many of my friends when the heroin had been at its worst, but I was slowly reaching out and getting reconnected with positive people. My mother paid off all my debt, and I had a payment plan set up with her. I got a job as an admin at a construction company, and since I had no living expenses and a minimal social life, I was pretty much signing my checks over to my mother for a while. That was okay, though, because I was getting a fresh start in life, and I was grateful. My mother and I agreed that as soon as I had paid her back, I would move out on my own again.

My best friend, Amy, had heard about my troubles and called me. It had been nearly three years since we had spoken, and it was like no time had passed. I was overjoyed to hear from her, and it was just another testament to our friendship. No matter how much time passes or what transpires, some things are stronger than any negative force in life, and our friendship has always been one of them. She had moved to Colorado with her boyfriend, Chris, and she was eager for me to come and visit. My mother was more than happy to buy a plane ticket for me to visit Colorado and see my dear friend. Our friendship never took a hiatus again.

I made plans to go back to college and get my bachelor's degree. I was interested in hospitality management, and UNT had a great program. It was decided that I should take baby steps and enroll in Weatherford Community College to get my basic classes out of the way. Moving off and going to college at a university probably would have been too much, and I wasn't sure anyway that I wanted to try to live on campus and do the traditional college route, as I felt like I had kind of "missed the boat" on that.

I started school full time at Weatherford Community College in the fall of 1996, so I had to find a part-time job rather than the full-time job I had. I applied for a job at Macaroni Grill, and a new chapter in my life began. The atmosphere and work duties suited me perfectly, and there was a lot of room for advancement. They had an extensive training program for new hires. I did well at my job, and I met a whole new group of friends through work. I had positive direction in my life and attainable goals. I was finally doing what other people my age were doing—working, going to school, and socializing.

I completed my first semester at Weatherford Community College in December of 1996. School was still something I enjoyed, and it wasn't overly challenging but enough to keep me focused. I had paid back my mother, and we decided it was time for me to get an apartment in Fort Worth. I found a cute, small complex where some friends lived, and they had studio lofts for the cheap rate of four hundred dollars a month. It was tiny but perfect, and it was mine.

After two semesters at Weatherford Community College, in 1997, I began commuting to UNT two days a week to attend classes, and I worked at Macaroni Grill the other days. I progressed and moved up quickly at work. Life was happy and fun for the most part, but I did still struggle with insecurities because of my past.

I had a few "flings" here and there but nothing serious. I thought being in a relationship would be nice, but I just didn't know if I was relationship material. Between the drug usage and past unhealthy sexual experiences, I wasn't really good at handling sexual relations in a proper, mature, and healthy way. It had only been a little over a year since I had stopped using heroin, broken up with Brandon, and basically started my life over, so I was still figuring out a lot.

I had genuine friends who were good people, cared about me, liked me for exactly who I was, and understood where I had come from, but I was still trying to accept where I had come from and the mistakes I had made. Every time I heard a story of a kid overdosing on heroin, I would just cry and cry and think about how easily that could have been me. I was grateful, but I also wondered why I'd been saved and what I could do to make every day count. What made me more worthy than any of those other people?

Then I had another life-changing experience, but this one didn't come from a place of negativity at all. It was pure and positive. I discovered Mother Nature.

Chapter Six

*I*n my late teen years, my father started a new business endeavor in Alaska. He was an avid fisherman and had taken many fishing trips to Alaska. In 1994, my father, always the entrepreneur, found property for sale in the heart of the Bristol Bay area in King Salmon, Alaska, and he built a brand-new, high-end, all-inclusive fishing lodge, complete with float-planes, boats, and everything to take people on their dream fishing vacations. He called it Rapids Camp Lodge.

I was too distracted and in too bad of shape to have any interest or concern about this new endeavor of my father's when it first started, but by the summer of 1997, I was ready to see it. The outdoors had not been my scene growing up, so I didn't know what to expect in Alaska. I hadn't fished since my early childhood, and I had certainly never fly-fished.

I was in awe when I first arrived in Alaska. It was a sensory overload. Everywhere I looked, there were limitless views. There was a pristine awesomeness that didn't exist anywhere else in the world. While flying over certain areas, I was looking at land that no human would probably ever touch. The vastness and raw beauty put everything in perspective regarding God, life, our foundation, and the gift we've been given to have this amazing earth to use and be part of. It is God's country, and you feel his presence and everything spiritual in the core of your soul.

Fly-fishing was pretty much a disaster for me initially. Although I was embarrassed because all the fishing guides were super cute, and I looked like a complete moron attempting to fling the line from the oversize rod, I still had fun. I got a little better as the week progressed, and when I finally caught a rainbow trout all on my own, you would have thought I had just landed the world record of Alaskan trout because I was so excited.

I had the time of my life, and being in Alaska made me feel complete and whole. I was in nature all day, I went to the bathroom in the tundra, I came within feet of grizzly bears, I wore waders and tromped through the rivers like a real wilderness girl—I felt in my element in the last place I would have ever imagined. I knew I had to go back and spend as much time there as possible, so I asked what I could do to make that happen the next summer. I was told, "You can clean toilets," which meant housekeeping. I was more than fine with that—I would have walked through sewage to stay there for an entire summer.

I continued going to UNT, and then, in the summer of 1998, I went to work at Rapids Camp Lodge. Not only would I be in a remote area of the wilderness for three months, but it was the first time I had gone far away from home on my own. My father and Cindy didn't spend the entire summer at the lodge, so I was on my own for the most part, working like all the other employees. I was twenty-two years old, and I was going

to the "last frontier" to spread my wings and fly and truly discover myself. It was all I could hope for and more. Not only
was I in this amazingly gorgeous environment, but I was also
experiencing a sense of freedom. I had a feeling that I could
be anything I wanted. I was having fun and felt an energy and
excitement I had never felt. It was a high greater than any drug.

I bonded with most of the staff, and we had a great time all
summer. It was only the second season for the lodge to be open
to the public, so the lodge wasn't completely booked and busy
all summer. That gave us time to go camping for three days,
where I had my first experience of existing in the wilderness
without any running water or electricity. It was me and four
guys, which wasn't nearly as scandalous as it sounds. We were
all friends, and the closeness and togetherness I felt in such a
remote area with people whose company I really enjoyed was
enlightening. I was so at peace with myself and with the world
around me. Everything I saw was fresh and new. It was a summer of joy.

My closest friends for the season were two guys, both named
Jason. One Jason went by "Chops," which was a nickname he
had gotten in high school. Chops was actually the stepbrother
of Cindy, my stepmother. I had known Chops since we were
young. We used to have family dinners together when he visited
from Missouri, but I hadn't seen him in years until that summer
in Alaska.

As always, God had a plan, and it was meant to be for
Chops and I to work together that summer and become such
good friends, because the greatest blessings in my life would
ultimately come from that friendship.

Chapter Seven

After my summer in Alaska, I went back to Texas but moved from Fort Worth to Dallas. I continued attending UNT and working at Macaroni Grill. I was given even more responsibilities and was eventually put in charge of all training and scheduling for my location, and I started traveling for the opening development team for new restaurants. I thoroughly enjoyed everything I was doing, and I soon moved into a newer, bigger apartment. I was progressing in life and accomplishing my goals, but I still felt a void. I had made more friends at my job, and there were a few casual relationships, but I was wanting to find "Mr. Right." I thought somehow that would fix whatever void I was still feeling.

I started seeing a new counselor to try to figure out what I was missing in life. I'd had this metamorphosis of sorts in Alaska; then there I was, back in Texas, still a little lost and confused. I had overcome my negative past, I was in school, and I had a job I loved. I had friends and a supportive, loving family, but I just didn't feel completely happy. The counselor recommended a book for me to read called *How to Be Your Own Best Friend*, through which I learned how to let go of negativity and stop being so hard on myself, but it was a long, slow process, as true growth typically is.

Chops—whom I called Jason by this point—and I talked regularly. He was living in Missouri, getting his MBA. Our conversations were friendly and innocent, but there were sometimes hints of flirting. I mentioned it to my counselor, who advised me that "if it ain't broke, don't fix it." I had a tendency to want to orchestrate and control everything around me, but my counselor encouraged me to just go with the flow.

I enjoyed Jason's friendship tremendously, and I looked forward to our phone conversations. Since his stepsister was my stepmother, the flirting could have been perceived as odd, but everything about my family was kind of odd. We were great friends, we enjoyed each other's company, we seemed to have enough in common, and we were at that age where our peers were finishing college, getting married, and moving forward with their lives. Even then, I was hesitant to get into a relationship with someone I was so close to as a friend. Plus, there was the family connection, which could get very uncomfortable if we dated and it didn't work out.

I put our conversations on hold for a while, and I dedicated myself even more to my career at Macaroni Grill, even temporarily quitting school because I was enjoying traveling with the company so much. It was a terrible decision in hindsight, but it seemed acceptable at the time because I was going to school for restaurant management, so I was pursuing my career goals before I had even finished the education. Not a responsible decision, but one that my manager at Macaroni Grill encouraged me to make.

After not talking for a few months and stepping back from the situation, in September of 1999, Jason and I resumed talking and finally decided to pursue our relationship beyond friendship to see where things would go. I visited him in Missouri, and he visited me in Texas regularly. In May of 2000 we got engaged, and I moved to Wichita, Kansas, where he had been hired for his first job after completing his MBA.

The first time I drove to Wichita to visit Jason was a huge deal because I had never driven that far by myself—the drive was a little over five hours. My mother was concerned and asked that I upgrade my cell phone to one that would have coverage everywhere rather than our simple plan that worked only in a limited radius. I was twenty-four, and for all the serious experiences I'd had, I was still rather sheltered and not independent in some ways.

It was dark and rather late when I got to Wichita. I'd never been to Wichita nor driven outside the state of Texas on my own, so I was not confident. I got lost, and this was way before the time of GPS on phones or in the car. As I tried to discern where I was, I heard a noise that sounded like a flat tire on the right side of my vehicle. I immediately pulled over, locked the car doors, and called Jason. Thank goodness I'd upgraded my phone like my mother had requested. I was exasperated. I described to him where I was, and he found me and came to my rescue. He immediately noticed that I did not have a flat tire. I had simply crossed over into the shoulder of the road and hit the rumble strip.

I still had a great deal to learn about life. Nevertheless, I felt I was ready to get married and move on with that phase of my life. Jason was a wonderful man—well educated, kind, hardworking, and loyal—and we were great friends with similar interests. We had a good time together. There seemed no reason not to marry him except that I really wasn't emotionally mature enough to be getting married, nor did I really know what I wanted in life for myself—but, always a headstrong one, I forged ahead.

Our wedding took place in Texas at a Methodist church I had attended with my mom and JB in Weatherford when I had lived with them. I had not gone to church growing up, but ironically, both my parents and their new spouses joined the Methodist faith. I attended with both sets of parents at each of their respective churches and really enjoyed it. While living in Weatherford and attending church with my mother, I had been baptized at twenty-one years old. It was special because it was a choice I'd made independently as an adult. So that was the church where I wanted to get married.

It was a huge affair—traditional and somewhat formal but laid back. We had about 275 guests. Our wedding invitations read "Today I Marry My Friend," which was probably the most accurate way to describe our new union. Jason had been one of my closest friends for three years leading up to our wedding, and being friends as well as lovers is important for a successful marriage.

After the wedding, we continued our life in Wichita, but I didn't really enjoy Wichita. I tried to make the best of it, but it was ugly and cold, and there was not much to do. I went back to school and finally finished my degree at Friends University of Central Kansas (think of the acronym and the fact that it's a Christian school—it's ironic and funny). I got my bachelor of science in business management. I was just glad to be finished with my degree after starting and stopping so many times. I also made some great lifelong friends—Chris and Gayle. We had regular small dinner parties with them, and that was when I officially became a foodie, and my love for cooking really developed.

We moved back to Dallas in December 2001. I missed my family terribly, and Jason's job in Wichita wasn't going the direction he wanted. He found a great job at a hedge fund in Dallas but had to move a month before I was able to leave my job in Wichita.

I made weekend trips to Dallas throughout the month of December before I officially moved back, with improved long-distance driving skills and an awareness of rumble strips. The first weekend I drove to Dallas was the weekend of the holiday party for the hedge fund where Jason had started working. Even though I had grown up in a privileged environment with many nice things, I had never experienced anything so glamorous and fabulous. Everything his company's management did was over the top—not quite to *The Wolf of Wall Street* level, as I never saw illegal drug usage, but there were plenty of overly lavish dinners, parties, bottle service, private jets, and suites at all the big concerts and sporting events.

Even though I had grown up with many nice things, and Jason and I enjoyed the benefits from my upbringing, the actions of Jason's management were unlike anything we had experienced. Jason came from very humble beginnings in the Ozarks of Missouri. He had been raised by his mom, who had worked and gone to school, and his stepdad, who had been disabled and hadn't worked, and money had always been scarce. This new world was foreign to him, but he deserved the rewards. He had worked very hard to better himself and leave his childhood environment, and he was achieving his goals. That was and is one of the things I have always respected most about him.

We moved to an apartment in the Uptown neighborhood of Dallas. Uptown was the hottest new neighborhood in

Dallas and was where all the postcollege twenty-somethings lived. Back in 1996 when Uptown was being developed, I had worked for a company that had been developing the neighborhood. I'd worked there right up until when my apartment had been raided by the DEA. I had come full circle.

We had a great social circle. We worked hard and played hard. I got a job at a health-care recruiting firm. It wasn't the job of my dreams, so eventually I decided to go back to school at UNT so I could get a teaching degree. I quit my full-time job and went back to work part time, managing the training for a Macaroni Grill in Dallas, not because I had to work but because I missed the restaurant industry.

Life seemed great except that Jason and I fought, and we fought excessively. We fought in private; we fought in public. We were that couple that everyone always knew was going to have some blowup. That's not to say that we didn't have fun, too, but I still didn't know how to really be in a healthy relationship, and I was still trying to figure out who I really was.

In the summer of 2002, my father and Cindy ended their relationship. It was Cindy's decision, and my father was heartbroken. I was furious. They had been together for nearly ten years, and I had finally convinced myself that she wasn't just a gold digger, and now I didn't know what to think. He absolutely adored her. To this day I don't fully know the story, and their story is not mine to tell. But as time went on, many years later, I started to understand a little. Cindy had been twenty-six when they'd gotten together, and my father had been nearly fifty. She probably hadn't known what she wanted long term in life. I realized later that I didn't really know what I wanted at twenty-six either.

My father was emotionally crushed, and I wanted to be there

for him. It was such a shock to him. Nobody had seen it coming. And the divorce seemed to go on forever, much longer than my parents' had, which I couldn't understand because there was a lot less to sort out financially between him and Cindy. Complicating matters even further was the fact that Cindy was Jason's stepsister. They hadn't been overly close growing up, but they had become closer when he and I had gotten married. It made for an awkward situation, which added more stress to our already strained marriage.

My father was more present in my life after the divorce. Jason and I took trips with him and had dinner with him regularly, which was fine with me because I immensely enjoyed my father's company. We formed a new bond, and it was the beginning of a new relationship for us. We really got to know each other as peers and became companions and confidants.

The bickering between me and Jason escalated, and it seemed neither of us could make the other happy. My biggest issue was that I wore my emotions on my sleeve. I always wanted to talk and hash things out. I was passionate and demonstrative and had no problem telling people exactly what was on my mind. If Jason made me mad, I would tell him. If I made him mad, he wouldn't tell me, but I'd still know because he would act negatively toward me. We didn't know how to communicate well. We had a really big argument in May 2003, right after our second anniversary, and then we called a truce. Things seemed okay for a while—good enough that we talked about having a baby.

Other people we knew were starting families. I turned twenty-eight the summer of 2003, and I had always thought I wanted to have kids before I was thirty. One day that summer Jason and I were enjoying a beautiful day with cocktails and friends at my childhood lake house and it hit me: "I'm ready for more than this; I want something more fulfilling. I want a baby."

When I became pregnant, I knew instinctively before I took any test. I had this tingling inside me. It was like I could already feel life growing in my womb. A few weeks later, without even telling Jason what I was doing, I took a pregnancy test. I don't know why I didn't tell him. I think I just wanted that moment to myself. The test showed positive—I was pregnant. I went out to the living room, where he was on the computer, and said, "I'm pregnant." He hugged me and said congratulations.

I just happened to have an upcoming appointment to go to the doctor because I was also due for my annual exam. I was about six weeks pregnant, and the doctor offered to do a sonogram. What I saw during that sonogram I would have never imagined in my wildest dreams. I was pregnant with twins!

The doctor confirmed that my due date was in mid-August, but since I was having twins, I wouldn't be allowed to go past thirty-eight weeks. That meant the babies would be born the day before my birthday. Everything he said to me was kind of a blur. I couldn't believe I was having two babies. I just kept thinking, "Okay, God, I guess you think I can handle this." It was daunting and unbelievable, but also exciting. The doctor explained the possibility of absorption, where one twin literally absorbs the other during the very early stages of pregnancy, or one of the fetuses is reabsorbed into the mother's own body, but if this didn't happen in the first ten weeks of pregnancy, it wasn't going to happen. That was kind of creepy and bizarre sounding, but it was also the first time I felt the enormous amount of love for my babies. The thought of losing one of them was already overwhelming.

Jason and I began looking for a house. "Our overpriced box"—as I liked to call our trendy, small apartment in

Uptown—was not going to provide nearly enough room for a family of four. We found a neighborhood that we liked and spent our weekends going to open houses to find the perfect house, and we succeeded. It was a 1960s ranch-style brick home in the Devonshire neighborhood of Dallas, which was a popular neighborhood for couples and young families. It had four bedrooms, two living areas, and a large front yard, back-yard, and side yard. It needed some remodeling, but it suited us just fine.

I continued working at Macaroni Grill until February of 2004, when I was about three months pregnant and just beginning to show. I finished the spring semester of school as I had planned and then would take a break until the babies turned one. We moved into the house in March, and I began planning for the arrival of the greatest blessings of my life. Sitting at the kitchen table one day in late March, I felt the faintest movement in my stomach—my first time to feel them kicking. I cried tears of joy. It was the most amazing feeling knowing they were growing inside me

I had an incredible pregnancy. I was huge, and the end of the pregnancy was in the heat of the Texas summer, so I was uncomfortable and hot, but I was healthy, and the babies were healthy and growing well. I did prenatal yoga, I walked every day, I swam, and I cooked a lot and even baked, which was odd because baking had never been my thing. I was nesting. I made sure everything was ready, or as ready as one can be, for the biggest journey ever in life.

The big day was scheduled for Friday, August 6. I was so ready. When I went in on July 28, I asked the doctor, "Please, can we go ahead and do this?" I was getting restless, big, and uncomfortable. He explained that regulations did not permit him to "take" the babies prior to thirty-eight weeks, but if I had any signs of labor, he would go ahead and do it. I was sent on my way.

July 30 is my mother and JB's wedding anniversary. My mother must have had "mother's intuition," because the morning of July 30, 2004, she asked me if I was going to give her the best anniversary present in the world by making them grandparents. By that afternoon, I was having signs of early labor. Jason's mother happened to be in town for a funeral, so the three of us went to the hospital. My mother, JB, and my father all got there just in time to see me whisked away to the operating room. I left the maternity room simply their daughter; the next time they saw me, in just a little over an hour, I was a mother with children of my own. It's amazing how quickly life changes.

The doctors had classic rock playing in the operating room. There was a big sheet raised between my abdomen and them, so I couldn't see the doctors but could hear them talking and knew they were beginning the surgery. As they cut me open, they were discussing dinner plans for later in the weekend, acting like it was another day at the office for them. I was somewhat annoyed at their attitudes about the whole thing, but I suppose when you had delivered countless babies and performed countless C-sections, it *was* just another day at the office. But for me, it was the most important day of my life.

They finally stopped their idle chitchat and announced that they saw babies. George Harrison's "My Sweet Lord" was playing, and there couldn't have been a more fitting song, with the lyrics repeating, "I really want to see you." Our baby boy came out first. I immediately heard him crying, which was the most incredible sound. They announced he was healthy, quickly cleaned him up, and gave him to Jason, who brought him over to me so I could see him. I couldn't hold him yet because there was still another baby coming. But I saw him, and he was perfect. We'd already decided on a name—Gavin.

The doctors announced that they saw "Baby B," and I asked if it was definitely a girl. All through my pregnancy, I'd been told "Baby B" was a girl, but only with 95 percent surety. They confirmed the baby was a girl, and they also announced that her head was flat because her brother had situated himself on top of it in the womb. Her head ultimately turned out to be fine, but it was always a funny story within our family. They announced that she was healthy, cleaned her up, and gave her to Jason so he could bring her over to me. I saw Kieley (she was given my mother's maiden name) for the first time, and she was absolutely beautiful.

I finally got to hold them, and when I looked at both babies, I cried with an overwhelming joy and love that I had never felt in my life. I had read every book I could get my hands on about being a new mother; I had prepared in every way imaginable, but nothing that I'd read and nothing that anybody had told me could have possibly prepared me for that moment when I saw my children and held them for the first time. Suddenly everything in the world and in my life made sense. Everything I had done had somehow led me to this moment. My purpose for being in this world was right in front of me. The meaning of my life and of all life was crystal clear. God had given me the greatest gift of all, and my reason for living was more obvious to me than anything had ever been in my life.

Chapter Eight

As it is for all new parents, those first few weeks at home were a whirlwind of feedings, sleepless nights, countless diaper changes—our lives were not our own anymore.

With the exception of a few rough nights, I really enjoyed being a new mom. Gavin and Kieley were wonderful, angelic, healthy babies. Gavin was needier than Kieley and was the more high-strung baby. Kieley could soothe herself indefinitely in her swing and was always happy to be held but also able to be at peace on her own. She started sleeping through the night at seven weeks. With the Ferber method of letting him cry it out, Gavin was sleeping through the night at eleven weeks.

I loved being at home with the babies. We would have tummy time, music time, feeding time, nap time, and dance time, where I would bring them outside to sit on a blanket, and I would dance around in a goofy fashion to music just to watch the amused (and sometimes bewildered) looks on their faces.

That's not to say that I didn't have the stress that many new moms have—I certainly did. I wasn't perfect, and I lost my temper at times and wasn't always patient, but I embraced being a new mother. I made all the baby food from scratch, and I loved watching them do every single new thing, from rolling over, learning to sit, holding their bottles on their own, trying new foods—anything and everything.

We had the babies baptized in November of 2004. The baptism was a wonderful affair followed by a big celebration with a big luncheon at our house, even though the day had begun with Jason and I having a huge blowup. Poor Kieley, being the sensitive girl she is, had cried all the way to the church and during the ceremony. The baby who rarely cried was crying all morning during her big public debut.

As the twins got older and could sit up in the bathtub, we made a big production out of bath time every night. When Jason got home from work each day, we turned the radio on the "oldies" station and sang while we bathed the kids. It was a fun time of the day and some of the best memories of their infancy. We hosted Thanksgiving at our house that year, and it was a big, festive occasion with family members from both of our families. We drove to Jason's hometown in Missouri for the twins' first Christmas—a long six-hour drive with two infants, with both kids having bowel blowouts continually along the way. We laughed about it and chalked it up to the many experiences of being first-time parents with infant twins.

I consumed my days with taking the babies on long walks and jogging with a jogging stroller. It eventually led to me training for my first marathon, which then led to a full-time hobby with multiple 5Ks, half marathons, and marathons over the years. As the babies got older and approached toddler age, I would take them to the neighborhood park. One day I met another mom who invited me to the neighborhood playgroup. I never understood the dynamic, though, because I liked spending time with my kids and interacting with them, and the purpose of the playgroup was for the moms to interact. I guess I was the weird one, though, because playgroups existed everywhere for that very purpose. I never felt a connection with the other mothers, but I guess the connection was that we all had kids the same age. At that stage in my life, I didn't understand the importance of connecting with other moms simply because we had kids the same age. I didn't understand the value in having other moms that I could depend on and vice versa. That, of course, was how kids at the infancy or toddler ages made connections for when they began school later, but I didn't realize the need for "networking" at that time.

The issues that Jason and I had before we had the twins were only magnified after we became parents. The fighting continued and even escalated, and now there were children present to witness it. We tried to do things to keep our relationship positive and connected, such as a weekly Wednesday date night, but the tension was always there.

My father was over for dinner one night toward the end of summer in 2005. I had stayed home for a full year, and I was ready to go back to school and finish the teaching degree I had started. I loved being a stay-at-home mom, but the twins were going to be starting preschool part time, and it was time for all of us to get out into the world. My father broached the subject of me coming to work with him. He felt the businesses could be run better; they needed a fresh set of eyes, a new perspective. In the back of my mind, I had always thought I would have some involvement in the family business one day. After all, I was an only child and would be the sole heir to everything, but it wasn't something I had given serious thought to recently. The legal concerns of the Gas Pipe weren't prevalent like they had been when I was a child, and the social stigma had all but disappeared. All our friends, even the highly educated elite of Dallas whom Jason worked with, thought that my family owning the Gas Pipe and my father's entrepreneurial skills were impressive.

I told my father that if I went to work for him, my children would always have to be the top priority, to which he told me he would have it no other way. He also knew what a driven person I was, and he suspected I would dive in and take on more than I expected. We worked out the parameters, which on my end meant having someone who could help with the twins while they weren't in preschool. My godmother, Emma, as fate would have it, was in a transitional point in her life. Just as she'd helped take care of me when I was a child, she came on board to help take care of the twins—and make yummy, delicious food for us and generally help manage the household. It was a match made in heaven.

I started work in October 2005. I really didn't know what I was doing at first. There was no real set plan or a definitive job description. I was told that Amy Lynn Inc.—the purchasing arm, distribution, and administrative support entity for the Gas Pipe stores—needed to be more profitable. There were six Gas Pipe stores at the time, as well as Amy Lynn Inc. and Rapids Camp Lodge. My father was a self-made multimillionaire and had done very well, but Amy Lynn Inc. needed a breath of fresh air. It was lacking in the human resource area, and generally the business practices were a little antiquated and needed to be modernized. I dove in headfirst and absorbed as much information as I could, then made some immediate, obvious changes such as updating the payroll process by contracting with a payroll company and getting everyone set up on direct deposit. We had a POS (point-of-sale) system that had never worked properly, and until we could get it working correctly and efficiently, keeping track of inventory in a modernized and accurate fashion was challenging.

Because the head-shop industry wasn't mainstream, products didn't have bar codes and PLU numbers like most products in other industries. These had already been created for our stores, but the software that had been bought to manage it didn't fully suit our needs. So, I brought in an experienced IT consultant, Ro Rojas, who was able to help us and would eventually create a customized POS software, and he would become more involved in a leadership role in the company in the following years.

It had been several years since a new store had opened, and I thought it was time we did just that. We began looking for a new location, and with my father's guidance, I picked a Gas Pipe location for the first time. I was a nervous wreck wondering whether the store would be successful, and thank goodness, it was. It was the first location where we rented the space rather than buying the building. My father was against renting, but real estate was harder and harder to come by, so renting was the only way to really expand. We eventually bought the shopping center where we had been renting the new store. My father had always believed real estate was the best investment ("You can't go wrong with dirt"), but years later, we would wonder if owning so much "dirt" made us a target.

The company was growing and becoming more profitable and successful since I had joined, and that's not to say it was because of me. There were a lot of factors. I think it was motivating for my father and the company to have some new energy in there, and that new energy wasn't just me—it was the policies and other new people I brought into the company. I had a lot to learn, but I was eager and ready to do whatever I could to make it even more successful.

Jason and I had discussed my return to work in depth, and we had both agreed it would be a good thing. When it actually happened, though, it brought even more stress into our marriage. The kids were still my top priority, but now I was a working mom with interests outside of the home. Jason and I became even more disconnected. Our Wednesday date nights were replaced with weekly marriage-counseling sessions.

As we continued to try to work on our marriage, I found confidence and enthusiasm in new interests, not just my work. I ran my first full marathon in December 2005, just a little after a year from when I'd had the twins. I continued running at least one a year, going to different cities each time. I ran with a running club, which gave me a new exercise and social outlet. I also joined a book club, which became one of my greatest sources of strength and enjoyment over the years.

In 2007, Jason and I stopped going to marriage counseling. We had been going for about two years, and although I didn't verbalize it at the time, I felt we weren't getting anywhere with it. Jason thought that we just didn't need to go anymore, and he understood my agreement to not go as my way of saying that we didn't need it anymore and that, inadvertently, we were fine. I had grown and changed, and while I loved my kids more than anything in the world, the person I had been when I'd gotten married at twenty-five was not the same as the person I was becoming. Jason was a good man, but the constant arguing and disconnect were becoming increasingly frustrating. When we stopped going to counseling, I resolved that I would either suck it up and do everything I could to stop arguing, even if I was unhappy about something, or I would end the marriage. I knew I couldn't live in limbo forever, and I would have to commit one way or another.

In December 2007, my father and I decided to expand our lodge business by opening a lodge in Santiago, Chile. My father had found a beautiful lodge for sale in the northern Patagonia region, so we decided to visit it.

I would be gone for a week. I was so excited but also nervous to leave the kids and go so far away, but at least I would have cell service. It was a ten-hour flight just to get to Santiago, and then there was another hour-and-a-half flight to Puerto Montt and then a lengthy drive to the remote lodge. It was going to be an adventure. I had always wanted to travel to different parts of the world, and I was finally getting to.

We flew overnight, and I woke up in Santiago—how amazing was it that just a few hours prior I had been on a different continent? We had lunch with a prominent attorney, whom we had been introduced to by our attorney from Texas. The two of them would facilitate the purchase of the property. Arturo, our Chilean attorney, was such a gentleman, and we had a beautiful lunch with fresh fish and Chilean sauvignon blanc, pouring freely, as well as the traditional Chilean drink, pisco sours. We dined alfresco, overlooking the expansive golfing green at the attorney's country club. I felt exotic and prominent just being there. Just the day before, I had been in Dallas with my children, living a normal life, and now here I was in Santiago, a Latin metropolis thousands of miles away, having an exquisite lunch and discussing foreign real estate ventures.

The next morning, we began our journey to Patagonia. I discovered quickly how differently things operated in Chile, particularly as we got to a smaller city. The town of Puerto Montt, considered the gateway to Patagonia, had the biggest airport in the area. But in 2007, tourism was just beginning to really develop there, so it still left a lot to be desired. Our rental car, which initially couldn't be located by the rental company, had a missing dashboard and was in very poor condition. Driving through the town of Puerto Montt was an adventure in itself. The streets were winding and crowded, and it was nearly impossible to tell the correct direction to drive on each street. We finally got out of the crowded town and found ourselves on a dirt road, which was barely a road as it had more potholes than not, but it was actually designated as a highway. Eventually we made it to the ferry, where we would cross the bay. While waiting for the ferry, we went to the local empanada stand, which was a traditional Chilean food. The crispy fried dough filled with cheese, *carne*, or *mariscos* (a mixture of local seafood) was gooey, delicious, and greasy in the best way possible.

We departed the ferry and began our journey into a really remote area of Chile. The poorly managed dirt road continued, with so many bumps that you could almost feel your internal organs moving out of place, but soon I was so mesmerized by my surroundings and the scenery that I didn't care about my comfort. We were slipping further and further from society, and everywhere I looked was lush greenness with beautiful flowers. It felt like we were slipping into another universe. It was paradise, and I had never seen anything so gorgeous.

We arrived in the town of Hornopirén. It was a picturesque scene—a small fishing village set on the bay, overlooking the Andes. If you stood in town and looked around, you would see water and the Andes everywhere you looked.

We finally arrived at the lodge just outside of town, and it looked like how I'd always pictured the Garden of Eden. There were vibrant flowers, fruit trees, and lush vegetation all around, surrounded by the Andes. It was absolutely spectacular.

We knew we had to purchase it. Apart from some remodeling and a few maintenance issues, it was a perfect piece of property, and they were asking a reasonable price. We went back to Santiago and closed the deal at the attorney's office. Rapids Camp Lodge had now officially expanded into South America.

Just like when I'd gone to Alaska for the first time, going to Chile impacted my life. My eyes were opened to a whole new world and culture. I had never experienced anything like that—the land, the food, the people. Everything was so different from anything back in Texas, and I loved it. As foreign as it was, I somehow felt right at home and at peace there. Nobody spoke English, and my Spanish, which I had studied for four years in high school and had spoken sparingly since, was in pretty bad shape at that point, but somehow we managed to communicate. Everyone greeted each other with a polite kiss on the cheek. I loved the warmness of it, and I loved the beauty of everything there.

When I returned from Chile, I had changed even more and felt even more disconnected in my marriage, but I wasn't ready to give up on it yet. I had children to think about, and I didn't want them growing up with divorced parents. Although my parents had had an amicable divorce and an ongoing relationship as friends, I knew many divorced parents did not. I struggled with the idea of which was worse—growing up with divorced parents or growing up surrounded by constant arguing and negativity.

I made a second trip to Chile in April 2008. The weekend before I left, Jason, the kids, and I went to visit Jason's family in Missouri. On the way back, Jason and I had a huge argument in the car. There was yelling and name-calling, and the kids were crying in the back seats. That night, as I was getting the kids ready for bed, Kieley asked me why we yelled so much. My decision at that moment was clear. She was only three years old and didn't understand the impact of what she was asking, but I knew we couldn't go on like that any longer. Yes, I hated the idea of divorce, but I just didn't see our marriage getting better and didn't want my kids witnessing so much negativity.

I left for Chile the next day, knowing most likely what I was going to do when I returned from the trip, but I didn't talk with Jason about it prior to my departure. We went to bed that night not speaking, on the eve of me leaving for a weeklong trip overseas.

During that trip to Chile, I went on an incredibly beautiful and challenging hike. Even though I had run numerous marathons at that point and exercised regularly, I had never done anything like this hike, either physically or spiritually. It was a strenuous four-hour hike uphill and then downhill on the return. It was steep in many parts, muddy and slippery, and even scary in parts. I wasn't alone—I went with a friend who was working at our lodge, and he was much more experienced in that sort of terrain. I didn't want to seem incapable, so I continued to forge ahead, panting and gasping for air all the way, trying to keep up with him, not wanting to appear like a wuss or pathetic city girl who didn't know her way through the wilderness. The farther we went on the hike, the farther we slipped deep into the forest, where I felt as though I was going into another world, almost a magical world. It was almost mystical. The locals in the area actually did believe that the forest was enchanted and haunted with special spirits and powers, both good and bad. I felt absorbed into a new realm of existence, and with every excruciating step and each breath I took, I felt powerful and renewed. As we descended and made our way out of the forest and back into reality, I felt cleansed and stronger than I had ever felt in my life.

That hike brought me great clarity. I had already made many mistakes in life, but I had been given a second chance at life. I had been given the greatest gifts from God with my two children. I had thought, seven years prior, that I was ready to get married, but I hadn't been. I had tried my best to make it work and honor my commitment, but we weren't happy, and it couldn't go on like that anymore. I had been too young, at least emotionally, when I'd gotten married. I hadn't been "made" yet, and I had still been trying to find myself. As I did find myself, I realized my needs were different than I had thought, and that wasn't Jason's fault. It was time to part ways. I had my children and my job, and I was finally figuring out who I wanted to be in life. I was becoming comfortable and confident with myself. I knew I was about to make a decision that would be hurtful and cause grief and pain, but I believed, after lots of thought and prayer, that it was the right decision and needed to happen.

I came home from Chile and told Jason I was filing for divorce. I outlined my reasons and a summary of all of our arguments and disagreements, which I don't feel the need to disclose publicly or harp on anymore. We are still good friends to this day, and I value that. I don't see any point in airing the details of our dirty laundry publicly. We do an excellent job of co-parenting and consulting each other regularly on decisions involving the children, and since we don't live together, we get along just as we did as friends before we ever got married. Divorce is not ideal for children, but I like to think we've made the best of it.

Chapter Nine

I spent April and May of 2008 adjusting to my life in Dallas as a single mom. Jason moved to a nearby apartment, and I stayed in the house. I started seeing a counselor, and she helped me greatly through the transition. She asked me about dating, and I was adamant that I had no desire for that. I still wasn't officially divorced, and I didn't trust myself to make the right decisions for dating. Besides, I was really happy with just being me and being a mom. She encouraged me to be open to the possibility; after all, I was young, and even though I was just now getting divorced, I had kind of left my marriage a long time ago. It would be good for me to learn about healthy dating. To help me sort out my feelings, she told me to try writing a list of what I would want in a partner so that if I ever did date, I would know what it was I really wanted. This sort of exercise would help me make good, sound decisions instead of just getting swept away for the wrong reasons. I followed her advice. I put my list away in a drawer to reference later should I ever start dating anyone, and I wouldn't look at it again for a long time because I wasn't planning on dating or pursuing any sort of romantic relationship.

I was getting more involved in the operation and management of Rapids Camp, and I made plans to spend several weeks in Alaska with the kids in the summer of 2008. I had been taking them there every summer for a week since they were one, but this would be our first time to spend extended time. The kids, Emma, and I left for Alaska in early June. I was ready to have the best summer ever, and it started off amazingly. I began the summer running my fifth marathon in Anchorage. It was completely different from any other marathon I had run. Less than a year prior, I had run in the New York City Marathon, and now I was running in Alaska on trails and gravel roads, and I even saw a moose along the way. The two marathons couldn't have been two more diversified scenes—a parallel for how my life had changed in the past year and how different I felt.

I loved being at the lodge. It was exactly what I needed: the energy and closeness among everyone and being back in the last frontier, working in the place I loved so much. I wasn't cleaning toilets anymore, although I was willing to jump in and do whatever was needed. I was in a managerial role, and I was excited to help make Rapids Camp the best lodge it could be. It had a strong foundation, and the business had grown considerably since I had last worked there, but I wanted to make it even more organized. Dan Herrig, the lodge manager, was eager and happy to have someone to share the responsibilities.

My father had told me that in Dan Herrig, he had finally found the guy he had been looking for to properly run the lodge. There had been a string of managers come and go over the years. My father needed someone who fully understood the industry and was dedicated and responsible enough to manage things properly. Dan had been working in the Alaska fishing-lodge industry his entire adult life, and he had more of a passion for fishing and the outdoors than anyone I had ever met. My interactions with Dan prior to the summer of 2008 had been limited to a very negative miscommunication we'd had a couple of years previously when I had been complaining about something I shouldn't have been. Later, we visited some when he came to Dallas to work with my father on preseason lodge preparations, and we had spent time together within a group when I had been in Chile. As I had taken on more of a role in the lodge management, that had meant communicating with Dan more as well.

Dan offered to take me, the kids, and Emma fishing one day. He was such a gentleman, and it was generous of him to offer to take two ladies and two three-year-old children fishing. The kids knew him as Mr. Dan, and he never lost his patience with them throughout the day as they said "Mr. Dan" repeatedly, followed up with questions or silly kid comments. He was calm and kind and fun. We had a storybook fishing day where everyone caught big fish. I caught the biggest salmon I had ever caught in my life. I was so excited and caught up in the moment when I saw the size of the fish that I jumped up and down, screaming, and then reached up and gave Dan a surprise peck on the cheek to show my gratitude. I don't know what possessed me to do it, but I was giddy and having fun.

Later in the day, as I was daydreaming and watching from afar Dan clean our fish, Emma asked what I was thinking about. I think she somehow already knew. I said, "Honestly, I'm standing here thinking what a great guy Dan is, and it's too bad I'm not ready to date, but I'm not, and I can't even go there right now." Whether I was ready or not, he had me hooked that day. I had never met a guy like Dan. He was strong, both inside and out, and he had an integrity and character about him that was a rarity. He was fun, compassionate, respectful, passionate about life, positive, and upbeat, not to mention very handsome. More than anything, though, he was beyond amazing with my kids. That day of fishing was beautiful and so smooth and easy. I felt like we bonded. It felt the way I had hoped a day of fishing as a family would feel. It just felt right.

I had no idea if Dan felt the same way or if he was just being a stand-up guy by showing us a nice time. Even if there was something between us, no way would I let myself go there. I wasn't divorced yet, even though in my heart I was, and it was absolutely too soon. While I was very comfortable, confident, and happy in my own skin and where I was in life, being newly separated and almost divorced meant I was kind of a mess, and I could not bring someone like Dan into that. He was a good guy, a really good guy.

We were scheduled to go back to Dallas the day after our perfect day of fishing, but Emma pointed out that I should stay because the kids were going with Jason to Missouri to visit family immediately upon their return home. She could see how happy I was in Alaska. It made sense, and I made arrangements to change my ticket, and she and the kids would fly home. I cried watching them board the plane without me. They had never gone anywhere without me, so it was emotional.

That decision to stay would change my life forever in a wonderful way. We had a staff night out at the local bar in town. It was a typical evening of drinking, dancing, and fun. Dan and I spent much of the evening talking and flirting, and I was excited but had trepidation. I didn't want to do anything stupid that could have negative consequences. I didn't completely trust my judgment and didn't want to rush into another relationship, but I felt this very real attraction to him. It was not a feeling I had ever felt before. It wasn't just a physical attraction or a crush. I was deeply attracted to him as a person.

After we returned to the lodge, Dan suggested we go somewhere and talk in private, which was somewhat difficult to do in the close quarters of the lodge. We drove to the nearby boat launch, where we stayed until the wee hours of the morning, talking and getting to know each other more. That night, we had our first kiss. He likes to say *I* kissed him, and I say *he* kissed me. To this day it's an ongoing joke between us, but no matter who kissed whom first, I knew then that I never wanted to kiss anybody else again. I felt the kiss all the way down to my toes, and I still feel that way every time we kiss. I knew that night what it truly felt like to be falling in love.

Dan and I wouldn't ride into the sunset together immediately. There had to be some holding back and reevaluating things before we made our relationship official. The night at the boat launch was magical. We shared a lot, discussing our faith in God—his was a little more of the traditional church type than mine, and mine was based on life circumstances, but nevertheless we shared a deep faith. He told me that he loved the kind of mother I was, and that was something that attracted him to me. I told him that the way he'd interacted with the kids was so attractive and important to me. I told him I trusted him and felt safe with him. At one point he looked at me and told me he could get lost in my eyes forever. The night was full of sweet memories that left my heart glowing. One of the most important things he shared with me that night was that marriage was very important to him and that he didn't date just to date, and although he wasn't a virgin, it had been several years since he'd had sex, and he was now waiting for marriage. That one kind of threw me for a loop, and I told him that I had no intention of ever getting married again because I just didn't think it was for me, and the "no sex" situation was a new concept. I usually had sex with guys and then figured out the emotions later. Things with Dan would be different, and that both intrigued me and scared me.

After I left Alaska to go back to Texas for a few weeks, Dan learned through the grapevine that I wasn't officially divorced, which was upsetting to him because he would never intentionally be with a married woman. I explained to him that in my heart and mind, I was divorced, but he was not accepting of the situation. He also wasn't sure if I was someone he could see a future with, and he didn't date just to date. I was devastated. The sadness I felt surprised me. It made me realize that I really, truly did have feelings for him, but he appeared to not be returning them. I was shocked because I believed that he was such an honest guy who would never say the things he had said to me that night if he hadn't truly meant them. I just couldn't wrap my head around the situation, but I had to accept it and not dwell on it because we worked together, and I couldn't let anything affect that negatively.

The kids, Emma, and I went back to Alaska in September of 2008.

Other than the required communications about work-related things, Dan and I hadn't really talked in weeks. I had sent him a couple of personal emails but had never received a response with any substance. About a week before my September trip, Dan emailed me. There was nothing at all about the email that was work related. It was just a friendly email asking how I was doing. I couldn't believe it, but I was cautious. I thought maybe he was just trying to break the ice by being friendly so things wouldn't be negative when I got there.

When we got to the lodge, I couldn't wait to talk and figure out what was going through his head. Toward the end of the night, Dan suggested we go to the office and talk where we could have some privacy. The first thing he asked was if I was officially divorced, which I was. He told me that he couldn't get me off his mind, and he wanted to give things a try. I told him he had really broken my heart. I was nervous now. I hadn't expected him to have such an effect on me, and I really hadn't wanted to get my heart broken, but in a way, it had been a blessing because it had shown me just how serious my feelings really were for him. That reassured me in my decision to be with him. We talked for a while and then decided it was time to go to bed, in our separate places, and we would reconvene tomorrow. I had taken my shoes off at the beginning of our talk that night, and when it was time to go, he reached for my shoes and gingerly placed each one back on each foot. It was such a small gesture but was so caring. It was, and still is, the simple things like that about Dan that make me feel so loved by him.

Things between Dan and I progressed quickly after that. We spent a day fishing again with Emma and the kids, but it wasn't like the magical day we'd had earlier in the summer. Both of the kids had complete meltdowns; it was stressful, they were unhappy, and I was a little nervous that Dan would have second thoughts. But if he was going to be part of our lives, this was real life some days, meltdowns and all. He handled it all with grace and compassion.

We spent several nights together, but I would sneak out of his cabin early and go back to my father's house, where the kids and I stayed. We couldn't spend every night together because we needed to get sleep at some point. Even though we weren't having sex, there was still plenty of physical attraction and lots and lots of talking. Nobody had ever been so interested in really getting to know me, and Dan had a way of making me feel like the most important person in the world. He wrote me love notes and poems and got my plate for me during meals and always made sure I had something to drink. Although we were in remote Alaska and didn't go on any actual dates, we were still dating and having a better time getting to know each other than any actual date I'd ever been on. I was floating on a cloud twenty-four seven.

We finally told my father what was going on with us, and he wasn't shocked. I think Dan and I were so into our own little world and so distracted in our new relationship that we hadn't realized that what we thought was a secret was obvious to all. My father was happy and said he couldn't think of a better guy for me to be with.

After spending two weeks in Alaska, I went back to Texas, and Dan stayed the remaining two weeks of the season. We made plans for me to visit him in early October in Oregon, where he lived when he wasn't working at the lodges. This was going to be the one big issue for our relationship. I lived in Dallas and was committed to being there for my kids and my job, as that was where most of our businesses were headquartered. Dan lived in Oregon and was an avid steelhead fisherman who spent his time surrounded by the mountains of the Northwest and fishing the plentiful streams. He was never going to move to Dallas, where it was hot, crowded, and ugly, with no mountains and certainly no steelhead fishing. This was one of the obstacles he had mentioned when he had been explaining to me why we couldn't be together, but I had said we could work that out somehow—I had tons of airline miles. I was determined not to let that be a negative factor in us being together, because in my mind it was better to be with someone part of the time than not be with them at all.

I had never met anyone like Dan. I was attracted to everything about him from the inside out. His faith was an inspiration. We had a genuinely fun time together, either being romantic or being completely silly and laughing. In addition to the romantic side of our relationship, he was also my friend and confidant. It had only been a couple of months since the finalization of my divorce, and I was obviously aware of that, and it gave me reason to pause, but the attraction between Dan and I and our desire to be together was too strong. Our attraction was like magnets or two pieces of a puzzle that fit perfectly together. I had spent a lot of my life not knowing what I truly wanted or needed, so even if the timing wasn't ideal, I finally knew and understood exactly what I wanted and needed, and there was no real reason to wait. One day I pulled out that list my counselor had encouraged me to write about what I would want in a partner; Dan and the list matched.

A few weeks after my trip to Oregon, Dan came to Dallas to spend a few days with me and the kids, who truly loved him. We then went on a trip, just the two of us, to Los Barriles, a small town in Baja California Sur, Mexico. This would be the final test for our relationship. Traveling can be stressful and intimate. The ability to be able to travel together is a true testament to any relationship. Other than the normal early dating insecurities—such as having privacy to go to the bathroom, hoping there wouldn't be embarrassing noises or smells—the trip was perfect and beautiful. We went fishing, cooked together in the little casita we were renting, frequented the local bars and restaurants, and took long walks on the beach. During one of those walks Dan said that he wanted to walk on that beach together when we were eighty and eighty-three. I knew then I would spend the rest of my life with Dan, and I never looked back or had one ounce of doubt. Next to the love I have for my children, my feelings for Dan are the surest thing in my world. I felt it that first day we went fishing together and the first time we kissed, and it just continued to blossom and grow from there. He became my rock, and his presence in my life and the children's lives has made us all better people. He is the strongest person I know. None of us had any idea how much his strength and all our faith would be tested in the years to come, yet Dan never faltered.

We spent the next year working and traveling. In the spring of 2009, we took the kids to Chile and on a trip to the Oregon coast, where we rented a house. Dan's brother also came to the coast, and the kids quickly grew to love Uncle Mikey. Dan came to Texas for our first Christmas together, which we spent at my mom and JB's house, where he met them for the first time. Like everyone else, they loved Dan. I had met Dan's parents a couple of times, and I took the kids to visit them in Washington so they could meet them. They couldn't have been more welcoming and accepting of the new blended family dynamic. They welcomed me and the kids with open arms and immediately referred to the kids as their grandkids.

Even though Dan and I were raised extremely differently, the commonality in our childhoods was that our parents were unique and had done things differently than most. My parents had been liberal hippies who had been different from just about everyone in Clifton, Texas. Even though I'd had rules and strictness and order in the home, I had known the ideology and belief system of my parents were very different than those of my friends' parents. Then, of course, there was the Gas Pipe, which was extremely different than what anyone else's parents did for a living. Dan's parents were unique in a different way. When he was in fifth grade, his mom turned off the cable service, so the only thing they used the TV for was to watch rented movies. Friday nights, even when Dan was in high school, were always family movie nights. His parents were very protective of him, and he wasn't allowed to go to many social functions. They've said since that they were maybe too protective. Dan has always said he is grateful for how he was raised because that is why he learned to love the outdoors so much and find joy in more intrinsic things. I would have to agree that his parents did an excellent job because I know the man he is today.

My kids couldn't ask for a better stepfather. From the day Dan came into their lives, he has treated them with love and kindness. His patience and ability to talk to them is something I personally strive to be able to do. Dan loves kids, but he never expected to have any of his own because of his career and life-style. He's on the go constantly and always traveling some-where. Gavin and Kieley were three when Dan became a part of their lives. They really don't remember life without him, and while he's not around all the time, the time he does spend with them has had a marvelous impact on their lives. They have an excellent father, and Dan has never tried to replace him. He's just a wonderful, blessed addition to the "village" we all are part of in raising the kids.

On November 3, 2009, Dan and I got married. We wanted to get married on the beach in Los Barriles, where we had taken our first trip together, but to make our marriage legal, we had to get married stateside. We made our marriage official with a very small, intimate church ceremony in Dallas. It was just our parents, Dan's brother, Emma, and the kids. It was a sim-ple religious ceremony, and after the ceremony we all went to lunch. Everyone got along beautifully, the conversation flowed, and I was the happiest girl in the world. My mom and JB took the kids with them after lunch.

Dan and I had both been anxious and excited for the wed-ding day and couldn't wait for the lunch to be over so we could go home and be alone. Dan had insisted we remain true to his vow to not have sex until marriage, and although I had strug-gled with it at times, I was ultimately glad that we waited. It gave our relationship a depth and foundation that I realize now can be muddled and confused by having sex too soon, and it made our wedding day extra meaningful. The details of such a special occurrence should be kept private, but it's important for me to recognize that it was special, unlike anything I had ever experienced. To know that someone made a vow to wait for that certain someone, and that I was that certain someone—that another person would consider me that valuable and sacred, even after all the negative stuff I had done in my life (and Dan knew about it all)—was a love unlike anything I had ever felt. Dan had chosen me, and I had chosen him, too, but he had been waiting patiently a long time. When we came into each other's lives at the right time, he picked me to be that person for whom he had waited, and I was so grateful because he was exactly what I needed and wanted, even if it had taken me a while to figure that out in life. It's the kind of love that is almost overwhelming, in the best way possible. It's a gift from God.

We followed up our church ceremony with a ceremony on the beach in Los Barriles four days later on November 7. We've often said that our love is so strong it needed two weddings. It was a beautiful, festive affair with our families and about thirty of our close friends. Gavin walked me down the aisle, and Kieley was the flower girl. The four of us stood hand in hand while the ceremony was performed, and we each had a container with different colors of sand that we poured into a giant glass heart, symbolizing all of us coming together as one.

Chapter Ten

Marriage with Dan was everything I'd hoped for and more. It was fun and easy and full of positivity and love. That's not to say that we didn't have disagreements—every couple does. But Dan's ability to resolve things calmly and maturely was so different than anything I'd ever experienced. He made it known early on in our relationship that he wouldn't participate in yelling or angry behavior. It has been a work in progress for me, but I've made improvements, and he has been an excellent influence.

Because of Dan's schedule of working in Chile for two to three months in the winter and being in Alaska all summer plus still keeping a residence in Oregon, not much changed officially in our living arrangement when we got married. We continued with the same schedule, with him being in Dallas half of the year. I would make trips to Oregon on the weekends when I didn't have the kids, or sometimes I'd take the kids. We missed each other when we weren't together, but it was good to have our space. It was a balancing act for sure, but one that, for the most part, we achieved well.

I continued to pursue my hobbies as well. In October 2010 I ran my sixth marathon in Portland. My father and the kids traveled with Dan and me, and we made it a family vacation. My fifth marathon had been the year previous in San Diego, and my father and I had done it together, which was beyond special. We had made that a family vacation as well, taking the kids to SeaWorld, Legoland, and the San Diego Zoo. Dan was such a trooper going on all these trips and taking care of the kids while cheering me along during the races. He never complained or seemed overwhelmed by any of it. He was thrown into parenting full force with a set of lovable but strong-willed and energetic twins. They all embraced each other and welcomed the addition to their lives.

The kids began first grade in the fall of 2010. I lived in the same house as I had when the kids had been born, which was in the Dallas school district. The public schools were not good in our area. The area of town right next to where we lived was called the Park Cities, and the community had excellent schools. Jason made the decision to move there. This was great with me because the kids could go to an excellent school, and I wouldn't have to move.

I was more nervous than the kids were for their first day of first grade. I don't think they thought too much about fitting in, making friends, or the various insecurities associated with a brand-new school where they didn't really know anyone, but I was very concerned with all those things. I was concerned about them going to a new school where most of the students would have already spent a year together in kindergarten. I was also concerned about how I would fit in with the other mothers.

It seems so silly to be thirty-five and be concerned with all the things you think you left behind in high school, but I was. My kids were now attending school in the elite Park Cities, an area of Dallas that my parents would have never moved to when I was child. During the 1980s, Dallas had been very conservative, and Park Cities had been the mecca of that conservatism. The neighborhood had been filled with the elite, old-money families of Dallas, and it had certainly not been an area for hippies who ran a chain of head shops. While I knew the societal views on the Gas Pipe and that industry in general had become more liberal, I was still very insecure about the opinions people may have had of me as well as trying to fit in when I wasn't actually living within the community.

I had it in my mind that I would have to work very hard to be accepted in the Park Cities. My first way to try to find this acceptance was to get involved in multiple volunteer activities at the school, and that was actually a win-win because it meant I was involved with my kids' school lives as well. I became room mom, volunteered in the cafeteria, volunteered in the teacher workroom, signed up to read to the kids' classes regularly—if there was an opportunity, I did it. I loved being involved and being there for my kids, and I was very blessed because I had a flexible work schedule with my father, so I could work and volunteer.

Even with all the volunteer work, I still felt like an outsider. I had preconceived notions about what people from Park Cities would be like, and while some may have fit the mold, my ideas were really based on my own fears and insecurities. Nevertheless, I projected a standoffish attitude, as people often do because of their own issues. The opinions I had formed of the Park Cities throughout my life, coupled with the fact that I didn't actually live in the Park Cities, made me feel that I simply didn't fit in. I desperately wanted my kids to prosper and make friends, yet I didn't know how to make friends myself within the community. I would go to Gavin's sporting events and sit on the sidelines, but I was often on my phone, checking email for work and not engaging in the social interactions going on around me. I knew I should be involved socially and try my best to do so, but I felt I was different than many of the other moms and just didn't know how to initiate the social interaction. And I worked, while many of the other moms didn't, so I often was juggling checking emails or taking a work call while simultaneously trying to be supportive of my kids' extracurricular activities.

At the end of first grade, we hosted a big end-of-school party at our house, where we had a huge blow-up waterslide in the front yard, and kids swam in the pool. We grilled hot dogs and hamburgers, and everyone seemed to have a wonderful time and thought Dan and I were awesome hosts. Dan was a trooper that day. It was so hot and miserable. Dan had never been a fan of the Texas heat, and there were nearly a hundred people at our house—it was overwhelming, and he was not concerned one bit about trying to achieve the social status I was working so hard to achieve. He was way too comfortable in his own skin to worry about impressing people for the wrong reasons, but he was very supportive that day. First grade ended, and I felt I had accomplished enough to not feel like a complete outsider. The irony was that at that time I really had nothing I should have felt insecure about, and then years later, when I was at my worst and shamed very publicly, I was still accepted and defended by many. Sometimes it takes hitting rock bottom for us to find our true confidence and security.

Work was getting much busier during this time. In December of 2010, we purchased the Ridglea Theater complex in Fort Worth, Texas—a historic theater adjoined to a retail and office complex. The theater was an amazing piece of architecture that had been built in 1949, but over the years it had been neglected. It was the oldest movie theater and shopping center in the Fort Worth area, but it hadn't been used as a movie theater in nearly thirty years. It had become a distasteful venue for low-budget heavy metal acts, and a building that should have been the jewel of the community was becoming an eyesore that attracted unpleasant patrons coming to see vulgar musical acts. There was a huge battle within the community to either destroy the theater and replace it with new construction (a bank, specifically) or to save the theater and restore it to its original beauty. Restoration, though, was costly and time consuming, and there weren't many people willing to take on a project of that magnitude, except for someone like my father.

The restoration of the theater and the entire complex began in 2011. My father was thrust into the spotlight in a favorable way. The last time he'd had articles written about him was in the 1980s during his fights with the government regarding the alleged illegal activities of the Gas Pipe. Now, he was being proclaimed a hero for saving Fort Worth's historic landmark. It would become a true labor of love for him. He poured everyone ounce of time and energy he had into bringing the theater back to life, and the initial restoration encompassed and absorbed over two years of his life. The end result was worth it, though. The theater received national historic status and will never be in danger of demolition. It once again became something for Fort Worth to be proud of, and it continues to gain recognition as one of the top venues for performances, weddings, and private events in the Dallas–Fort Worth area.

All things in life were going great. The Gas Pipe stores were growing, the newest having opened in the complex with the theater. The bookings for Rapids Camp Lodge were increasing steadily each year, the lodge in Chile was developing, and we were beginning to add to our real estate holdings by purchasing shopping centers throughout the Dallas–Fort Worth area. I was married to a wonderful man whom I loved more and more every day, and the children were funny, intelligent, happy, well-rounded little people who were the continual lights of my life. Financially we were in a position to take amazing trips during the holidays—Hawaii, multiple trips to Baja California Sur, trips to South America for work and fun, and a hunting trip to Africa. Dan and I fulfilled a lifelong dream of mine to go to Machu Picchu and do a challenging but revitalizing four-day trek into the Inca ruins. I was getting to enjoy so many new experiences and so much of the world, which is what I'd always wanted to do. It was really hard to find anything to complain about, as life was beyond blessed.

By the end of 2013, we had expanded to twelve Gas Pipe stores, bought a group of existing fishing lodges called Deneki Outdoors—which would double our lodge business and give us multiple lodges throughout North America, including Canada and the Bahamas—and we had started a new corporation called Ridglea Complex Management Inc. that owned and managed our rental properties. Dan and I bought a house in Oregon, and we also bought a house in Baja California Sur, right on the beach, almost in the exact spot where Dan had said he wanted to walk with me when we were eighty and eighty-three. We also built our own house at Rapids Camp in Alaska so we didn't have to share space with my father any longer. We also bought a much bigger house (way bigger than necessary) in the actual Park Cities, so I was officially no longer an "outsider." We had also bought four additional airplanes so that we could start a small charter air service in Alaska, where airplanes were a primary method of transportation due to the limited road system. Dan had a small plane as well because he had started working on his pilot's license. Everything seemed great and was moving along more than comfortably. The only issue, which we didn't know was an issue at the time, was the phrase that would haunt us for years, changing our lives unimaginably and bringing more stress, problems, and trouble into our lives than

I'd ever thought possible: herbal incense.

In the fall of 2013, the kids began fourth grade, which would be their last year in elementary school. Gavin had become very active in sports. We'd discovered that he was a runner, and a very fast one. Kieley was more of the artistic child; she loved to perform, play the piano, sing, and dance. They both were doing well and loved school. Their teachers loved them and commented regularly on what adorable, smart, sensitive children they were.

I continued to be involved with the school. Over the years we had become one of the top donors for the annual school fundraising auction by donating trips to Rapids Camp. People were fascinated by the idea of my family having a lodge in Alaska. While some knew about the Gas Pipe and just didn't care or even thought it was cool as they had shopped there in their younger years, people were always more interested in my life of travels and having businesses in faraway places. I had become known as one who traveled extensively and had this incredible life of adventure. The traveling and adventurousness had almost become like an addiction for me. I wanted to go as much as possible. I was always juggling a hundred different things, and I loved it when people would continually tell me, "I don't know how you do it all" or "Your life is so exciting," because that somehow made me feel worthy and important. Being busy and always on the go made up for any shortcomings I may have felt for my shameful past (even though I typically didn't share my past with people, it was always in the back of my mind) and not attending college on the traditional path or pledging a sorority at one of the universities that it seemed everyone from the Park Cities had attended.

I had a wonderful life with two smart, loving, talented, beautiful children, a husband who absolutely adored me and whom

I adored in return, a great career, and wonderful extended family and friends. Everything that truly mattered in life was right in front of me. I didn't have to pretend or work for their approval—they loved me unconditionally. Nevertheless, I was caught up in the rat race. I was enamored by the life that surrounded me outside of my family. I began to think prestige and status mattered, and I wanted to matter in that regard. I valued the intrinsic things in my life such as family and relationships, but I also valued things of monetary value. It was an unfortunate part of our society, particularly in Dallas, Texas, and the Park Cities. We were inundated daily with a lifestyle driven by money—Wall Street, Hollywood, *Fortune* magazine—everywhere we looked, there was always something or someone living a life of glam that was made to look desirable. "Keeping up with the Joneses" had become *Keeping Up with the Kardashians*. That, in a nutshell, explains a good deal of what's wrong with society today.

The Park Cities were often referred to as "the bubble." It had become more diversified over the years, but even though it was located in the middle of the city, it was anything but "inner city." It was an upper-class neighborhood with its own police department, mayor, and city ordinances, located right in the middle of Dallas. It truly was not a place I'd imagined myself living, but the quality of the schools and the security of the area were appealing to me, even though there was a huge lack of culture and diversity. I had made some genuine friends in the area, but it was always very clear to me why it was called "the bubble." However, I was determined to live there and do what I thought I needed to do to fit in, even if that was only my misperception. And so I bought a big house located on a huge triangular lot on a major street corner. It was the equivalent of having a neon sign that says, "Hey, look at me!" By the summer of 2014, just about everybody in Dallas would know of the house, and it wouldn't be for a positive reason.

The pinnacle of my misguided actions in my effort to be accepted in the bubble of Park Cities was a party we hosted in May 2014. Every year one of the most coveted items at the school live auction was a dinner prepared in the winning bidder's home by Mico, the former chef of the popular Mi Cocina restaurant chain. I was determined to be the winning bidder for the last year I would attend the auction. It was a huge splurge, but I wanted to host that party. It would be the event of the spring. We had been in the new house for about six months, and it was officially ready for company now that the pool and landscaping had been completed.

I did my best to convince Dan it would be a fun affair, and while he was excited about the food, as we both love good food and are self-professed foodies, the pressure I was putting on myself and therefore him to have this perfect party was ridiculous. I invited parents from the kids' school, some of which had become true friends, and others were invited because they were friends with the people I was friends with, and I felt they had to be invited—it was a social move on my part and was phony and silly. I can't even say whether I enjoyed myself—the evening flew by, and everyone said it was a fabulous evening. But a week later, when my life turned upside down and I was publicly ridiculed and humiliated, I only heard from a handful of the party attendants. I am beyond grateful for those who did reach out, and maybe those who didn't just simply didn't know how or didn't know what to say. I get that—it can be an awkward situation and certainly beyond what many people can even begin to relate to. I knew people were talking about me—I'd hear things from time to time. Fortunately, nobody ever said anything hurtful directly to me; that would have been rude and improper, and if the bubble was anything, it was proper.

I'll never know or understand fully what other people think, but I was about to start learning, in a very extreme and painful way, a lot about myself and what really, truly matters in life. My life was about to take an unexpected new direction, and I was going to embark on the most intense and grueling journey of self-discovery and growth and a metamorphosis like never before.

Chapter Eleven

*T*he months leading up to June 4, 2014, were action packed and exciting, but there was a constant angst accompanying that. It was the opposite of the calm before the storm. It was more like a big volcano that had so much activity swirling inside of it that you knew eventually it was just going to explode. I was living life at an unbelievable pace, and nothing in my life had my undivided attention. Vacations were spent fielding calls and emails. Quality time with my kids was constantly interrupted with a phone call or an email I had to answer right then. The previous year, when Dan and I had taken our fabulous trip to Machu Picchu, I had been cut off from the world without technology, and I'd decided I would never do that again because I had missed too much. I thought that validated my relevance in the world in some way, but now I know it's ridiculous to not be able to "tune out" for a couple of days.

Our businesses were growing rapidly. The Gas Pipe business was getting stressful because the laws surrounding one product we sold—herbal incense—were always changing, and we were always scurrying to keep up. We always believed everything we were doing was legal, but staying on top of the legality of it was exhausting. One day a product would be legal, and the next day it wouldn't, but nothing had happened that ever made us think we had done anything that would cause our entire world to come crumbling down.

I'm sure there were many reasons that the events of June 4, 2014, happened, but what happened was so overwhelming and unbelievable that I had to use the experience to look at myself and what I should and could do differently in my life to learn and grow from the experience. The United States government did not initiate its action against us so that I could learn to slow down and be a better mother, wife, employer, friend, and person in general. They had a very different agenda, but to be able to cope with what was happening to me and my family, I had to look for a reason I could grasp and what I could learn and gain from the experience. I would have to remind myself constantly of that philosophy in order to make it through each subsequent day for the next few years.

Dan, my father, and I went to Alaska on June 3 and began the preparations for the beginning of the season. The kids and Emma would join us later. The majority of the staff would arrive the next night, June 4, in our new Pilatus airplane. The Pilatus was the newest addition to our fleet of aircraft we had acquired in recent years. It was so new that even though I had negotiated the purchase of it, I had yet to see it.

We woke up the morning of June 4, and I checked my email. There was an urgent email from our office manager Carolyn saying that she had been trying to call me, but the phone on our end wasn't working. I was able to get the phone to dial out, and I called her immediately. She informed me that she had gotten a phone call from our pilot in Anchorage telling her that one of the floatplanes that had just been purchased the previous fall and hadn't even been moved from Anchorage to the lodge yet was being seized by federal authorities. I told Dan, and we called our pilot, who confirmed what Carolyn had told us. He said that he wasn't given any detailed information from the authorities other than that they had a warrant to seize the aircraft. Dan and I couldn't imagine any reason why the aircraft would be getting seized, and we assumed that it must have something to do with the previous owner, since we had just purchased the plane within the last year. To this day we laugh about how we sat in our kitchen commenting that the previous owner must have done something sketchy and that there must have been confusion about whom the plane belonged to and its background; we were certain it would all be sorted out soon.

As Dan and I sat there drinking our morning tea and discussing the bizarre situation, we got a phone call from our pilot, who informed us that they were seizing the new Pilatus. This was shocking, and we knew then that it had nothing to do with a previous owner because two planes being seized meant that it had something to do with us, but we couldn't understand why. Our pilot gave us a contact number from the seizure paperwork, and I immediately called our attorney in Dallas, who said he would make some phone calls to determine what was happening.

I called Carolyn back and asked her if everything was okay at the office, and she said everything seemed fine. We were perplexed at this point. About fifteen minutes later I got a phone call from the manager of the Ridglea Theater. He told me that DEA agents had surrounded the entire building and were raiding the attached Gas Pipe store. My heart practically dropped to the bottom of my stomach, and I got a sickening feeling. Something big was going on, but I still didn't understand what. I tried to call Carolyn back at the office, and there was no answer. I called every Gas Pipe store, and nobody answered. I continued dialing numbers frantically, just hoping someone would answer. I was standing outside, staring at the river, with my cell phone in my hand, just praying that if I kept dialing, someone would pick up the phone and tell me everything was okay, but they didn't. I knew something really bad and of astronomic magnitude was happening. I was breathing hard and felt like I was about to hyperventilate. I knew the stories from the 1980s when the Gas Pipe stores would get raided by police, but I had never experienced it, and I couldn't understand why it would be happening now. There hadn't been any problems for years, and we weren't doing anything illegal.

Our attorney finally called me back and explained that he had talked with Brian Poe, the AUSA (assistant United States attorney) who had been assigned to our case. The DEA had several controlled buys of illegal substances that had been purchased from the Gas Pipe. This, I suppose, explained why they would feel compelled to raid our stores, but I didn't know of any time we had intentionally or knowingly broken a law by selling an illegal substance. I was sure there was a mix-up, and I certainly couldn't understand how any of this would give them the right to seize our aircraft that belonged to Rapids Camp Lodge. I understood that if a person knowingly sold something illegal, then there would certainly be consequences, but we hadn't knowingly sold anything illegal at the Gas Pipe, and Rapids Camp was a separate company, so I couldn't understand how everything fit together.

I pulled myself together and got in one of the trucks to drive to my father's house and tell him what was happening. On the short drive, my cell phone rang. It was a friend of mine who had driven by my house in Dallas, and he was calling to ask if everything was okay. He explained that there were police cars and DEA agents everywhere, an armored car, and yellow tape around the entire yard. The street had been blocked off. All I could think was, "Please don't let Emma and the kids be there." I called Emma, and she answered her cell phone and confirmed that she and Kieley were at the house. She told me they were both okay and that she believed the authorities were going to let her leave in a few minutes to pick up Gavin from his lacrosse camp. I had a thousand questions for Emma, first and foremost being, "What are they doing there? What is it they are looking for?" But she couldn't really talk. They told her that she had to hang up the phone immediately. I was shocked and confused. I couldn't understand what they were doing in my home, and I was beyond scared and concerned for my children, particularly Kieley because she was there to witness it all.

I informed my father about what was happening. I hysterically yelled, "They are at my house!" I was panicked and in a complete state of disbelief. I couldn't wrap my head around what was happening, and unbeknownst to me, it was only going to get worse. I tried to call Emma back to confirm she was going to pick up Gavin, but she didn't answer her phone. I learned later that the authorities had taken her phone and forbidden her to talk to me. I had to call Jason to tell him what was happening. He was understanding and supportive and said he would do whatever he could to help with the kids.

I didn't know if anyone was going to get Gavin from camp, and for all I knew, the authorities had taken Emma and Kieley somewhere. I wouldn't find out until over an hour later that Emma was forbidden to leave the house with Kieley to get Gavin because they were seizing her car, which was registered in my name, and they would only allow her to leave if she left Kieley at the house with them, or they could drive her and Kieley in one of their cars to pick up Gavin. They wouldn't allow her to answer my calls or call me to tell me what was happening with my own children, and they wouldn't allow

her to make contact with Jason either. Jason went to pick up
Gavin, who had already left camp with Emma in the DEA's car,
but neither of us knew that at the time. Then he went to my
house, where he finally found them all. Not knowing for over
an hour what was happening to my children, while I knew they
were experiencing an extremely terrifying situation, and not
knowing if they were safe or who they were with had to be the
most horrible feeling I had ever experienced.

Later I would learn that the agents took pictures of the children holding up signs with their names on them. They questioned my daughter about hidden rooms in the house, and
they aggressively tried to pull my bookshelf off the wall, insist-
ing there was a hidden space behind it. My daughter eagerly
showed them the "hidden door" in the floor of the guest-room
closet, which was nothing but an access point to the crawl space
underneath the house. It was clearly obvious that my children
had nothing to hide and lived in a home where they were loved
and comfortable. Regardless, the agents told Emma that their
lives were going to be changed forever. They were threatening
and intimidating to my godmother and my children for absolutely no reason. They found nothing that they were looking for
in my house—no guns, safe, hidden piles of cash, drug-manu-
facturing facility—nothing. The only illegal thing they found
was a very small, personal usage, misdemeanor amount of marijuana in a drawer in my closet. Yet they continued with their
demeaning and hostile behavior.

Things got progressively worse throughout the day. We
got phone calls informing us that our other airplanes had been
seized, including Dan's personal airplane as well as our for-
ty-two-foot ocean vessel that we used for our halibut-fishing
program at Rapids Camp. I called our investment broker and
learned that they had seized all our funds—my father's and the
Gas Pipe's entire savings (way into the millions) as well as my

personal savings. They were taking everything my father had earned over forty-four years and what I had earned in the last nine years because for three years we had allegedly sold something that was illegal.

After a few hours, our employees were able to call us. Nobody had been arrested, but many of them had been handcuffed while authorities scoured the Amy Lynn Inc. office, distribution warehouse, and all the stores. They took all the money from the stores, down to the very last penny. They also emptied the funds from all the operating business checking accounts. A few hours later my father and I went into the town of King Salmon, hoping we could access funds from our personal checking accounts via the ATM. When we tried to do so we learned that those had been emptied as well. Even though I shared an account with Dan, who had nothing to do with the Gas Pipe, the government had completely wiped out the account.

We were able to finally determine that the government was investigating, not charging, us for "distribution of a controlled substance, money laundering, mail and wire fraud, maintaining a drug-involved premise, and defrauding the United States," none of which made any sense to us. The investigation stemmed from one product line we had sold, even though we sold over two thousand product lines.

Herbal incense—also known as Spice, K2, and synthetic marijuana—had been on the market widely since about 2010 and was openly sold in gas stations, in smoke shops, in head shops, in adult shops, on the internet, and in various other places. We followed the trend and began selling it due to customer demand. We displayed it in our showcases in a way we believed to be legal—in the open, just like any other product. We rang it up, documented it, and paid sales tax and income tax based on the sales of it. There was nothing hidden about what we were doing. As my attorney would explain to a jury years later in trial, there are things drug dealers don't do—they don't pay taxes, they don't advertise their business publicly on billboards, they don't sell their products openly in a retail store, and they don't keep records of their sales in QuickBooks. None of our actions were indicative of people who thought they were breaking a law.

We were not ever told we were breaking a law, we were never warned, and we were never told to stop, but our government doesn't have to prove that someone has broken a law before they come in with guns drawn, handcuffing people and seizing everything they own. They can go to a federal judge and get a search and seizure warrant based on hearsay and what they portray to the judge as "proof," but the judge only gets the benefit of hearing the government's side. The accused doesn't have an opportunity to present their side prior to a seizure warrant being issued. And even after an accused gets to file something with the court, if they are fortunate enough to be able to hire competent legal representation after having absolutely everything taken, the government is almost always given the benefit of the doubt. The accused only finally gets to be truly heard in a trial, but often the accused is forced to settle or take a plea deal because they can't properly defend themselves after having everything taken. Yes, this is how things really work in the "land of the free."

The herbal incense business was really this phenomenon that came out of nowhere. It wasn't a product that we initially pursued. Everything that has ever been sold in the Gas Pipe is because of customer demand. In 2010 we had been contacted several times by Lawrence Shahwan, who was the largest vendor of the product in Dallas. At the time the product had been called K2, and Lawrence relentlessly pursued us to carry his product. Finally, after continually having customers request the product and then leave to go shop at our competition, we started carrying his product. Other vendors and suppliers of the product would come and go over the years, but Lawrence was the main supplier for Gas Pipe and other stores throughout Texas, particularly the Dallas area. The name K2 eventually couldn't be used anymore due to a city ordinance, and Lawrence felt that the name itself had been tarnished due to other suppliers copying it and producing an inferior product, so new products were developed with lots of different names, but the product itself never really changed.

There may be those reading this who have never heard of herbal incense or any of the other names I've referenced. It is a substance made of a leafy plant material that has a chemical—a synthetic cannabinoid, to be specific—mixed in with the plant material. The final product—the plant material combined with the synthetic cannabinoid—is then put in little mylar packages, typically in three-gram quantities, and sold under ridiculous names such as Scentsi Star, I-Blown, 42 Degrees, and countless others. The product is easily made, but getting the ingredients and the packaging for the product were not as easy. Lawrence Shahwan was a master at it, and Gas Pipe, because of its customers, was very dependent on Lawrence.

The product is not typically used as an actual incense. I suppose it could be, and we even burned it as incense at our office. It wasn't like the typical stick incense. It was more like potpourri that could be put in a dish and burned. But people bought the product to smoke it and get a high similar to marijuana. I realize that may sound negative and illegal, but a substance isn't illegal just because it makes people high. It was never explicitly sold for that purpose, at least not at Gas Pipe, and everybody believed that it was legal so long as it wasn't directly sold for that purpose. The packaging described it as incense and had "Not for human consumption" written on the packaging, and it was referred to as incense. There was never much discussion with customers beyond that. To us, it was no different than many of the other products Gas Pipe sold. Bongs, for instance, are pipes most typically associated with marijuana smoking, but for years, after the 1980s, Gas Pipe had successfully and legally sold bongs as long as they weren't sold with the specific verbalized intention of using them for smoking marijuana. And when the DEA came in and raided all of our businesses and seized everything because of the herbal incense, they said nothing about our other products—such as bongs. They told us we could continue our business, although we wondered how since they had taken all of our money and put liens on all of our properties, and they proudly stated the latter.

There was a fair amount of negative press associated with K2, which became the generic name for herbal incense products regardless of the name on the actual package. There were stories of overdoses, but the products were made by so many different people and with so many different chemicals (sometimes not even a synthetic cannabinoid—there were people known to use formaldehyde) that we never believed any of the dangers were associated with our products, and we never had any confirmed reports saying they were.

One thing that was undoubtedly risky about selling the product was the ever-changing law regarding the chemical that was in the product. The DEA was constantly scheduling chemicals, which meant making a chemical illegal by placing it into schedule I of the list of scheduled drugs. The DEA would post a notice to the public announcing that a ban was to take effect in thirty days, giving retailers, distributers, and manufacturers time to rid themselves of product. Then the ban would officially take effect thirty days later, and once it did, the product was then deemed illegal. Anybody with any common sense would interpret this to mean that prior to the ban taking effect, the product had been legal. So every time a chemical was banned, we would throw away hundreds of thousands of dollars of product so that we wouldn't be in possession of or selling an illegal product. This was something else a drug dealer doesn't do, as my attorney would later tell a jury. Drug dealers don't care if their product is legal or illegal. In fact, a drug dealer is usually dealing an illegal product.

The "catch," according to the government, was that people would soon find a new chemical for the product. And yes, this process of buying product, selling it, destroying it when it became illegal, and then finding a new, legal product was something we did time after time. The government would later tell a jury that our process of destroying product when it became illegal and then selling a new product that contained a new chemical that wasn't banned was proof that what we were doing was illegal and that we knew it. Somehow, complying with the law as we understood it meant we were actually breaking the law. If the government's theory sounds confusing and nonsensical, don't worry—it is.

For someone to be accused and convicted of selling an illegal substance, there is a very important word in the Controlled Substances Act—*knowingly*. There must be knowledge and intent to sell a controlled substance. Most of us think of controlled substances as things such as heroin, cocaine, and even marijuana in some states and at the federal level. We all know those are banned substances—they are controlled and illegal. There is no question in anyone's mind about that. We had never knowingly sold a controlled substance.

What we didn't fully know or understand was the Federal Analogue Act, which was a subsection of the Controlled Substances Act. The Analogue Act stated, "A controlled substance analogue shall, to the extent intended for human consumption, be treated, for the purposes of any Federal law as a controlled substance in schedule I." That was the main sentence of the act, but there was also prong one, prong two, and prong three after that pertaining to what also must be proven for something to be an analogue. It was long and complicated and dealt with chemistry, something I never understood even in high school, when I got grounded majorly for the only time in my teen years because I almost failed that class. At the inception of our herbal incense business dealings, we didn't even know about the Federal Analogue Act nor what would make something an analogue per prongs one, two, and three. As time went on, the law surrounding the Analogue Act and how it could be enforced changed as well. On June 4, 2014, unbeknownst to us, the government believed they had enough evidence against us to seize everything we owned based on the parameters of the Analogue Act and the mishap of when we had unknowingly sold an actual controlled substance. They somehow grouped all of that together to label us money launderers and a full-fledged drug cartel that had also allegedly committed mail and wire fraud and defrauded the United States by misbranding a drug.

The government said we had committed misbranding and defrauded the FDA because of improper labeling on the herbal incense packaging, although we were never investigated by the FDA, and typically the FDA sends warning letters when there is a misbranding. We never received a warning. It's unfortunately true that we did commit misdemeanor misbranding—during the selling of herbal incense, we didn't even know about laws regarding misbranding, which would make it a misdemeanor and not a felony. There was no criminal intent, and nobody was being defrauded. But we weren't accused of misdemeanor misbranding. We were accused of a conspiracy to defraud by misbranding—a felony. We had never even discussed or thought of the FDA in our herbal incense business. It wasn't even on our radar. We simply sold a product that was labeled a certain way industry wide, and that was it. But mislabeling—either as a felony or a misdemeanor—doesn't lead to forfeiture, so the government had to make all the other accusations so they could seize our assets. Even though my father, the Gas Pipe, and all his other businesses had been successful for years prior to selling herbal incense, the government thought they should take everything we owned.

Weeks, months, and even years passed as the accusations against us continued to unfold and as I came to fully understand the government's case against us or at least understand what they were alleging. I had never even heard of many of the statutes they were accusing us of violating, much less understood how they applied to us. What I did know was that the government had declared war, and I didn't know how we were going to do it, but we had no choice but to fight back.

I was asked several times after June 2014 if I wished we hadn't sold herbal incense. Of course, knowing what I do now and all the stress and heartache it ultimately caused for so many people, I wouldn't have sold it. But at the time, it was a business decision—nothing scandalous or devious, just a simple business decision that seemed to make sense at the time in accordance with what we were seeing in our industry. And when we were selling it, we had law enforcement in our stores regularly for various reasons, typically because we had called them to report a nuisance, break-in, or theft. One time we even reported the theft of herbal incense, and law enforcement ultimately arrested the thief and ordered restitution—not something that happens when someone's cocaine, a clearly illegal substance, is stolen. I doubt a drug dealer would ever even report his cocaine stolen.

We were consistently given the message from local law enforcement that what we were doing was perfectly legal. We had no reason to think what we were doing was illegal. This wasn't the 1980s, when law enforcement harassed Gas Pipe regularly. They were helping us regularly. I wish we hadn't sold something that caused me and, even worse, my family and our employees so much stress. I wish we hadn't sold something that caused us to almost lose everything, including—and most importantly—our freedom for the rest of our lives and other people's freedom, jobs, and everything they owned. I wish my children and husband hadn't had to go through everything they did because of the legal action taken against us, and I wish we hadn't sold something that ultimately was negative for the community. But I never thought in my wildest dreams the selling of herbal incense would lead to what it did. However, as things continued to unfold and transpire over the next few years, I slowly and gruelingly learned that I could and would become a better person because of it. Things would get worse before they got better, and even more challenges would come our way, but I, along with my family, would find a strength I never knew I had.

Chapter Twelve

*T*he day after the raids and seizures, my father and I left Alaska to go back to Dallas. I needed to be with my kids, and our employees needed us. Everyone had been traumatized. My father and I were in denial about the severity of the situation. We were just sure it was a big mix-up and that once we explained our side of things, everything would be cleared up. We hadn't broken a law, we had never intentionally done anything wrong or illegal, and in our minds the government had made a big mistake.

Emma had cleaned the mess at my house, so there wasn't any evidence of the destruction from the raid. I had been spared from living through what she and my children had had to witness as well as what all our employees had had to witness at the office and stores. I wasn't grateful for that, though—I would have traded places with any of them. It wasn't right that the raids had occurred while my father and I were away. I'm not sure why they felt compelled to go to my home in the middle of the day when my children were there. One of the agents reportedly said she believed the children would be in school. It was June—summertime—and if the agents had done even a minimum amount of research, they could have verified before-hand that school was out just by looking at the district calendar. They simply didn't care, and to this day I really don't know why they thought they needed to search my home at all.

Our story was all over the local news, and we were being referred to as the Gas Pipe DTO (drug trafficking organization). I was mortified. This was way worse than any of the Gas Pipe legal issues from my childhood. The government and the media weren't just saying we sold pipes that people could possibly use to smoke marijuana, which had always been the allegation in the 1980s. They were now calling us actual drug dealers. People began reaching out to me immediately. I heard support from people I'd talked to daily, and I heard support from people I hadn't spoken to in years. I heard support from people in the Park Cities whom I didn't even think I knew that well, and I received support from people whom I knew well, though I wasn't sure what they would think about this current ordeal.

Jason brought the kids over the following morning. I was a wreck and hadn't slept for the past couple nights, but seeing the kids gave me strength. They had lots of questions, and I did my best to answer them. I didn't fully understand what was happening, so it was hard for me to explain it to them. I repeatedly told them how sorry I was they had to endure what had happened and that we were going to get it cleared up because we hadn't done what we had been accused of doing. Kids are resilient, and Gavin and Kieley are incredibly strong human beings, and they showed me nothing but love, forgiveness, and understanding.

While the government had seized or restrained all our money and airplanes, they had only put liens on our real estate, which meant we could stay in our home and still had the ability to operate and manage our real estate and operate our stores, even if we didn't have any money to resume operations. The only properties they didn't attempt to put liens on were my father's house in Dallas—presumably because he had bought it prior to the commencement of the alleged illegal activity, and they couldn't attempt to tie it to alleged illegal activity—and our real estate that was outside of the United States, presumably because they didn't have a way to seize something outside of the country. Not only were they attempting to take nearly everything we owned, but they told us they would be backing up these seizures with a federal indictment very soon. I didn't even really understand what it meant to be federally indicted, but I would soon begin learning more than I ever cared to know about our federal legal system.

Frank Shor, our attorney who had represented us for years, explained to us that my father and the corporations could share an attorney because he was the sole owner of the corporations, but I would need my own. And because I had young children and the most to lose (money aside, losing freedom and being taken from my children superseded everything else), I was being referred to the person Frank considered the best criminal attorney in the state of Texas, David Botsford. I was still in denial that I needed a criminal attorney. I hadn't broken a law. These were overzealous actions being taken by the government, and it would be resolved before it got worse. I retained the attorney just to make sure my bases were covered. I had zero dollars—not a penny to my name—and the attorney would be expensive, but thankfully my mother was there to help.

I don't know how we made it those first few months; it is truly a miracle. In addition to taking every penny, they took every computer and register, so we had no way to ring up sales in the stores. Until we could get new pieces of technology, the stores accepted cash only and kept track of sales with pen and paper. It was archaic and chaotic, but somehow everyone pulled together and made it happen. The sense of family and camaraderie among all our staff was inspiring and comforting. We all wanted to prove we could survive. The office computers had been taken, too, so we couldn't reference QuickBooks for any of the payables. It was as though the businesses started new as of June 5, 2014, except there were outstanding bills and checks from prior to that day. There were about $250,000 in bill payments that had been mailed in the days leading up to June 4, and those wouldn't clear because the bank accounts had been emptied. Payroll was due in about ten days, and that was the most important priority. We also had a sales tax payment due of about $250,000 at the end of June. We didn't know if we could even use our business checking accounts and didn't for a few days, but after about a week we were told by the bank that the accounts, which had a zero balance, were available to use. We had no money, no "hidden" savings, nothing to fall back on, and it was our most expensive time of the year with the lodges being in operation for the summer.

People were supportive and understanding. We had vendors that were willing to work with us and extend terms. It was humbling and humiliating, but there was a strength found through it. If we could somehow overcome the financial earthquake we had experienced, then we would know that we had taken the government's best shot and still persevered. It wasn't easy, and it was very much one day at a time, often feeling like we wouldn't make it to the next day, but we kept moving forward. The government had intended to shut us down, but they didn't succeed.

Personal finances were a struggle, but they were almost too much of a struggle to even worry about—we were beyond a budget or any sort of manageable situation. Dan, my father, and I didn't take a salary for a couple months so the companies could cut back on expenses. We lived off credit cards, which of course led to a good deal of debt. I had kids and living expenses that had to be taken care of, so I just spent what I needed to spend. I was still sure that the government would see the error in their ways soon and that funds would be released. I kept wishing that I had saved more or somehow been more prepared, but then I realized that it wouldn't have mattered because it would have just been that much more the government would have taken.

The stress was a true test for my marriage. Dan and I had certainly had disagreements over time, like all couples do, but our life had been very good and relatively stress free, other than being way too busy. Dan didn't have any involvement with the Gas Pipe—he solely worked for Rapids Camp—but we weren't sure if they were going to try to involve him somehow from a criminal standpoint. Nothing that the government had done so far had made any sense to us, so anything they would try to do wouldn't surprise us at that point. They had certainly involved Dan from a financial standpoint by seizing our joint bank accounts and his airplane and putting liens against our homes, and the seizure of the lodge airplanes and ocean vessel made his job at Rapids Camp much more challenging, as the equipment needed for the lodge to function properly wasn't available. Dan was left fielding questions from lodge guests all summer, and it was awkward and uncomfortable.

The kids began middle school in the fall of 2014. I was grateful they were going to a new, bigger school. It was within the same district, but it was larger than their elementary school and could be viewed as a fresh start. I thought this was great timing because hopefully many people in the new school wouldn't even be aware of the ordeal my family was experiencing. The kids seemed to like being at the bigger school. Other than asking me for updates every now and then on the situation, the kids seemed to have moved on and were as happy as they could be, but none of us believed things were going to get progressively worse.

By September there were still no indictments, and it didn't appear that there would be anytime soon. The prosecutor ensured our defense attorneys that indictments were imminent, but time went on with nothing happening. Things were normalizing somewhat, or maybe it would be more accurate to say we were finding a new normal. The Gas Pipe had always been an incredibly successful business, and we had a strong customer base and were able to generate an income. We had replaced all our computers one by one and were functioning, but we were constantly playing catch-up due to falling so far behind from the abrupt seizure of everything. The lodges, theater, and rental-property businesses suffered because many people didn't want to book expensive trips or reserve a space for an event or lease a space for their business because of a potential forfeiture that would lead to the business not being in existence. We forged forward the best we could and thankfully had many past customers who were loyal and others who were willing to take a chance on us.

The Gas Pipe had always been like a family, and everyone felt very close. Lunchtime at our office had always been a fun time where we all gathered around the table and had many laughs. That had subsided somewhat after the raids. There was paranoia, and nobody knew who could be trusted and what was really happening. The government was making a lot of accusations, and it wasn't clear if people might be "cooperating" with the government, since they had threatened all our employees. Then, as time went on, we found our comfort zone again, and work was the fun place it always had been. We got into a new rhythm and felt like everyone was genuinely pulling together to defeat the government because we all felt we had done nothing illegal. Later, we would learn we were wrong and that almost every person had cooperated with the government; I know now people got scared when they were being threatened constantly, so they had to do what they thought was best for them and their families. I held grudges for a long time, but I learned a great deal about true forgiveness and compassion over the years—a wonderful lesson and blessing from a bad situation.

The banks we used for all our business and personal banking no longer wanted to have our accounts. We were disappointed but assumed we would just find another bank, but we had no idea how the banking world really worked and how leery banks would be to work with a business—or people associated with that business—that was being investigated by the federal government. We were completely innocent, and we hadn't even been charged with a crime. Even if we had been charged, we were supposed to be considered innocent until proven guilty. We were turned down by more banks than I can even recall. Some said it was because of the accusations that had been printed in the media, and some actually said it was because we had a high volume of cash deposits—our store sales are half cash and half credit cards—but that made zero sense to me. Isn't having a place to deposit cash the reason one needs a bank? Who knew? We also had similar issues with merchant services processors, and for months, off and on, we couldn't accept credit cards. Finally, after over two years of being dropped by countless banks and merchant services providers, we were connected to a "friend of a friend" who helped us find solid financial relationships and also became a dear friend. These friends, and others like them in our lives, would become people I would refer to as "angels on earth" in the years to come.

In many ways it was like we were starting a brand-new company: new bank accounts, new merchant services, new processes, and reformed policies. I tried to look at the whole ordeal as an opportunity for growth—both for the company and for me personally. I had always let everyone at the Gas Pipe function in their roles independently, but now I was getting involved in everything I could. We had to operate on a very strict budget to be able to overcome things, and I began overseeing all the bills payable and gained my own access to QuickBooks. I got more involved in the ordering of inventory and understanding our cost and profitability. Even though we were starting to get ahead again, and business was good, we had residual expenses and debts (mainly a huge federal income tax payment and property tax payments) from the previous year, and the government was holding all the money we would have used to pay that.

Fortunately, we didn't have to make loan payments on any of our real estate, as they had all been paid for in cash—probably another reason they were so enticing to the government. We had no real debt except for our gigantic tax bill, but we couldn't borrow against any of the properties either because the government had liens on all of them except for the foreign ones, but those couldn't be borrowed against since they were in a different country. There was an angst for us to get some movement on the case and have a judge look at what was happening to us.

Toward the end of 2014 we had a big meeting with all our attorneys. By this point we had retained six attorneys, one of whom was Steven Kessler, the leading forfeiture expert in the country, and as time went on he would become a very dear friend. Frank Shor, who had been our attorney for years, had very suddenly and very sadly become terminally ill, so we had to find other attorneys to replace him. That is how we got connected with George Milner and Michael Mowla, who would also become dear friends over the years. I was still represented by David Botsford, and we had two attorneys in New Mexico who were representing us for the Gas Pipe stores in Albuquerque—John Boyd and Nancy Hollander.

We had the big meeting at my house in my dining room. This would become our meeting place for years to come. We had several meetings over the years, and the attendees would change over the years, but these meetings were always long and emotionally draining—all-day discussions about strategy and possibilities, with tears and anger from me. The attorneys all had brilliant minds, and it was quite fascinating to hear them talk, but the circumstances were nothing but stressful. At the first meeting we discussed the pros and cons of either filing motions to hopefully get our assets released or waiting a little longer to see if we could settle things amicably with the government. The ultimate consensus was to wait a little longer. I didn't know how we were going to keep our heads above water if we didn't get at least something released, but I had to have faith, and I had to learn patience, which had never been a strong characteristic for me. Oh, how I would learn!

The holiday season arrived, and we made an effort to try to mentally put everything on the back burner temporarily and enjoy time with family. I always loved being with my family, but just a few months previously I hadn't known if I would be spending Christmas with them because I was sure we were going to be indicted, so this Christmas was extra special and felt like a victory. It was the first of many Christmases that I would spend wondering whether it was going to be my last.

We also went as a family to the house in Baja California Sur to celebrate the New Year. We were trying to live life as usual, even though the big dark cloud was constantly hanging over our heads.

At the beginning of 2015 we were told about a Supreme Court case—*McFadden v. United States.* This case would change the future of Federal Analogue Act prosecutions.

There was discrepancy across the country in different circuits about what had to be proven to show that someone knew they were selling an analogue. Many people think that if a law is a federal law, it is enforced uniformly across the country, but different circuits can interpret and prosecute a law differently unless it has been clearly decided by the Supreme Court. In the Fifth Circuit, which is where Dallas is, I had learned that all the government had to prove in previous analogue cases was that the defendant knew that the substance being sold or distributed was being done so with the intent for people to get high. Even though that was not exactly what the Analogue Act said, the jury instructions given in these cases said so. Stephen McFadden, who had been charged and found guilty of an analogue violation in the Fourth Circuit, had gone to trial with jury instructions that mirrored what had been used in the Fifth Circuit. His appeal was being taken all the way to the Supreme Court, asking the Court to clearly define what *mens rea*, a legal term basically meaning "knowledge," a defendant has to have to be found guilty of violating the Analogue Act. Although it would be months before the Supreme Court would issue their opinion on McFadden, all the briefs and information leading up to it appeared very positive for McFadden and therefore us.

Our attorneys finally decided it was time to file some motions to get some of our assets returned. Except for my three cars that had been seized, nothing had been returned. It was time to get aggressive and see how things would unfold. It was late March 2015, and it had been nearly a year since the raids and commencement of the civil lawsuit. There seemed to be no immediate sign of indictments, even though they kept threatening it, so we went for it. I had never read legal motions prior to this, but even I could tell that these were well drafted and should give us a good chance at getting some of our stuff released, or so I thought. We knew that a potential consequence of filing the motions could be the prosecutor coming back with indictments to help substantiate their allegations and increase the chances of holding on to our assets, but we were very confident in our innocence, particularly with the pending Supreme Court case, so we felt that it was the right move to make.

The motions were filed, and within a week we heard that Lawrence Shahwan, our main herbal incense vendor who had originally been arrested for charges that had nothing to do with us or herbal incense, made a plea bargain for an analogue charge related to our investigation. His other charges would be dropped, and he was pleading to a charge that had to do with analogues and would be willing to testify against us. A few days after that, our attorneys received an email from the prosecutor, Brian Poe, saying he was ready to move forward with indictments, but he would meet with us first to see if there was any way to resolve the case.

Although the prosecutor invited my father and I to the meeting, we didn't go. The attorneys would handle any discussions. We had never knowingly sold an analogue or a controlled substance, so with the pending Supreme Court case and our willingness to pay a settlement just so we could move forward with our lives and put the ordeal behind us, we were sure things could be resolved. We decided to go away for a few days to our house in Baja California Sur to decompress and relax while waiting for what we were sure would be positive feedback from the meeting. We were going to get our lives back on track and start to put this ordeal behind us. We were in for another shock.

Chapter Thirteen

e were on pins and needles in Baja California Sur on the day of the meeting, waiting for the attorneys to call. We got the call. The government was playing hardball. They wanted to keep everything they had taken—so there would be no more Gas Pipe or our other businesses, I would be homeless, and my father and I would be pretty much penniless except for the little amount of money we had earned since last June, which wasn't much because of the debts and legal bills. They wanted both my father and me to plead to some twenty-year count—it could be an analogue-drug count or money-laundering count—they didn't necessarily care so long as it carried a maximum sentence of twenty years. If we didn't do that, they would move forward with indicting us with multiple charges that could lead to life in prison as well as indicting twenty-plus other people, but they wouldn't say who those other people were.

We still hadn't seen any actual evidence against us. The government had yet to produce discovery, which is all the information, evidence, interviews, etc. pertaining to the case. Other than knowing undercover officers had come to the Gas Pipe and purchased herbal incense products, which we believed to be legal, we didn't know anything about their investigation. We certainly didn't understand how they were going to claim we had committed money laundering. We kept meticulous books and records. We paid taxes on every dime we made. Nothing was done under the table or in a scandalous way. The only issue we'd had was when we had mistakenly and unknowingly sold an actual controlled, banned substance, but we had corrected the error as soon as we knew about it. We believed if we could just explain that, then all would be understood. The government, though, wasn't interested in our explanations. They were only interested in punishing.

We didn't know exactly when we were going to be indicted and arrested. Brian Poe would only say that it would be sometime before the end of May. He also wouldn't allow us to self-surrender, even though our attorneys made this offer several times. The government wanted to surprise us so they could have a public display of us being taken away in handcuffs. I was adamant that my children had already been traumatized enough by watching their home get raided by the DEA. I was not going to let them watch me be taken away in handcuffs. According to Brian Poe, though, the only way to avoid this scenario was to plead to something, to make a deal, and then we would have the opportunity to not be arrested in such a humiliating manner. We were learning if we weren't going to play by their rules, we weren't going to be cut any slack.

We spent every day waiting for the "surprise." Every time a car I didn't recognize pulled up in front of our office, I wondered if they were there for us. I was looking over my shoulder everywhere I went. I didn't know how to prepare to be indicted. I didn't believe I would be detained (held in custody until trial) when we were arrested, and neither did our attorneys. After all, we had gotten on a plane from Baja California Sur when we had been told indictments were imminent. That was not indicative of someone who would flee the country, which was one of the reasons the government could move for detention for a defendant who is awaiting trial. The other reason they could move for detention was if the defendant was a danger to society. That didn't apply to us either. We had been continuing to run our businesses for almost a year since the raids, and we clearly weren't criminals or hurting anyone. I was a responsible, loving mother and a positive member of my community, and apart from the mislabeling of a product, which I hadn't known was illegal, I had done nothing wrong. Nevertheless, my attorney had me ask friends and family to write character letters expressing their belief in me as a person and how I would never flee and leave my children.

I didn't really understand what it meant to be detained, and I really didn't think it was going to apply to me anyway. I didn't prepare the kids because I didn't think I needed to. I believed I would be arrested and immediately let out while awaiting trial because there was no logical reason that shouldn't happen, and I still believed that somehow things were going to be resolved sooner rather than later. We did inform all our managers that although we didn't know for a fact who was going to be indicted, we suspected it could be all the managers because the prosecution had told us it would be around twenty people. Some had already retained attorneys the previous year when everything had commenced because they'd had concerns. Some had done nothing, though. And some, although we didn't know this for a fact at the time, had already been working with the government—negotiating toward a plea deal even though nobody had even been charged with anything yet—and even though we were told from day one to be leery of this, we didn't want to believe it. The Gas Pipe was like a family, and nobody believed they had done anything illegal. We were naive.

Dan was supposed to leave for Alaska upon our return from Baja California Sur, but he stayed longer so he could be with us for support. I cried and cried, constantly expressing my disbelief at what was happening. It was like a bad dream—an extreme nightmare—that I was surely going to wake up from soon, but I didn't. The nightmare continued and would for a very long time. He always encouraged me and told me how strong I was and that I was going to have to fight this thing. He never once wavered in his belief in me. I loved that everyone around me thought I was so strong, but I wasn't feeling so strong. I had spent the past year putting on a brave face for everyone—I was a cheerleader at work, I stayed positive for my kids, I tried to maintain normalcy in life—but I was starting to crumble. I really didn't know how much more I could take, and I had no idea that I was going to have to face much more than I'd ever imagined possible.

Because the prosecutor would not agree to let us self-surrender, my attorney David Botsford had the brilliant idea of my father and I going down to the US Marshals Office in the federal building downtown to attempt to self-surrender. This would accomplish two things: we would avoid being arrested in public, and it would prove we weren't a flight risk because people who were going to flee didn't self-surrender. Although David and I would eventually part ways and he would no longer represent me, his advice regarding this is something that I will always appreciate. He advised us to go to the US Marshals Office, give them our names, and explain that we had been told we would be indicted soon and that we were there to see if there were warrants for our arrest because we wanted to turn ourselves in. We did that the first time on Thursday, May 7, 2015, and after talking with four different people, who all seemed shocked that we would actually bring ourselves down there to surrender, we were told there were currently no warrants.

Dan had to leave the following week for Alaska. It was time to get things going for the lodge season, and there wasn't anything he could do for me—he couldn't make it go away, which was all I really wanted. Sure, I loved just having him with me, but it was inevitable that he was going to have to go and that the businesses had to continue operating. I thought I would be joining him in Alaska that summer as I always had because I knew people traveled all the time while they were under federal indictment and awaiting trial. I would learn later I was wrong.

On Wednesday, May 13, 2015, I took my kids to school, and we decided to grab a quick breakfast at Chick-fil-A on the way. As we sat there eating our chicken biscuit sandwiches, I was overwhelmed with a sadness. My father and I would be going back to the US Marshals Office again that day. I didn't want to believe it, but somewhere in my psyche I think I knew it was not going to be a good day. I wanted to give the kids a big goodbye, but they didn't know what was happening, and besides, even if we were arrested, it wasn't as though I wouldn't be seeing them again very soon. They were going to be at their dad's anyway from Wednesday evening through the weekend, so even under normal conditions I wouldn't see them until Monday. Kieley's piano recital was that Sunday, so I would actually get to see them before Monday. I wouldn't be in jail that long. I didn't even think the prosecutor would really move to detain us because there was no real reason to do so. But still, my heart ached when I dropped them off at school that morning. I guess a mother should always listen to her intuition.

That afternoon my father and I went to make our second attempt at surrendering ourselves at the US Marshals Office. Once again, we had to talk to a few different people before anyone could determine whether we indeed had warrants for our arrest. They asked us to go wait on the wooden bench in the hallway, and it seemed like we waited forever, watching different people walking by—it was not a happy place. People often got bad news there, and we could see evidence of that all around us. My heart was racing, and my mind was racing too. I didn't fully grasp what was happening, but I had a sickening feeling, and I could feel that things were about to change for the worse. A crying woman, escorted by marshals, walked by us in shackles and a yellow prison uniform. Then the marshals came out to talk with us. Life as I knew it immediately changed forever.

We were informed that yes, we did have warrants for our arrest. We weren't told what the charges were, but we were told that since it was the end of the day, if they took us into custody right then, we would have to stay the night, or we could leave and come back in the morning. I immediately said we would stay because I didn't want to chance being arrested the following morning at my house. Even though my children wouldn't be there because they were at their dad's, I wanted to surrender right then and there and be done with it and not have a spectacle in my neighborhood. There had already been enough of that the previous year.

I had been in jail briefly twice before; years ago, I had written some hot checks that had gone unpaid so long that law enforcement had finally issued arrest warrants. I'd found out I had warrants and turned myself in. My attorney had already lined up everything, so I'd just had to stay in the holding tank for several hours while my paperwork was processed. I naively and incorrectly thought this time would be the same way, except I did realize, according to what the marshals told us, that I would be spending the entire night in jail. I thought *jail* meant a holding cell right there in the federal building. I assumed I would go in front of the judge for my arraignment the next day, plead not guilty, and then be on my way until we went to trial or finally got this mess—and what I still saw as a big misunderstanding—resolved.

We followed the marshals and entered the custody area. The marshals were very courteous and considerate. They allowed us to call our attorneys, whom I immediately asked to call my mother and Dan to tell them what had happened. They also allowed me to make a call to our office so I could let them know what had happened and make sure someone would take our dogs home, who were at the office since we brought them to work with us daily. The marshals then put us into separate holding cells. The cell was minimalistic with a metal bench and a toilet and a small sink in the open—pretty much what I'd expected. There was a lady in there—the one I had seen walking down the hall earlier in a yellow prison uniform and shackles. I asked her if she had just been sentenced, as I had seen her crying earlier. She confirmed she had; it was for a drug charge. She was going to prison for nine years. It was my understanding that she was waiting in the cell to be taken back to the prison, wherever that was, and I would be staying the night alone in the cell, but I didn't verbalize that to her. Had I, she surely would have corrected me and explained the "law of the land."

The marshals came to get me, and they took me to a small room, along with my father. They gave us paperwork to fill out and took all our personal belongings, and then they explained we would continue the booking process when we were brought back tomorrow because it was getting late in the day. *Brought back?* I asked where we were going. They said we would be going to Kaufman County, as if I was just supposed to know what that was, which I didn't, and nobody was telling me anything.

I then heard the female guard asking if I was supposed to leave my clothes there for the night and change into prison clothes so that my clothes would be there when I returned the next day or if I would change into prison clothes at Kaufman and just bring my clothes back with me. I tried to ask, "You mean I don't get to wear my own clothes to my arraignment tomorrow?" but nobody heard me. In my previous jail experience, I'd never changed clothes. I had appeared at my arraignment in my own clothes. I was slowly figuring out that this was going to be very different than my previous experience.

It was determined that I would wear my clothes to Kaufman County and then change there, and they would determine at Kaufman County whether my clothes would travel back with me the next day or whether I would have to go back to Kaufman the next day to be released and get my clothes. It was all so confusing and overwhelming, and there wasn't anyone explaining things. At this point my mind was kind of starting to go someplace else. I was going on "autopilot" mode; by the grace of God, that would carry me through the next few days.

I heard the guard say, "Okay, I'm going to get them chained up." I looked around at the prisoners who had been brought out of the other cells and knew immediately what she was referring to by "chained up." They all had shackles—a set of handcuffs connected by a chain—on both their wrists and ankles. I was getting the shackles that I had seen the lady in the yellow prison suit wearing, and I was also going to get a yellow suit when I arrived in Kaufman County.

The guard told me to turn around and put my hands on the wall. She then put a metal cuff around each ankle, and because I had on sandals with no socks, the metal dug into my skin, making immediate red marks. I hadn't prepared properly for that part of the indictment or really any part of it, and I wished

I'd worn socks. She told me to turn back around; then she put a metal cuff around each wrist. We were told to get in a single file line and follow the guards. We all shuffled to an elevator, which we took down to a parking garage. There was a big white bus with bars over all the windows waiting for us.

The men and women were separated on the bus. I spent some of the ride talking to my new friend, Virginia, the woman who had just been sentenced to nine years. She had spent the past few months in Kaufman County while waiting to get sentenced to prison. She would now be going back to Kaufman County until they determined the prison where she would serve her sentence. She told me everyone at Kaufman County was nice, but the food was horrible; it wasn't like federal prison where prisoners had access to amenities such as makeup and physical activities. It was just a holding facility, not the place where federal inmates ultimately ended up. She was looking forward to being moved now that she had been officially sentenced. I wasn't overly concerned because I didn't think I would be staying there more than the one night anyway. Our arraignment was the next day, and even if the government moved to detain us, we would fight the detention immediately and be on our way because there was no logical reason we would be detained. I believed, wrongly, the government would see it that way. I would learn over the next few years that the word *logic* had little to no meaning in our situation.

Kaufman County Detention Center was far—nearly an hour away. And we had to stop at another detention center on the way to drop off some prisoners. Everyone in the bus with us had come in from jail that day to go to their sentencing hearing, and now, like Virginia, they were going back to the jail until they moved on to a federal prison to serve their sentences. Some of these people had been stuck in the county jails for many months awaiting sentencing, and the county jails were not designed for long-term living, as I would soon witness.

We finally arrived at Kaufman County, and I said good-bye to my new friend, as it seemed we were going to separate places for the night. She had asked the guard if I could be in the cell with her, but the guard had said she didn't even know if I would be going into "population" since we were going back for our arraignment the next day. I had no idea what she meant by "population," but I would soon learn. A male guard and a female guard checked my father and me into Kaufman County. There were a ton of questions to answer and paperwork to be filled out, but they did that all for us since we were in hand-cuffs. I was sitting there, next to my father, being checked into a county jail because we were under federal indictment. It was surreal and just didn't seem right. We had worked together, traveled together, done a marathon together, had many good times together, and now we were going to jail together.

I tried to keep a smile on my face and a sense of humor about the whole situation. It was the only way I knew how to cope at that point, along with a lot of prayer and faith. The guard asked me what I weighed, and I noticed a scale in the corner of the room. I asked if she was going to actually weigh me—I hadn't weighed myself in probably a year because I found it depressing that no matter how much I worked out, the scale never said what I thought it should.

She said, "No, but I can if you want me to."

I said, "Yeah, now would probably be a good time because I wouldn't be too upset no matter what it says since I have bigger problems on my hands now." She laughed. Anyway, I opted not to weigh.

The guard took me into a room and had me change into the yellow prison suit. It was scratchy yellow material made into something like hospital scrubs but not near as comfortable, and on the back of the shirt, "Kaufman County" was spelled out in big black block letters. There was not a bra issued, and I had to turn mine in with the rest of the clothes I had worn there, so I wouldn't be wearing a bra (a bra could have been purchased from the commissary, but our accounts wouldn't be funded until after one week). I was issued the most hideous underwear I had ever seen in my life—I couldn't even call them panties. They were big, white, cotton underwear that looked similar to an adult diaper. I did have to be strip-searched, but that part wasn't as bad as I thought it would be. It wasn't an invasive strip search where they look into your most private areas. The guard was actually very kind. I was given prison footwear—a pair of orange rubber slip-ons—but no socks were issued. Those too could have been purchased through the commissary. I always hated wearing socks and had always preferred flip-flops or sandals, but for the first time in my life, I really did not like having my feet exposed.

I was instructed to grab a dingy blue mattress from a pile of mattresses as well as a scratchy gray blanket. I was issued a plastic bag that contained a flimsy plastic comb, a bottle of shampoo, a bar of soap, a toothbrush, toothpaste, and a roll of toilet paper. The guard then walked me over to a cell door, opened it, and told me, "Here's your home for the night." It was pretty much just like the cell I had been in briefly at the federal building, but it had a thick metal door that I couldn't see out of, and there was a window that had mini blinds on the outside that were shut. The fluorescent lighting in the cell was blinding, and I could hear all the noise outside of the cell, which was right by the guard station. I wasn't going to get any sleep that night, for several reasons.

They came to get me a few minutes later to continue the booking process, which involved taking my mug shot. There is no "say cheese"—I found it very uncomfortable and exposing and didn't know what expression should be on my face, fearing it would be displayed publicly throughout the media. The guard asked me what I'd been arrested for, and I couldn't tell her because I didn't know. Nobody had told us our charges yet. They let me have my one phone call, and I called my mother. I would have called Dan, but I knew he was in transit to Alaska. She was relieved to hear my voice, and we had talked several times in the previous days about the indictment, so she had been prepared for it. She said she would get in touch with Dan to make sure he knew, and she said she would tell Jason what had happened so he could be prepared for the kids should the arrest be publicized.

I was brought back into my cell, where I tossed and turned on the flimsy mattress on the floor all night, and the bright fluorescent lights remained on all night. I was isolated and in shock. I had spent the last year of my life wondering if this would ever happen, and it finally had.

I lay in that cell all night long, my heart racing, feeling sick to my stomach, thinking that if I could just make it through this one night, then I would go home tomorrow, and we would begin really preparing for our case and get everything resolved sooner rather than later. I didn't think it would really be all that bad once I made it to the next day.

At some point during the night they brought me out of the cell so a nurse could check my vitals. My blood pressure was skyrocketing. The nurse asked me if I had children. I said yes and that I was very worried about them. She said her blood pressure would be high, too, if she were in my situation. While I was with the nurse, I saw on my paperwork that the charge against me was "defrauding the United States government." I didn't fully understand what that charge meant, but I thought it had to do with the misbranding allegation, which I knew was the least of all the charges they had threatened, with a five-year maximum sentence. I went back in the cell and thought maybe it wasn't so bad. Maybe they were starting out small, hoping to get us to come to the table and make a deal. Unbeknownst to me, the paperwork I saw that night only listed that one charge because it was the first of several charges in the indictment, not the only one.

I was called out of my cell around six o'clock the next morning. I saw my father, but we were not permitted to talk. We just sat and waited in silence for nearly two hours until it was time to be shackled up and loaded on the bus. I asked the guard if they could wrap the cuffs around my pants instead of directly on my skin because they had been digging into my ankles, and they said that regulations didn't allow for that. Why would they care whether the cuffs were wrapped around clothing material rather than directly on the skin? Was it just to make it as uncomfortable as possible?

I was in shock and sleep deprived. When we arrived at the federal building, I was taken back to the holding cell where I had begun my imprisonment the night before. The wrist shackles were removed, but the ankle shackles would remain on all day. There were two girls in there already, but they were in orange suits. They had come in from another jail and were there for their sentencing hearings.

Their stories were sad. One was only nineteen and had found herself with a drug problem and a bad boyfriend, which had led to her ending up in the current situation. I thought how easily that could have been me at nineteen and how grateful I was that it hadn't been, yet look where I was now. The irony was that at nineteen, I'd known I was breaking a law with my drug usage, but now I didn't understand what I had done. The other girl was older, and this was her ninth time to go to prison—every time for dealing meth. She explained that it was a vicious cycle for her—she wasn't a criminal, but she was an addict, and for her the two had started to go hand in hand. Every time she got out of prison, she would try to do the right thing but couldn't get a job due to her felony conviction, and any job she could get wasn't enough to keep her afloat. Then the addiction would set in again and the dealing, and, well, the saga continued. She knew right from wrong—she wasn't defending her actions—but she did say her life was doomed after the very first conviction. People were supposed to go to prison to get rehabilitated and learn to live a better life, but that was often not what happened. There are success stories out there, but I would learn over the next few days that there are many stories like the one I heard from this girl who had been in and out of prison her entire life.

About an hour before our arraignment I had my interview with pretrial services; I met with a government official whose job was to meet with people who had been arrested to determine whether they should be released on a personal recognizance bond. The federal system didn't have a monetary bond like the state system. I had been prepared for this by my attorney. I was told it was very important because this was the person who would write a report for the judge, and this report would say whether I was a good candidate to be released. I was told to be completely honest with pretrial services—I would be asked about any drug usage, past criminal record, and my personal data.

She asked at the beginning of the interview for a name and phone number of someone who could be contacted to verify everything I would tell her, so I gave her my mother's information. She asked me about drug usage, and I said I smoked marijuana some but not habitually. She was very concerned with how often I smoked, and I reiterated that it wasn't all the time. I thought I was going to have to take a drug test that day, and I even offered to, but she didn't want me to. I thought that was odd because I would have passed a drug test, which would have substantiated my statement that I wasn't a habitual smoker. She asked if I had ever done any other drugs, and I was honest and discussed my late teen years briefly. It was a laundry list of drugs I had tried, but I knew I was supposed to be honest, and in my mind that had all happened so long ago that it was a positive I had made it through and overcome an addiction. I knew she was going to call my mother, and my mother would tell her all the same information, so it was best to be honest. I was also asked about my job and the fishing lodges and where those were located, whether there were bank accounts in foreign countries, and whether I spoke a foreign language—the last two questions I said yes to because I was being honest. Little did I know what the government was trying to establish by taking me down that path of questioning.

We had our arraignment, and it was a whirlwind. Almost a year after the civil case had commenced, we were finally presented with our charges, and it was everything that they had threatened us with since June 2014: distribution of a controlled substance and a controlled substance analogue, importation of a controlled substance analogue, money laundering, maintaining a drug-involved premise, conspiracy to defraud the United States government (which was the misbranding), and a few other minor things thrown in there just to make it all sound even worse. It was seventeen counts total. It was overwhelming, and still none of it made any sense to me. The government was moving to detain us, and because my attorney happened to be out of town for the weekend and couldn't be there to represent me, our detention hearing would have to be postponed until Monday. I would spend the next four nights back in Kaufman County. I was in shock, and I couldn't understand why one of the other attorneys on our team couldn't just represent me so we could get the hearing over and done with, but I didn't realize what a complex ordeal the hearing would be.

I sat in silence on the bus ride back to the jail. I was exhausted because I hadn't slept, and I was so sad. I was going to miss Kieley's recital because our hearing wasn't until Monday. I was devastated, and then as I thought about that, I started thinking about the idea of possibly not even getting out on Monday and all the things I could miss. The reality of the situation was starting to hit me, but I didn't allow myself to think that for very long. I was going to be positive. I decided for that night, since I assumed I would now move into "population" in Kaufman County, I would just be happy to move into a cell where I at least had a bed, some people to talk to, a TV, and a hot shower—I had confirmed already that at least those things existed in Kaufman County.

I was brought into my new cell that would be my home until Monday (I hoped not one day longer). The girls all welcomed me enthusiastically. There were five of them, and the first question they asked, which I had already learned was the first thing everyone asked in prison, was "What are you in here for?"

I started to explain my rehearsed answer: "We operate a store where they said we sold something illegal." I had been coached by our attorneys to keep conversation regarding the charges as simple as possible because you never knew what people may misconstrue.

One girl immediately said, "Oh my gosh; we just saw you on the news! We love Gas Pipe! This is such bullshit what they are doing to you!" I guess I had stupidly hoped the ordeal hadn't made the news, but of course it had. I asked my new roommates what the news had said and whether it was bad. They assured me it was shown briefly, and it wasn't too bad. I think they were downplaying it, or maybe their idea of "not too bad" was different than mine, because I would later learn the news coverage was bad.

After some begging, I was allowed one phone call upon my return to Kaufman County, and I called my mother. I was able to give her the number she could call to set up an account so I could call her regularly from the phone in the jail cell. There were two phones in the jail cell, and I called her constantly. Sadly, for the other girls, I never had to fight to use the phone because I was one of the few who had anyone to call, especially someone I could call as much as I wanted. Dan also set up an account, as did my godmother, Emma, and my cousin Jessica. I was blessed I had so many people I could reach out to, and I even solicited help from Emma to call some of my roommates' family members and give them the number to call and set up an account so my roommates could call their families too. Many of them had not been able to call their families when they had arrived in Kaufman County, so they hadn't set up accounts and therefore hadn't talked to family members in months. I was glad we were able to help them reconnect with the outside world.

I didn't talk to my kids while I was there. That would have been too difficult. I had been told by my mother that Jason had explained to them where I was. It was heartbreaking to imagine what they must have been feeling and thinking. My mother had talked to them, and she assured me they were good. I was adamant I was getting out Monday, or at least that's what I would say out loud. My mother would say she was sure, too, but I could tell something was off in her voice. At the time I tried to attribute it to the stress she must have been feeling knowing I was in jail, but later I would learn that when the pretrial services officer had called her to confirm all my information, she had told my mother that she was going to recommend I be detained until trial because I was a flight risk due to our businesses outside of the country.

I literally ached for my children. Every fiber in my being hurt at the thought of not seeing them or holding them. I hadn't even told them goodbye or explained what would be happening. All I could think about was hugging them. I daydreamed about it constantly. It was a pain and longing unlike anything I had ever experienced. Of course, I missed Dan, too, but he at least could understand, as best as any of us could, what was happening. And I always saw Dan as so strong. When I called him from jail, he was as strong as ever and quoted Bible verses for me, encouraging me to be strong and pray and know that God would see me through. Little did I know—until he told me much later— that every time we hung up the phone, he would cry.

The next four days were spent in a bit of a daze. Unbelievably, I didn't cry once. It was like having an out-of-body experience— like I was watching myself from the outside. I prayed and read the Bible, which was one thing that was provided, thankfully. I was not in charge of myself those four days—it was God. I was weak, but I went through the motions from day to day and was propelled forward by prayer, faith, the phone calls I was able to make to my family, and the one fifteen-minute visit that was permitted with my mother. I made friends and interacted with the other girls, many of whom asked if I would give them a job when they got out because, like I had already heard from other prisoners, getting your life on track after going to prison and having a felony on your record was difficult. Many of my roommates in Kaufman County were unfortunately repeat offenders—all very nice people who had gotten into trouble at a young age and had never fully found their way out of it.

We played card games, and I led everyone in yoga a few times. There was also a television in the room. All my cell-mates slept all day and then would be awake all night. I didn't understand why, but that was the routine they had established. I think part of it was the massive amounts of antidepressants they were given daily to help them cope. I was told by new friends that I, too, could get evaluated for those after I was there a certain amount of time. There wasn't any counseling or programs for rehabilitation at this facility, but there were drugs handed out daily.

Most of the girls had been together in that cell for months, and some even over a year. The positive part of them being asleep all day was that I could watch whatever I wanted to watch on television. The negative part was at nighttime, when I was trying to sleep; they would be up and talking all night, laughing and having a good time, and cooking food they'd bought from the commissary in the coffeepot they had bought from the commissary. They had all stopped eating the jail food some time ago. Most of it was unidentifiable and highly processed, with minimal to no fruits and vegetables. Anyway, sleep, even with silence, would have been challenging because the bright fluorescent lights were never turned off. I didn't complain to the girls about their noise, though, because I admired their ability to stay positive and seemingly have fun, knowing where they were with no end in sight. All of them were there because they'd already been sentenced, but there wasn't room yet for them in a federal prison, or they were awaiting sentencing, but all had been detained when they had been indicted either because they had met the profile for someone who should be detained or more commonly because they didn't have the resources to hire a capable attorney who would argue for them not to be detained. There was also this theory, as explained to me by one of the girls, that if defendants didn't fight detention and instead agreed to be detained, the government would be more lenient when it came time for sentencing. The problem was that facilities such as Kaufman County, where defendants are detained indefinitely, are not designed for people to live there for months and even years while waiting to be sentenced or transferred to a federal facility.

At detention centers such as Kaufman County, there are no rehabilitation programs for federal inmates. There is no exercise or outdoor activity. We would get to go to another cell once or twice a day for thirty minutes, and this was called "outside," but it was nothing more than another concrete cell with a chain-link fence as a ceiling so that some air could be felt. There was nothing to do in this "outside" area except walk around in a circle and play "sock ball"—a game the girls had invented by wrapping a bunch of socks together in a ball and then volleying it back and forth. Inmates were only allowed one visitor once a week for fifteen minutes, and the visiting was done through a glass window. There were not any work programs, counseling, computer usage, or the advertised ability to make a phone call. Had I not begged to call my mother when I had returned from our arraignment and asked the guards for the information I could give her so she could set up an account for me to call, I would have had no way to contact my family. My cellmates had not known to do this, and that was why few of them had been able to make calls to their families.

There was one girl in my cell who was incoherently out of her mind. She stayed in her bed almost twenty-four seven, and when she did get up, she babbled about her dog that was missing. She obviously was mentally ill and needed help. When I mentioned my concern for her to one of the guards, I was told, "There's nothing we can do; we see it all the time."

People have a way, I suppose, of convincing themselves that if someone has committed a crime, they shouldn't even be treated as humans any longer. People have a way of justifying the inhumane treatment individuals go through as criminals who are perceived as bad people, never once thinking maybe they are just flawed, imperfect human beings, like we all are, who made a mistake and, if given a chance, could be better. Never once during our entire legal ordeal did I ever hear anything from the prosecution along the lines of wanting to help people become better or be rehabilitated. All dialogue was always geared toward the greatest punishment possible, and I heard the same story from all the girls I met in Kaufman County. It was evident by the way everyone was treated and left there, forgotten. It's not natural to stay confined in one room twenty-four seven, with the exception of maybe an hour a day in an area that was called "outside" but wasn't really outside. The body and psyche are deprived of so much—the lack of sunlight, vitamin D, fresh air, feeling the grass, seeing something besides the same four walls or whatever happens to be on the TV—it's not healthy. Violent offenders serving hard time in prison get better treatment than that.

One thing I learned is that you quickly bond in a situation like that. You are with the same people all day and all night, and even though we may have had nothing in common on the outside world, and we were all very different people, we were in there together. You learn to make the best of it. You share stories, and you share what few belongings you have. I didn't have anything from the commissary because I hadn't been there long enough, but everyone was happy to share their nicer toiletries with me, and they would share their commissary food with me. There was a unique support system and sisterhood there that I would have never expected. It was humbling and equalizing.

Chapter Fourteen

*I*t was finally Monday morning and time for me to go back to the federal courthouse. Once again, I was pulled out of the cell at six o'clock in the morning only to sit and wait in silence. I saw my father for the first time since Thursday evening. He looked tired and worn, and I wanted to hug him, but we weren't even allowed to talk to each other at that point.

A guard we hadn't met before came to prepare us to get on the bus, which meant the shackles again. He put the ankle cuffs on tighter than anyone else had previously. They were so tight that it went beyond leaving a red mark—they actually squeezed the skin as he locked them, and when I said, "Ow, that hurts; can you please loosen them?" he actually replied, "You should have worn socks."

I tried to explain that I didn't have socks because I hadn't arrived with socks, but he then said, "Well, next time you'll know if you're going to be arrested to be prepared with socks." Well, there were a lot of things I would have done to prepare differently had I had any idea how the whole indictment process was going to play out.

We arrived at the federal building and were taken back into holding cells at the US Marshals Office. I was alone in a cell for about an hour, and then Carolyn, our office manager and dear friend, came in. She had been indicted, too, but she was just now turning herself in. I was able to find out from her who else had been indicted and when—our retail managers, our corporate buyer, and our operations manager had all been indicted and arraigned on Friday. The government had not moved to detain anyone but me and my father.

I was so glad to have somebody to talk with from my regular daily life. It helped the time go by—of course, I was counting down the minutes. I had my crappy bologna sandwich sack lunch that had been sent for me from Kaufman County, but I wasn't hungry. The DEA agents had treated Carolyn to a cheeseburger and fries, accompanied by a conversation they had with her in hopes of trying to get her to make a plea deal—how nice of them. She kindly offered to share it with me. Even though it was the first "real food" I had seen in days, I could barely eat. I had a couple french fries, which were delicious, but my stomach was a wreck. My immediate future was at risk.

My attorney came to meet with me briefly. He explained that the pretrial services had recommended I should be detained because I was viewed as a flight risk. I had traveled extensively out of the country the past year and always returned, knowing that an indictment was looming. We had even gotten on a plane to come home from Baja California Sur immediately after learning we were going to be indicted. I had young children whom I would never voluntarily leave. There was no way I met the definition of a flight risk, but the government was taking the position that because I helped operate businesses in foreign countries and remote Alaska, that meant I would flee. It made zero sense to me. Also, my honesty about my late teenage years was now being used against me so I could be described as someone with "lifelong drug usage." The most negative spin possible was being put on my life, even though I had been drug free for over twenty years, except for occasionally smoking marijuana.

I was shocked, scared, and in complete disbelief. My attorney assured me he was going to do the best he could. I knew I was in good hands, but I had never expected to be portrayed the way the government was portraying me. I was desperate to go home, and my attorney asked me if I would be open to the idea of some sort of house arrest if that was what it would take to get me out of there. Of course I said, "Yes, just get me out of here."

I was told I would see a lot of people I knew who were there to show support when I went into the courtroom. I knew my mother, stepdad, and cousins would be there, but I didn't know who else. I was grateful they were going to be there, but I was nervous and already humiliated that they would see me in such a state—a yellow prison suit with shackles. It was disgraceful. I would not be able to wave, say hi, or give a hug or any acknowledgement, and I needed to try to contain all emotion during the hearing.

Several defendants from different cases would go through their arraignments in the same courtroom before my father and I would go through our detention hearing. We were chained up in our shackles, loaded onto the elevator, and sent to the floor where the courtroom was located.

We got off the elevator and shuffled to the courtroom. There were people everywhere. The hallway was packed. I saw so many people—more faces than I could count. My mother and stepdad were there, coworkers who hadn't been indicted, family friends, friends of mine from childhood, friends I had only known for a short period, my cousins, my godmother, and even my favorite teacher from fifth grade. There I was at my absolute worst—in that awful yellow prison suit and shackles, humbled to my core and stripped of almost all dignity—yet I had never felt so loved. I knew Dan had wanted to be there, too, but there were strategic reasons he had stayed in Alaska. Our defense attorneys accurately suspected that the government would try to claim Dan could help us flee because he was a pilot, even though the government had seized his airplane, and we had no money to obtain another airplane. The lack of logic wasn't missed on anyone, most importantly the judge.

Our attorneys were amazing during the hearing. It was brutal with the government putting a DEA agent on the stand who had all kinds of interesting stuff to say about me, my father, and the Gas Pipe, most of which couldn't be substantiated. The government tried their best to talk about what an unfit mother I was who didn't deserve to be back home with her children because marijuana (a misdemeanor amount) was found in my house. They glossed right over the fact that they didn't find anything they were actually looking for in my house such as massive amounts of drugs, guns, or hidden money. They stressed how confident they were that my father and I would flee if given the chance, even though we'd had ample opportunity to flee the past year or even the night we turned ourselves in at the US Marshals Office when they had told us we could go home and come back the next day to be arrested. That would have been a great time to flee, but we hadn't.

The DEA agent the government used for their one witness at our detention hearing must have been confused or very forgetful. He had been the one to sign the original civil complaint, which he had to sign as a sworn affidavit, and within that

document there were a litany of products and synthetic cannabinoids listed by name that we had allegedly sold. Yet during
cross-examination by our attorneys at the detention hearing, he
claimed to have never heard of some of the products.

After lengthy testimony, Judge Horan, who was the magistrate judge for our case and not the one who would be conduct-
ing the main trial, took a short recess to make his decision on
whether we would be released. After what seemed like eternity,
he came back with his decision. He said we were not a danger
to society, there was no evidence of any ongoing illegal activity
at the Gas Pipe (there you go—a federal judge was saying the
Gas Pipe was a completely legal business, something my parents
had longed to hear for years in the eighties), and we could go
back home and go to work. But we would have to wear a GPS
monitor and be basically tied to our homes with the exception
of work, school, church, doctor and attorney appointments,
and any other activities approved by our pretrial services officer. I didn't fully understand what a GPS monitor would entail,
but I was going home. I cried and said out loud, "Thank you,
God." I will be forever grateful to Judge Horan, who over the
years to come would preside over other helpful hearings.

We had to be transported back to Kaufman County, where
we would wait for our release paperwork to be processed. I
thought we would just get to walk out of the courtroom, but
once again, I was wrong. We had been registered as property of
the US marshals and were being held at the Kaufman County
Detention Center, so that was where we had to officially be
released from. Our clothes were there, too, so if nothing else, we
had to go back for those. That meant another bus ride back to
Kaufman, and it also meant being put back in the shackles, even
though we weren't going to be detained any longer. It didn't
make any sense to me, but I was just relieved to be going home.

It took hours for the paperwork to be processed, and it was nearly midnight when we were picked up by my mother and stepdad. They were such troopers. They brought my godmother, Emma, with them, and they brought us delicious food—pizza and fresh pasta from a Dallas Italian restaurant. We ravenously stuffed food in our faces in the back seat of JB's Suburban, but we really couldn't eat much, as our stomachs were not accustomed to such yummy, rich food after the cuisine we'd had the past five days. Even better than the food, though, was being able to give everyone hugs. It was so nice to have the feeling of closeness with people we knew and loved. I learned quickly while I was detained that the thing I missed the most was the touch of a loved one.

By the time I finally got home, it was close to two in the morning. I took a shower and crawled into my bed with my cotton sheets, down comforter, and multiple pillows. I didn't know if I had ever felt anything so exquisite and comfortable in my life, even though I'd had bedding like that for years. It felt new and different now.

I called Dan before I fell asleep, and it was so great to hear his voice from my own phone and not the jail phone. He was loving and encouraging as always, but all I could feel was guilt and shame. He deserved so much better than me. I didn't know how I could stay with someone who was such a good, strong, decent person. I didn't believe I had done what I was accused of, but I was starting to realize innocence didn't necessarily matter. I had been treated like a criminal already, regardless of my innocence. The whole "innocent until proven guilty" rule did not seem to ring true for me the last five days, but for the time being, I was free, and I needed to focus on that. Dan believed in me, and even though I felt unworthy of someone so wonderful, he was not going to have any part of that negative thinking. He was with me for the long haul. I was grateful but ashamed.

I was scheduled to report to the federal courthouse promptly at eleven o'clock the next morning to meet my pretrial officer. My father and I were both assigned to the same person, Eric Zarate. Coincidentally, I'd heard about Mr. Zarate from one of my cellmates. She had told me to hope to not get him. From the instant I met him, I couldn't understand why she had said that, and me being the outspoken person I have always been, I felt compelled to tell him that. He told me that my former cellmate had given him a hell of a time, so he wasn't surprised that she wasn't a fan of his. For me, though, he was so nice and easy to talk with, and he made an unpleasant situation much more bearable.

Eric seemed sympathetic to our situation, but he made it clear that it was simply his job to enforce the parameters of what the judge had given. We were to be monitored twenty-four seven and could only leave our homes for approved activities. I would have to submit a weekly schedule letting him know where I would be at all times, and I would have to wait to hear back from him to know if my schedule was approved. He explained that the monitor would be kept loose enough so I could clean underneath it while I showered, and I was shocked. I had assumed the monitor could come off and on while I was at home. Once again, how wrong I was. This contraption was going to practically become part of my body, and it was big, cumbersome, and hideous. I wouldn't be able to wear fitted jeans because there was no way to get jeans over or under the monitor. It would be very obvious when seen on my ankle, so unless I didn't want to make a spectacle of myself in public with people possibly staring, I would want to wear something that would cover it—thank goodness for maxi dresses! I had always been a fan of them, and I already had a few, but they would become my fashion staple of the summer, to the point I would be sick of them.

I asked about all the activities that would be approved. I explained how I always worked in Alaska in the summer, but I was beginning to suspect I wouldn't be going there that summer. He said I only could go if the judge approved it.

It was finally time to pick up the kids. I had never seen a more beautiful sight in my life. I gave them the biggest hugs I had ever given anyone. I had spent five days wondering if or when I would get to hug them again. They of course had questions, and they wanted to know what had happened. They told me how their dad had explained things to them, and my heart ached that everyone had had to go through that experience. I told them that I refused to admit to something I didn't do, and I was fighting this thing, and part of that was that I'd gone to jail for a few days because the government was trying to coerce us into pleading to something. I also told them that jail was somewhere they never wanted to go. While I was trying to be positive about my situation and put on a brave face, jail had not been a good experience, and I wanted them to learn that they should never do anything that might cause them to go there. I had to find a balance of remaining upbeat and portraying the idea that everything was going to be okay while also using the situation as a teaching moment for what could happen if we messed up, even though I still wasn't sure how I had broken a law.

The kids were interested in my new ankle accessory, and I explained that things were going to be different around the house for a while. We would be very limited in where we could go, but the alternative was me not being home at all. They were very understanding. I told them I would understand if they wanted to spend more time at their dad's while I was under these restrictions, but they wanted to be with me.

My actions, although I didn't believe them to be illegal, were causing so many people in my life to be hurt, scared, and stressed. I was really beginning to doubt myself as a person and finding it hard to like myself. I was in for a long journey of self-discovery, reevaluating myself and everything I believed in, and learning about patience, compassion, grace, and forgiveness for myself and others.

Chapter Fifteen

*I*f I was going to give this chapter a title, it would be "My Life with Bertha." I could probably write an entire book entitled that, but certainly an entire chapter of this book should be dedicated to Bertha, which is the name the kids and I gave my ankle monitor. Thankfully we were all able to have a sense of humor about it. I wasn't always humorous in private or when I was complaining to Dan or our attorneys, but with the kids I was because they seemed to be handling it all so well. Why should I be negative in front of them? The first thing they did when they saw the ankle monitor was laugh and talk about how awful and big it was. That was when we decided it should have a name, and its name should be one typically associated with something big, so we collectively agreed on Bertha.

Life with Bertha definitely forced me to slow down, something I needed to do. In the year between the raids and the indictment, I had thought I had slowed down, but I really hadn't. Being arrested and then monitored twenty-four seven changed my outlook on everything. It wasn't that I had anything to hide or anything I didn't want the government to know; my life was pretty much an open book. But my life was now limited, and things I had taken for granted were now privileges.

The first place I went with Bertha that wasn't related to work or taking the kids somewhere was the grocery store. Grocery shopping had to be approved as part of my weekly schedule, and I had to get everything I needed because I would not be permitted to go to the store again until the following week.

The upcoming weekend was Memorial Day weekend, and the kids were with me for the weekend. I wanted to make the weekend as fun as possible. We had people coming over throughout the weekend, so that would keep everyone entertained. There were definitely worse places to be stuck than our home—we had a beautiful, spacious home with plenty to do to entertain ourselves. We had never spent enough time at home anyway. I'd always felt that the big, beautiful house I'd wanted so badly had gone somewhat wasted and unappreciated because we had always been on the go.

The week after Memorial Day was the last week of school, and then summer break would begin. The kids were leaving on a school trip to Washington, DC. I was permitted to take them to the airport, but I was nervous because I would see their teachers and the other kids' parents. I knew that so far nobody had said anything rude or hurtful to the kids, but my situation had been all over the news and internet. My mug shot had been shown in multiple places, including the front page of the *Dallas Morning News*. When the civil case had been initiated the year prior, people had reached out and been supportive, and everyone had said, "Oh, they just want your money." Once it had turned into a criminal case, I feared some people had a different opinion. Suddenly we were labeled as potential felons, not just people who were being taken advantage of financially by the government, but things went fine when I took the kids to the airport. Everyone was friendly and acted as though nothing had changed.

The reality of what was happening was starting to sink in. My attorney filed a motion for me to be allowed to travel to Alaska and work. The motion was denied. I was completely devastated. The court didn't feel that I could be trusted to go so far. It felt like a punch to the gut. The job and place I loved so dearly were not going to be part of my life that summer. Alaska gave me clarity in life. It was always such a special place to me, and I loved working at the lodge with Dan, but it wasn't going to happen. I was supposed to feel lucky that I was home and not in jail, and logically I knew that was accurate, but also logically I didn't think any of this should be happening.

The kids still went to Alaska with Dan, and they went to summer camp, as they had for years. Although I missed them terribly, I was glad they had so many plans throughout the summer because I was very limited with what I could do with them outside of the house. I had a lot of downtime to reflect. The error of my ways was starting to have an effect on me. While I knew I wasn't guilty of the charges against us, I was definitely beginning to realize that selling herbal incense was one of the worst decisions of my life, and I had made some pretty bad ones prior to that. I had the opportunity to read and research a lot; it was a nasty business we had gotten caught up in, and I was so glad to not be part of it anymore. It took me a while to be able to say that because I was initially so angry about what the government was doing to us, and I was adamant that we hadn't knowingly broken a law, but I slowly realized I could say that I had made a very bad decision, even though I hadn't believed it to be illegal. There are legal laws, and there are moral laws. I had broken a moral law without a doubt.

I spent a lot of time reading and writing while I was at home. I wrote my first memoir, which was really a babbling emotional purge of my entire life, not really designed for the public to read, but it was cleansing and therapeutic. I also wrote a fiction novel, something I'd wanted to do, but I'd never had the time. I also had the drama and excitement of the primaries for the upcoming presidential election, which was surely going to be the most exciting in years, between Trump and Clinton. I had plenty to keep me occupied and tried to use the time to get things organized around my home and do some much-needed soul-searching, but it was hard, and it was lonely.

The weekends were particularly challenging, especially if the kids weren't there, since their activities were pretty much the only reason I could leave the house other than work and a few approved errands. I would get home from work on Friday and know I wouldn't be leaving again until Monday morning. I was often solitary for extended periods of time. I had friends and family who came to see me regularly, and I was so appreciative of that, but the situation itself was lonely. I couldn't fully talk about what was happening because the case and our defense strategy were confidential. Nobody I knew had been through anything close to what I was going through. When I would try to share my feelings with some of my closest friends, it was usually a very short conversation. It wasn't that people didn't care or didn't want to help, but they usually just didn't know what to say. I couldn't blame them. I wouldn't have known either had I not gone through it. It was a very isolating situation that nobody could have even begun to comprehend. I had a hard time comprehending it myself.

My attorneys were very supportive, and I'm quite sure they thought I'd lost my mind at times. I would call them and yell, cry, and completely break down. I was a bit out of my mind. I felt stuck, like I couldn't go anywhere. I was very limited where

I could physically go, but it wasn't just that. I was mentally stuck. I couldn't think about my future because I didn't even know if I had a future. I was facing life in prison—for selling a product in the wide-open retail environment, paying taxes on every dollar made from it, and even being told by local law enforcement that it was a legal product. I couldn't wrap my head around it. Nothing logically made sense about the situation, and I tried so hard to focus on the fact that I knew we were innocent, with the exception of the product being mislabeled, which was only a misdemeanor offense that should not lead to any sort of forfeiture nor life in prison. But I also knew that the odds were against us because our federal justice system was never in favor of defendants. Most cases never even went to trial, and those that did ended in favor of the defendant only about 3 percent of the time. The stakes were high, but we were being given no choice but to fight.

The reason most cases never went to trial was because most defendants took some sort of plea deal. As the months continued postindictment, the majority of our codefendants made a deal with the government, all agreeing to testify against us. We were shocked. Everyone who had been like family to us for so long, everyone who had believed we were all innocent and had continued happily working at Gas Pipe even after the government had come in and seized everything, everyone who had said Gas Pipe was the best job they'd ever had—they were now going to testify against us to save themselves, mostly out of fear of going to prison for a very long time, not because any of us ever believed we were breaking a law.

I understood the fear; I had the same fear, but I also knew I couldn't say I'd done something I hadn't done, and the government wasn't offering me or my father a reasonable plea deal. I knew more about our case than any of the people who had taken deals. I understood the complexities of it and how the

Analogue Act wasn't being applied to our case correctly. It wasn't a black-and-white situation. Nobody, not even chemists, understood what an analogue was, and there were discrepancies throughout the country about this; hence the McFadden case being taken all the way to the Supreme Court. During my summer with Bertha, the Supreme Court ruled unanimously in favor of McFadden, which was at least something positive for me to focus on. That would change the trajectory of our case, and I believed the government would realize that sooner rather than later, but unfortunately, they didn't.

As a condition of my pretrial release, I wasn't permitted to discuss the details of the case with any of the codefendants unless in the presence of our attorneys, and we certainly couldn't help our codefendants pay for the best attorneys, both because we weren't in a position to do so financially, and it wouldn't have been permitted legally. We would have been accused of trying to coerce people to stay on our side. Initially some of the codefendants were in a joint defense agreement with us, meaning we were all working together on defending the case with each of our attorneys, but then the government started offering deals that appeared too good to refuse, and the joint defense agreement went from several to a few. After that we couldn't share our strategies. I would have been hit with obstruction of justice and thrown in jail immediately. I didn't like the idea of people testifying against us—and potentially lying—but I could ultimately live with that. The idea, though, that people were pleading to something none of us even understood was hard for me to watch because I hated watching them go down that road.

There were a handful of our codefendants who stuck it out and would ultimately go all the way to trial with us. Their courage gave me courage. Most of the employees who had made a deal resigned per the advice of their attorneys. And then there were those who made a deal but still continued working for us. What a big emotional internal conflict that caused for me. I wanted to fire them. I couldn't stand the fact that they were going to say we all knowingly broke the law together, yet they still wanted to work for us—because they said it was the best job they'd ever had, and they loved working for me and my father. I was livid and just sick over it, but we were advised by our attorneys to not fire them because that could be viewed as retaliation, and retaliating against anyone was strictly prohibited in our pretrial release guidelines. Yes, we could potentially be put back in jail for choosing to terminate people we didn't want to work with anymore because they were going to potentially testify against us in federal court. I found that very bizarre, but it was even more bizarre that people would want to keep working for us if they felt we had all knowingly broken a law together. Ultimately, I'm glad we didn't fire them. Being forced to continue those relationships and continue to work together was one of the greatest lessons I've ever had in forgiveness and acceptance. God has an amazing way of teaching us things.

The worse part of Bertha and house arrest was the inability to exercise and go outside and feel the sunshine. Going to the gym or taking a walk were not permitted activities. This I never understood because even people in prison get to exercise. I had a treadmill in the house, but the size and placement of Bertha made it difficult to do any vigorous exercise. I tried and ended up with massive welts and blisters from Bertha pressing against my skin. Bertha could be submerged in water, so swimming was permitted, except my backyard was too far away from the antenna in my house that connected the signal to Bertha to confirm I was home when I was supposed to be. So if I went swimming, it would send a signal that I had left the house.

Our regular officer, Eric, was wonderful and understanding—he was another angel on earth. If Eric received a signal, he would always go online, locate me via GPS, and determine I was just in my backyard, but the weekend officer wouldn't do that, so there was no weekend swimming. I had been a marathon runner and had worked out religiously for years. I wasn't thin or overly fit because I always loved good food and wine, but I was healthy. I had great cholesterol and vitals and always had a tan and glow to me because I spent so much time in the outdoors and exercising. Now, the only time I went outside was when I walked from my car to a building on one of my approved outings.

Since I wasn't traveling and on the go constantly, and I couldn't do any of my previous hobbies such as running and exercising, I tried to find other things I could do. Cooking had always been a hobby, and I cooked a lot that summer, but it was mostly for myself.

I'm sure I could have organized dinner parties, and my book club was kind enough to always make the drive to my house for our monthly gatherings, but it was summer, and most people were gone. I was kind of in a funk anyway and wasn't really in the mood to entertain. Besides, I needed to find something outside of the house that could give me an outlet. Church was an approved activity, and the year prior we had joined the Highland Park United Methodist Church, which was walking distance from our house. I wanted the kids to go through the confirmation program beginning in sixth grade, and the church was convenient and had a minister whom I thought was one of the best speakers I'd ever heard. I thank my cousin Amber for first introducing us to that church.

I started adding church services to my weekly schedule. The church became a refuge for me, a place where I felt complete and protected. Every week that I went, I felt the sermon had been written just for me, and I don't mean that in a narcissistic way but in a way that I felt God knew exactly what I needed to hear in that moment. It was healing and rejuvenating, and I would often sit in the service with tears streaming uncontrollably down my face. I had found a connection with God that I'd never known. I'd always believed in God, but I felt a true connection that summer. I learned—and believed—that even though I felt very isolated and alone at the time, I was never truly alone. God was always there. The girl who had felt uncomfortable in church as a child now felt—in her darkest moment, filled with shame and regret—the most at home in church and with God.

Prayer became a need and source of daily fulfillment. I learned how to pray differently, and I began a habit of beginning and ending each day with prayer. I couldn't wait for the end of the day when I could crawl in bed in my dark, quiet space and have time with just me and God. I learned to pray for acceptance, strength, patience, and gratitude rather than praying for what I thought I wanted or needed, but I wasn't perfect at it and struggled with asking God for what I thought should happen. I also prayed for a lot of forgiveness and grace, and grace was something I had never really understood. I was beginning to learn how to give grace and also how to receive grace. I learned from a counselor through the church that it was okay to be angry at God. We get angry at our parents or our family, but we still love them. God is no different. Being angry at God is recognizing God, and we can then work through that anger and come to a place where we know it's not God's fault. God has a plan for us, and it is always a loving plan, even if we don't see it that way or if it's not the plan we want. Our anger may seem like it's directed at God, but it's really toward ourselves, and as we work through it and recognize and process the anger, we can let go of it completely. That concept was astonishing to me. It gave me a sense of peace, but it also intimidated me because I had always been one to hold on to anger and negativity toward myself and others. I was beginning to learn a lot about anger, forgiveness, kindness, and patience. I was slowly starting to learn that life is not about what happens to us but how we react to what is happening to us. And it's not always about being right—it's about being kind to ourselves and others.

I turned forty the summer of 2015. Although I didn't celebrate in Italy as I had planned to do for years, I was lucky enough to have two big celebrations. My mother, stepdad, and Dan planned a surprise party for me in July, a few weeks before my actual birthday so it could take place when Dan was in Dallas. He wouldn't be able to be there for my actual birthday because August was the busiest time of the lodge season. Dan, the kids, and I came home from church, and the house was filled with my friends and family. My mother had gone all out with a wonderful brunch, a video of my life set to music, and my favorite cake. I had been home with Bertha for about two months, and it was just the boost I needed. I celebrated big, as one would do for a big birthday. I was an emotional mess already, and the alcohol didn't help matters. I went from being the life of the party early in the day to having a very big emotional meltdown in the pool with my mother that evening, after the kids had left to go to their dad's.

I'm embarrassed to say I don't remember the details, but I remember I cried a lot and talked about the possibility of going to prison for the rest of my life. My mother helped me out of the pool and up the stairs to my bedroom, which says a lot about how bad off I must have been because my mother doesn't do stairs well herself due to a bad back. I woke up in my bed hours later—feeling sick—to my phone ringing. I had been in the pool earlier in the day, and Bertha was losing its power. It was sending a signal to the weekend monitor that I wasn't where I was supposed to be and that I had possibly disabled the monitor. Today I laugh at the memory, but it was a disaster at the time. Bertha had to be charged regularly, so I would always plug it in when I went to bed at night. I had, even in my drunken stupor, plugged Bertha in when I had crawled into bed, but the charge wasn't working. Mr. Perez, the weekend monitor, had been trying to call me to see what the problem was and to see if I was around and hadn't decided to up and flee the country, but I hadn't heard the phone ring at first. I had to wake up Dan so he could communicate with Mr. Perez, and luckily, after what I'm sure was a very disjointed conversation, we convinced Mr. Perez that I would check in with Eric the following day to get Bertha fixed. Eric came over the following day, and I got a brand-new Bertha.

My second birthday celebration was on my actual birthday and was a little more low key. I planned a pool party at my house and had several friends come over for the day. My father was even able to get permission from Eric so he could come over too. I notified Eric in advance that I would be in the pool most of the day so he could give notice to the weekend monitor. It was a gift to be able to actually go in my own backyard for the day and not have to worry about Bertha. I had gone from years of fantasizing celebrating my fortieth with a trip to Italy to just being thankful I could go in the backyard and swim with friends without setting off an alarm and getting in trouble. My perspective was slowly changing in life.

In an additional effort to find fulfillment and do something worthwhile with myself outside of the house, I started volunteering at the North Texas Food Bank. For years I had volunteered at my children's school, and I had always talked about volunteering more somewhere within the community, but I had never made the time to do it. I had been too busy traveling and doing other things that were, in hindsight, not that important.

Eric allowed me to add volunteering to my weekly schedule, and I soon became a regular at the food bank. I loved interacting with all the people. Going to the food bank quickly became a highlight of my week. I would continue to volunteer at the school as well, in the cafeteria, which was staffed by volunteer parents, and I did it even with Bertha (covered by pants, of course). I enjoyed being at the school and getting to see my children, but the food bank gave me a real sense of contribution, joy, and gratitude for all I still had in my life, despite so much being taken.

The kids were such troopers throughout the summer. They never made me feel guilty or inadequate as a parent for not being able to take them somewhere. There were no last-minute errands or quick spontaneous outings or plans with friends, because if it wasn't prescheduled, it wasn't going to happen. They understood, and they complied. They didn't complain. I had to have talks with them that no parent is prepared to have. In all the reading I had done in preparation for having children and raising teenagers, there was never a section on how to explain to your children that you could be going to prison for the rest of your life. I was able to tell my children candidly and honestly that we sold something that in hindsight was bad and not something we should have sold, and if I could have gone back in time and done it differently, I would have. Yet with the exception of mislabeling the product, I didn't understand how what we had done was illegal, and it certainly didn't warrant life in prison and me living with Bertha while I awaited trial. My kids believed in me, and if it hadn't been for my children and their belief in me, I'm not sure how I would have continued moving forward. Their grace and support taught me a lot about unconditional love, and their faith encouraged my faith. I remember them even telling me one night at dinner that maybe one reason everything was happening was to bring me even closer to God.

The same could be said for Dan. My husband, one of the best souls I have ever known, was suddenly thrust into this horrible, unimaginable situation with me. He heard and saw every raw, ugly, real emotion I was having. Part of me thinks I wanted to push him away because I thought on some level that I didn't deserve to be with someone as good as him. Even though I was aggressively fighting to defend myself, I also felt that I had done something wrong—not something illegal but still wrong—and that maybe I didn't deserve to be with a human being the caliber of Dan. He never made me feel that way, though—not once. He nor his family. They all showered me with support and stood by my side. I was loved, and people were rooting for me, but I was falling apart inside.

Queen's "Bohemian Rhapsody" lyrics, "I don't want to die; I sometimes wish I'd never been born at all," played through my head continuously. I certainly didn't want to die, but I didn't want the life I was living either. My entire life had gone off track, and while I was digging deep into my spirituality and finding a relationship with God stronger than I'd ever had, I was also resisting depression and being dragged down into what felt like a big dark hole. It was as though I could feel good and evil fighting within me. The good was my increasing faith, giving me the strength and power to know that I could overcome anything, that grace is given when we ask for it, that change is possible if we want it and work for it, and that at least one reason for everything happening was so I could become a better person. The evil was the constant voice in my head telling me how much I had screwed up, how unworthy I was, and that I had made horrible choices throughout life and deserved everything bad that could happen to me. I wasn't even sure if I was worthy of this life anymore. Well, the government was telling me that, too, and if I ever tried to forget it, Bertha was right there to remind me.

Chapter Sixteen

Summer ended, and the kids went back to school. That made my weekly schedule more complicated, but thankfully Eric was understanding. Other than teasing me for having a schedule that was like "herding cats," he approved my schedule as much as he could, particularly if it was related to something for the kids.

Every time I left the house, Bertha beeped for thirty seconds. It was a notification that I had left the house, as if I didn't know I had left. It was always tense for me if it did it when the children had friends in the car with us. Yes, even with everything going on and a huge media splash about our arrest, people still allowed their children to come over to our house and go places with me. Some parents knew me well, so they understood the situation and supported me, but there were other parents I didn't know, and I guess they never knew about my situation or didn't care. Regardless, I was so thankful that the kids were prospering and making friends, and they could have people over without it being an issue. But it all had to be preplanned, and the arrangements of me taking their friends back home or wherever we were going had to be on my schedule, and when we would get in the car, Bertha would beep away. I learned early on to make sure music was turned up loudly so nobody would hear it, and thankfully nobody ever noticed. There is a positive to adolescents being absorbed in their own worlds.

The kids were in sixth grade. It had been a little over a year since the legal situation had commenced, but it had only been a few months since I'd been indicted. We were starting to adjust to our new norm with Bertha, and I was trying to adjust to the negative dark cloud constantly looming over me with the threat of going to prison for the rest of my life. I was still convinced that we would come to some sort of resolution, that we would be offered a deal that would make sense. I was convinced that between the Supreme Court ruling in McFadden and the lack of evidence against us, the government would eventually come to its senses, and we would make a global settlement that would involve pleading to misdemeanor misbranding and a large financial settlement. We still hadn't seen the government's discovery—all the evidence that had been gathered for the case— and while I was anxious to see it, I didn't believe there was anything damning in there.

We had an initial trial date set for May 2016, but it would change several times and get postponed due to another high-profile case being tried in front of the same judge around the same time that also kept getting postponed. Like our case, that case had issues with getting discovery disclosed. It turns out that the government has a habit of initiating huge, overreaching cases and then isn't prepared to properly back them up with discovery in a timely manner. We did finally get our initial disclosure of discovery in the fall of 2015, almost a year and a half after the government had initiated the civil case. I dedicated myself to absorbing all of it. I had plenty of time on my hands, still being under house arrest with Bertha. The discovery was extensive—thirteen terabytes—because not only did the government seize every penny we had, but they also seized every single piece of paperwork and had issued subpoenas to every bank and any other institution they could think of that would pertain to our business dealings over the years. We had been in business for over forty years and had three different businesses entities, so there was a lot to seize, although very little of it was relevant to the case. They put it all in there, though, and in an extremely unorganized fashion.

I got to work immediately reviewing the discovery. The kids were with their dad every other weekend, so on my free weekends I sat on a barstool at the kitchen counter for countless hours, reviewing every document in discovery. My dogs, who were practically my best friends at that point and my constant and sometimes only companions for days at a time, would sit at my feet, keeping me company. I would often lose track of time and would be up until the wee hours of the morning looking at documents, and I would make notes, charts, spreadsheets, or whatever was necessary to piece the details of the case together for our attorneys. I became obsessed. I ate, slept, and breathed the case. My life revolved around my children and defending our innocence. The case consumed my marriage, and I'm so grateful Dan was understanding. Our attorneys relied on me greatly to sift through the details because I had lived through it and knew more about it than anyone else. I was barely sleeping and could rarely think of anything else.

Not surprisingly, there wasn't anything especially incriminating in the discovery. My search was centered around piecing evidence and information together that supported our innocence. It wasn't difficult to find these sorts of things. Most importantly, there was nothing in discovery indicating that we ever knowingly sold a controlled substance or an analogue of a controlled substance. After the Supreme Court ruling in McFadden, it was determined that one must have known they were selling an analogue to be convicted under the Analogue Act. The only way that could be determined is if it could be proven that one knew the physical attributes—the actual chemical structure—that made a drug an analogue. And, to make it even more complicated, nobody, not even chemists, could agree on what made a chemical structure substantially similar to a controlled substance and therefore an analogue. So how could just a regular person know? The answer was simple—they couldn't. Based on how aggressively the prosecution was behaving in our case, I feared there was something in discovery indicating that someone within our company had cooperated and made up some gargantuan lie saying we all sat around and talked about chemical structures of substances and that we all understood the structures and that they were analogues. It would have been false but still hearsay "proof" that we knew substances were analogues, and that would have been a problem for us. It would have been a "he said, she said" situation. However, nothing in discovery indicated that anyone had said that, and that was because those conversations never happened. Nobody at Gas Pipe understood analogues.

There was also no proof or accusation that we knowingly sold an actual controlled substance. Once again, to be convicted of selling a controlled substance, the word *knowingly* was very important. One must have intentionally and *knowingly* sold a controlled substance. Someone couldn't be convicted for selling something that they didn't know was an illegal substance. This wasn't an "ignorance of the law is no excuse" situation. If someone was selling cocaine, and they got busted, they couldn't say, "Oh, sorry; I didn't know cocaine was illegal." First of all, everybody knows cocaine is illegal, and secondly, if you know what you're selling is cocaine, then you know you're breaking the law. However, if you are selling what you believe is baking soda to a bakery, and then at some point you get arrested for selling cocaine because the bakery is really a front for a drug operation, and you didn't know it, and the baking soda was really cocaine, then you can't be convicted of selling cocaine because you believed you were selling baking soda and had no reason to think otherwise. In discovery there was plenty of evidence that confirmed the unintentional mishap of the wrong product going on the shelves—what we would eventually call "the AB-Fubinaca snafu."

In a very unfortunate incident in March of 2014, the Gas Pipe employees thought that a certain product, which was legal and not a controlled substance, had been ordered and subsequently received. Every product was always tested to confirm that nothing illegal was in it. This product was tested, but mistakenly the product was put on the shelves in the stores to sell before the test results came back. The vendor had sent the wrong product, one containing an actual controlled substance. We had ordered THJ-2201, a legal synthetic cannabinoid, but we received AB-Fubinaca, a substance that had been made illegal weeks previously. The minute we discovered that it was the wrong chemical, it was pulled from the shelves immediately. Our buyer, Ryan, had a lot of back-and-forth communication with the vendor, who refused to believe that we had received the wrong product. It was a huge mess, and to magnify it even more, unbeknownst to us, the DEA had already been investigating Gas Pipe and just happened to come into every one of our stores to make their "controlled buys" during the very ten-day period we had the illegal product on the shelves. Coincidentally, or maybe not so coincidentally, the DEA knew exactly when to come to the store and buy product—specifically during the "AB-Fubinaca snafu." Agents hadn't been in the stores in weeks, and then the day the bad product was put on the shelves, they showed up. We would learn much later that the person who had sent us the wrong product had been cooperating with the government. It was a setup we could never definitively and directly prove, and ultimately it didn't matter because it also couldn't be proven that we knowingly sold a controlled substance.

During their entire investigation, the DEA had never once involved the FDA, the organization in charge of labeling food and drugs. The FDA could have issued a warning or citation to us for the mislabeled herbal incense products, as their policy dictates should happen when there is a mislabeled product. We had no idea about proper labeling per FDA regulations, and the FDA wasn't even on our radar or something we discussed. The product was labeled a certain way and had been for years as an industry standard.

Everything that I found and read as I reviewed the massive amounts of discovery confirmed what I already knew. Nobody had knowledge of anything being an analogue, and nobody ever believed we were breaking the law. Every cooperating manager talked about our policy of not selling the product to be smoked, but they also said everyone knew that customers were going to smoke it. Although we didn't know it while we were selling herbal incense, previous case law had allowed for that to be enough for a conviction under the Analogue Act—if the substance was intended to get people high like an illegal substance, then it was treated as an analogue—but the McFadden ruling in the Supreme Court changed how the law was enforced, requiring that defendants knew the substance was an actual analogue, and there was no proof of that in our case.

All the talk from the cooperating defendants about knowing that the product was intended to be smoked even though it was labeled as herbal incense and had the wording "Not for human consumption" on the package only proved that the product was mislabeled—or misbranded—and it only proved misdemeanor misbranding, nothing else. Felony misbranding requires proof of intent to defraud someone. Our customers weren't defrauded. They knew exactly what they were buying and why. And because we had never interfaced with the FDA nor had one single discussion about trying to defraud the FDA nor had ever even thought about the FDA, there was no proof of felony misbranding.

I was convinced after going through discovery that we had to resolve the case, not because I thought we were guilty and needed to take a deal, but because I just didn't see why this case needed to go to trial. I begged and pleaded with our attorneys to do whatever they could to get the prosecutor to see the error in his ways. It wasn't that they didn't want to try, but the government was not budging. I couldn't understand how we couldn't file something to get the case dismissed or at least get a resolution we could live with. What I really didn't understand, though, was our justice system and how it worked. While an indictment was just a charge and not a finding of actual guilt, no matter what we heard about "innocent until proven guilty," the government was given the benefit of the doubt leading up to trial. Pretrial motions were viewed in the light most favorable to the government and under the assumption that everything in the indictment was true, even though an indictment was obtained by only the prosecutor going to the grand jury, where the defense was not present and didn't get to present their side. Plus, grand jury proceedings were confidential, so anything could be said during those proceedings with any slant on it the prosecutor chose, and nobody would ever be the wiser.

I tried to stay calm and focus on my evolving faith and soul-searching, but I had major breakdowns from time to time and was crumbling inside. I would get lost in my own thoughts, and my mind would go to terrible places, thinking about my future or lack thereof. I read every case and article I could find online pertaining to analogue prosecutions. I was obsessed. I could barely focus on anything else, and had it not been for my kids, I think I could have slipped down a dark hole very quickly. That's not to say that Dan and other people weren't incredibly supportive and encouraging—they absolutely were—but my kids needed me, and I knew that. Even though I was starting to fall apart, there was this little voice, amplified by my family and our attorneys, reminding me that we were innocent and that we could prevail. There was also another voice, though, telling me that we could go to trial, and no matter how innocent we were per the law, the jury could think that we were awful people who sold an awful product and made a bunch of money off of it and that we should be convicted and go to prison for the rest of our lives. The selling of herbal incense was not a positive thing, and that was starting to weigh on me greatly. While I vehemently disagreed with how aggressively we were being prosecuted, I was not proud about what we had done. We had been told repeatedly that what we were doing was legal, but I was beginning to accept and realize that didn't mean it was a good thing to do, and if I felt that way, potentially a jury would too. We all believed, especially after seeing how bad the government's case was from a legal point of view, that the government was going to use fear tactics and claim we were awful people who sold awful products. The idea of being judged by twelve strangers from all walks of life and putting my life in their hands was unfathomable.

In January of 2016 we filed a motion to get some leniency with Bertha, and the motion was granted. I still had Bertha, but I could go where I wanted when I wanted so long as I was home by midnight and didn't leave the Northern District of Texas. This also meant I could be granted permission to travel from time to time if we filed something with the court. I was elated. I was going to be able to spread my wings again and fly a bit. This made life so much easier. Bertha was still there, and it was a nuisance having to constantly be covered by clothing to avoid public embarrassment, but the increased freedom was appreciated. I could even swim in my pool freely now and sit in the hot tub, so long as I was back inside by midnight.

I immediately scheduled a series of work-related trips to New Jersey and Colorado for fly-fishing conventions where we promoted the lodges. I took two trips to Austin for family weddings and took a trip to our home in Oregon. The real icing on the cake was that I got approval to go to Alaska the summer of 2016. Bertha would accompany me, but I was going back to the place that had captured my soul years ago and brought me so much peace and joy, I was going back to the job I loved so much, and I would get to be with my husband. When I arrived in Alaska that June, it was like seeing it for the first time all over again. I had a whole new appreciation for it. This was another instance of something I used to take for granted now having an entirely new meaning for me—a lesson and a gift.

It was a wonderful summer, far better than the previous one because now I was in Alaska. I had a wonderful birthday celebration at the lodge and left the next day to go back to Dallas, feeling like everything was ultimately going to be fine. Right when I landed in Anchorage for my first layover, Dan called. One of our floatplanes carrying six people had crashed, and it was bad. Plane crashes are way too common of an occurrence in the Alaskan bush, but we had never had a major one that involved people being hurt. We initially didn't know the severity of the injuries. I was flying from Anchorage to Dallas overnight, and I spent the entire night not knowing anything definitively. The next morning, I learned that fortunately there were no fatalities, but there were some serious injuries. Most importantly, nobody had died, so we were blessed in that regard, but it felt like a dark cloud was always looming over us—a constant feeling of waiting for the other shoe to drop.

By this time the trial had been rescheduled multiple times, and we finally had what seemed to be a firm trial date of September 2017. I was happy to be traveling and have more freedom, but any bit of happiness I had was overshadowed by the ongoing legal situation. Ironically, we were granted more leniency with Bertha and travel right at the same time the government superseded the indictment, taking away some charges but adding other more serious ones, presumably in an effort to put pressure on us to take a deal. They added a CCE (continuing criminal enterprise) charge to the indictment. This is the most severe of drug-trafficking charges reserved for the likes of Noriega, Pablo Escobar, and El Chapo, true drug lords. The government was charging us with a prison sentence carrying a mandatory minimum of twenty years and most likely life with all the charges combined. Previously we had been looking at multiple charges that each carried a maximum of twenty years, so if convicted, we could get a life sentence with all the counts combined, or, if the judge felt inclined, we could get less than twenty years. The prosecutor told our attorneys he was adding the CCE that mandated a minimum of twenty years so the judge would have no ability to be lenient and go below twenty years. I guess the court didn't put too much stock into the accusation or the idea of us being horrible, dangerous people because we still had fewer restrictions with Bertha—I was grateful, but it wasn't logical. Nothing was logical about the situation.

Keeping the businesses going so we could afford to go to trial was challenging. We had an amazing team of attorneys, but they weren't cheap, as good attorneys never are. We had recovered somewhat financially from the seizure of everything two years previously, but every extra penny we had went toward legal expenses. Plus, we had a mounting IRS bill and property taxes that we were still trying to pay off from prior to the seizure, and we had filed a motion with the court to at least have funds released to pay our taxes (which is money going to the government), but the motion was denied. Yep, we couldn't even get money released from the government to pay the government. It was beyond stressful. Every day was about simply surviving. That's not to say that I didn't have good times. I did. I had to get up each day, no matter how hard it was, and put one foot in front of the other and put a smile on my face and keep moving forward. I had kids to take care of and companies to run. I had no choice but to forge ahead, but there were many days I was on autopilot, relying on faith to carry me through.

My personal debt was mounting. I could have and should have budgeted more, but I had been behind the eight ball with credit card debt since the legal proceedings had started, and it was pretty much beyond a budget. It was probably not responsible, but it at least seemed logical to me that I could spend whatever I wanted because either one of two things would happen—I would be found guilty and would go to prison for the rest of my life (or at least a good portion of it), and it wouldn't matter if I had debt or no savings, or I would be acquitted, and we would have millions returned, and the debt could be paid. That was my only way to cope mentally with the financial situation. I had a mind-set, even if it was somewhat warped, that if I lived my life and spent money like everything was normal, it would create a sense of normalcy. My house, which was clearly too big and way more than I wanted to keep up with anymore, needed several repairs, but I didn't want to spend any money on that because I didn't even know if I was going to keep the house or if it would be eventually forfeited to the government. I would have sold it if I could have and downsized into something more affordable and easier to take care of, but because the government had a lien on it, I couldn't even sell it. I was stuck.

I had really let myself go physically. I had gained a significant amount of weight, my skin color was not good due to being inside so much, I couldn't exercise properly with Bertha, and stress in general wasn't good for my health. I was trying to get back into some sort of shape by walking when I could, but it was hard. It was partially due to Bertha, but it was also due to my funk and inability to think about a positive future. I was still struggling with the good and evil inside of me. I was worn out. It had been two years since this ordeal had started, and I was tired of fighting to survive. The idea that there was still another year until trial made me feel defeated from exhaustion. My friend Darlene said to me one day that I probably wished I could be put into a coma and be woken up once it was all over. Yes, that was exactly how I felt.

In October 2016 I got a little bright ray of sunshine when I officially got to say goodbye to Bertha. I couldn't believe it. For seventeen months I'd had Bertha on my ankle twenty-four seven. I would now be able to travel throughout the United States by simply letting Eric know when and where I was going. A court order was no longer needed, and Eric was of course accommodating. He had actually gone to the court on our behalf and vouched for why we didn't need to be monitored anymore. Not only was it a huge relief to not have this huge thing around my ankle anymore, worrying about charging it at night, being home by midnight, keeping it covered with clothing, and all the other inconveniences that came with it, but this meant the court thought I was trustworthy enough and a good enough person to no longer have to be monitored at all times. I took it as a very positive sign of things to come and thought surely that meant that the government knew I wasn't the awful, guilty person they accused me of being. Logically I knew that it changed nothing in the government's opinion of me because Brian Poe, the prosecutor on our case, had made an objection to the court regarding Bertha being removed. I guess the court had simply decided that wasting resources on monitoring me was no longer necessary. I went shopping and bought a new short dress so I could go to dinner that night with my husband, showing my ankles to the entire world.

The kids seemed to still be handling everything fine. I tried my best to hide my stress from them, but I don't know how successful I really was. I was distracted; no matter how hard I tried to be present, my mind was always elsewhere.

We took a family trip to the Grand Canyon that December because it was on my bucket list, and I was determined to mark things off the list while I could. It was beautiful, and except for the kids fighting a lot and me being too distracted mentally, it was a great trip. The kids had been starting to fight a lot, and I will always wonder whether it was just their ages or whether they were affected by the stress of everything and just didn't know it. Maybe it was a little of both, but part of me was relieved that they seemed to have some sense of normalcy, sibling bickering and all. We enjoyed the outdoors, and we did some great hiking. I tried to savor every moment I could, thinking it could very well be my last vacation with my family with a trial looming the following September that could result with me being taken away for life. It was bittersweet. I was happy to be with my family but felt constant internal turmoil. I felt trapped, like I was suffocating, and I was tired—really, really tired. I was certainly tired from the stress of everything happening, but I was starting to feel a different kind of tired. I tried to convince myself that everything was just starting to fully catch up with me: the stress, the sleepless nights, the constant mental anguish, and the analyzing of every thought and theory of the case. Coupled with the fact that I hadn't been taking care of myself properly with regular exercise, it wasn't surprising how I was feeling. On one of our hikes at the Grand Canyon, I really struggled physically. I knew I wasn't in the best shape of my life, but even so, the hike was much more of a struggle than it should have been. It wasn't just exhaustion. My body felt like it was functioning differently.

Chapter Seventeen

I had never thought about how I would feel if I heard the word *cancer* in relation to me. It was never on my radar. Even when I let myself go physically and was under an unbelievable amount of stress, I was still healthier than most. I'd always eaten a huge amount of vegetables and healthy food, and while I did like unhealthy foods as well, my diet was better than the average person's. I know all about antioxidants, cancer-fighting foods, and healthy habits. Prior to Bertha, I had always exercised religiously. I had never been a smoker except for the few cigarettes I'd had in my younger years, and although I'd always loved being in the sun, my dermatologist had even told me that there was nothing about me that appeared to be high risk for skin cancer. Cancer didn't run in my family.

In November 2016 I read a book called *Firefly Lane*, written by one of my favorite authors, Kristin Hannah. One of the themes of the book was breast cancer, and the author's note at the end discussed the importance of breast self-exams, which I had always done from time to time. I lay in bed that night after

I finished the book and realized with all the chaos in my life, and the extreme decrease in taking care of myself and my body, I hadn't thought much about checking anything on myself. I checked that night and felt on my right breast what seemed like a very small lump—certainly just a cyst, as I'm sure every woman would tell herself upon feeling something. At some point, I briefly mentioned it to Dan, and we both agreed it was probably nothing, but I hadn't been to the doctor in quite some time, and I needed to make an appointment and go in regardless. It was the holidays, and days turned into weeks, and by the time I finally got around to making the appointment, it was late January 2017.

Even though I was feeling tired, I never believed it was due to anything other than the stress in my life. I made the appointment because I needed to go to the doctor anyway, and I was forty-one and needed to get a mammogram based on my age, if nothing else. I didn't tell anyone other than Dan that I had a concern with a potential lump in my breast because I was sure it wouldn't be anything serious. The weekend prior to going to the doctor, I took Kieley to New York to see the coveted *Hamilton* musical. She had developed quite an interest in the arts, and *Hamilton* was all the rage. It was a ridiculous expenditure, but it fit right in with the do-or-die attitude I had about everything because of the upcoming trial in September. She really wanted to see the musical and experience New York together, and I really wanted to have the special time with my daughter. I was going to experience everything I could in case it was my last chance. I really had no idea that "do or die" was going to *really* become a reality for me.

The doctor remained very calm as she examined my breast, but I should have known something was amiss when she sent me down to the second floor to get a mammogram immediately and an ultrasound "if necessary." That wasn't really the norm.

It was also not the norm for the ultrasound tech to say she was going to get the radiologist immediately upon completing the exam nor for the radiologist to tell you immediately upon reviewing the exam results that they knew they were looking at cancer. If I had known that my lump was so clearly cancer, I of course would have brought someone with me that day, but I really hadn't expected it.

As I sat on the exam table with tears streaming down my face, the radiologist calmly and kindly explained to me that further testing would of course have to be done, but she was sure that what she was seeing was cancer. I made my appointment to come back for a biopsy. I got in the car and called Dan, who was in Oregon. He didn't answer, even though he knew I was going to the doctor that morning, but we hadn't really believed anything was seriously wrong with me. I then called my mother, who was supportive but couldn't believe I hadn't told her in advance that I had a lump. And then I called my attorney because I had the trial of a lifetime coming up in eight months, and I had just been told I had breast cancer. It was a hysterical phone call. I didn't yet know the details of my cancer or what type of treatment would be involved, but I couldn't believe that I was going to have to fight for my life in two ways simultaneously—one way potentially ending with losing my freedom and life as I knew it, and the other potentially ending in death.

Dan called back quickly, I told him what I'd learned, and he booked a flight to Dallas immediately. My mother and stepdad drove to Dallas that afternoon so they could be with me. My father, always the optimist, told me he was sure further testing would prove the initial tests wrong and that it was just a cyst. The children came home from school that afternoon, and I vacillated between telling them right away or not, thinking perhaps it would be better to wait until we had more information. Plus, they were taking the SAT the following morning (as seventh graders—have I mentioned yet how brilliant my kids are?). I didn't want to distract them, and they had already been through so much in the past two and a half years, but kids are perceptive, and they knew something was wrong. So we sat down with them and told them. There were tears and questions, most of which I couldn't answer at the time, but overall, they seemed to accept the news. At least cancer was something people heard about and talked about regularly. It wasn't like watching your home being raided by the DEA or having your mother indicted and forced to wear an ankle monitor.

Cancer, in many ways, was easier for me to cope with than the legal situation. I finally had a problem I could talk about, one that garnered support from everyone. While I did have support from people with the legal situation, it wasn't like cancer, where people came out of the woodwork to shower me with support. Cancer was something that didn't have judgment associated with it, and it was something just about everyone was familiar with, unfortunately. It wasn't anything I had to be ashamed or embarrassed about, and people wanted to help, and they knew how to offer help. It wasn't that people didn't want to help with my legal situation, but really, how could they? Cancer gave me something to focus on besides the legal ordeal. I know how ridiculous that sounds—because who wants to focus on cancer?—but you would have had to be in my situation to understand. Cancer made everything else stop. It superseded everything else in my life. It was a distraction from the other mess in my life, which I know seems absurd, but that was how frustrated I had become.

I certainly didn't want cancer, but for nearly three years I had faced the prospect of losing my life, or at least life as I knew it. I had been told for nearly three years that I could be taken from my children, miss watching them grow, miss their high school and college years, their marriages, their own children. I had been fearing that possibility since June 2014. When most people find out they have cancer, they immediately think about the fear of leaving this world and being taken from their loved ones, but I had already been dealing with that fear. Now, it was just for a different reason. The converse emotion to all of this was the guilt I felt for even thinking such terrible things, for thinking that somehow cancer was better than what I was already going through with the government. Cancer is absolutely terrible. There is nothing welcoming or peaceful about it, but for me it provided a reprieve from the daily grind and stress I had been experiencing. Cancer itself brought on a whole new series of exhausting and stressful tasks, but I understood it more than what I had been going through. Cancer had scientific statistics, proven methods, books, pamphlets, and doctors who could explain everything to me and give a prediction—not a guarantee, but a very good guess—of what my outcome should be. The legal situation was not like that at all. Our attorneys passionately believed in our innocence, but neither science nor medicine could cure our legal problem. It would be left in the fate of twelve strangers. When my life was at stake, I felt much better with proven science.

Two things had to happen immediately after my diagnosis was confirmed with a biopsy. I had to be referred to an oncologist, and my attorney had to file a motion asking for a continuance—extension—of the trial date. The motion was drafted quickly, but it didn't get filed immediately because it was ever evolving as we continued to learn more about my cancer and my course of treatment.

It was two weeks before I could see my oncologist. Cancer is a busy industry, and with one in eight women being diagnosed with breast cancer, there's always someone new needing an oncologist. Months previously, Dan and I had planned a trip for the end of January. We were going to New Jersey and Atlanta for the yearly fishing conventions we went to every year to promote our lodges, and we had planned to take a road trip in between the two shows to stop in Philadelphia, where we had never been, hitting all the other states in between on the way to Atlanta. Another bucket list item of mine was to see every state in the United States. There was no reason for me to cancel the trip. Why, so I could sit at home and think about my double whammy of a situation with a potential prison sentence for life and battling cancer with a potential outcome of death? I understood the odds of me beating cancer more than I did the odds of me beating the federal government, even though we were innocent, but both situations were crummy. What made the idea of battling cancer even more difficult and depressing was knowing I could go through the battle with cancer and all the undesirable stuff that comes with it and survive, only to have to turn around and go through a huge trial with the possibility of still being taken away from my life. I was motivated to beat cancer but demotivated by the lack of potential for the rest of my life.

I do believe there is a reason for everything in life. I had been praying constantly for something to stop us from going to trial, for the case to get majorly derailed in our favor, for some force to intervene and stop the direction we were going. We had a great defense team, but there were certain aspects of our defense strategy that I didn't like—with a trial approaching quickly, there hadn't been time to make changes or go in a new direction. Then I got my diagnosis, and it was clear that the case and trial were going to have to be put on hold for a considerable amount of time. My cancer diagnosis would ultimately lead to a series of events that saved me. But when I first got my diagnosis and was processing everything, I had a few talks with God, trying to explain to him that he must have misunderstood my prayers; when I had said I was tired of my life, I'd wanted something—anything—to stop these legal proceedings. I had been fed up and hadn't known if I could go on, but I'd never meant I wanted cancer. Eventually, though, I said, "Okay, God. I'm going to accept this because there has got to be some good here somewhere. My life can't be *this* bad."

I was a big ball of emotion throughout my trip with Dan—anxious, sad, angry, and kind of relieved at times, too, because I was glad to have the case put on the back burner, even if it was because I had cancer. I thought for sure that eventually my cancer would lead to the prosecutor having sympathy and being less aggressive.

My main purpose for going to Philadelphia was to see the *Rocky* statue because I was a huge *Rocky* fan. I fulfilled my wish, but other than that, Philadelphia was disappointing—dirty, ugly, and crowded with rude people. Neither Dan nor I had ever been a big fan of Philly cheesesteaks, so that was lost on us. We did meet a homeless guy whom we took under our wing for the few days we were there, putting him up in a hotel and feeding him, and we got him some proper pants and shoes so he could interview at Starbucks. We had really been blessed throughout our legal proceedings, being able to keep our heads above water, even if we barely did at times, so it was nice to be able to give back. Prior to our legal ordeal, I had never given money to people on the streets because I passed judgment on them. I now knew anyone could lose everything for any reason, and we all could use a helping hand from time to time. Since Philadelphia, I've had the gift and joy of helping many homeless people.

During the trip I read our monthly book club pick, Carrie Fisher's memoir, *Wishful Drinking*. She stated in the book, "I didn't necessarily feel like dying—but I'd been feeling a lot like not being alive." That was pretty much my sentiment and how I had been feeling from the funk of the legal mess, but cancer was forcing me to truly want to live again. It gave me a new purpose. I had to fight for my life, and even though I'd been fighting for my life in a different way with the legal situation, fighting cancer was a battle that the odds said I could win. I did briefly entertain the idea of holistic treatments, researching everything I could about how to combat the disease without the intervention of chemo, a nasty poison by anyone's standards. I had my own mental debate about how much we were supposed to interfere with God's plan, and maybe when we were diagnosed with something such as cancer, we were supposed to accept that it was our time to go and not put these awful, man-made, toxic chemicals into our body only to increase life when it was trying to be taken from us. But I had my kids and my family and friends, and nobody else—even Dan, who hated doctors and despised taking medicine—assumed I would do anything but fight the cancer with all the force I could, with toxic chemo at the top of the list.

Our trip culminated in Atlanta, with me being very negative and angry toward Dan. I was scared and frustrated, and the totality of everything happening was really weighing on me. Dan was, is, and always has been the most wonderful husband I could ever ask for, but he was there, so he got the brunt of it. Because he was a smart man and understood when to give someone space, he gave me time to process. He worked the convention that weekend in Atlanta. I showed up from time to time after I'd allowed myself a huge meltdown in the hotel room one afternoon. I got out of the shower and stared at myself in the mirror for a long time, contemplating all the ways my body would soon be changing due to the treatment I would be facing. I thought about how extremely defeated I felt. I went to the bed and lay there naked for what seemed like hours, crying hysterically. And then that was it. I pulled myself together and committed myself mentally and emotionally to saving my life, and except for one time early on in my treatment, I wouldn't shed another tear for the next year. I didn't consciously commit myself to not shedding another tear, but I went into survival mode. I was focused and didn't allow myself to have any sort of defeatist attitude. I think it was a combination of an emotional wall I put up to avoid dealing with feelings and an "I am a warrior and will conquer" attitude, depending on the moment and the day.

We arrived back in Dallas, and it was time to really face the cancer. I loved my oncologist. It was really luck of the draw because once I was diagnosed, I was funneled into the system with every other new cancer patient who had been diagnosed through Baylor Health Care. Going in for my first appointment, I was a ball of nerves. I really hated the cancer center when I first walked in, but what did I expect? It was a cancer center. There were visibly sick people everywhere, it was really crowded, and I felt like I didn't belong there because I wasn't *that* sick, was I? We started communicating with the people who worked there, and they were friendly and calming, so I felt a little better.

Dan, my mother, and my stepdad all went with me. We had our lists of questions ready and were anxious to learn what I was going to be facing over the next few months. I had previously been told by the nurse navigator, a nice lady whose job was to notify new patients of their official biopsy results and facilitate their appointments, that my cancer was invasive ductal carcinoma, and further testing with my oncologist would determine whether it was triple positive, triple negative, or a mixture of both and whether it had spread beyond the right breast. I didn't know what those terms meant, but I would soon learn everything I never wanted to know about cancer.

Dr. Pippen, my wonderful oncologist, explained to me during our first meeting that my cancer was triple positive. Breast cancer is positive or negative for estrogen, progesterone, and HER2, a protein we all have naturally. When the body produces too much of any of those, the cancer is considered positive for those elements. The opposite is true when the cancer is negative for any of those elements. I was positive for all, meaning I had an abundance of those things in my body. The cancer would be treated with six rounds of chemo over about five months, followed by at least five years of an oral medication to combat the overproduction of estrogen and progesterone, and an additional nine months of a medicine called Herceptin, administered intravenously to combat the HER2 overproduction. The HER2 aspect of my cancer made it very aggressive, and according to Dr. Pippen, five years earlier we would have been having a very different conversation about my treatment because Herceptin was a newer drug for treating HER2-positive cancer, making it more treatable. He told me his goal was to reduce the tumor—which had been about two centimeters at my biopsy and had now grown to nearly eight centimeters—to a size that could ultimately be removed by a lumpectomy. However, my age also meant I was considered high risk, and due to a chance of recurrence, I would want to consider a mastectomy. I was referred to Dr. Grant, a surgical oncologist, who would guide me through the surgery process. Dr. Pippen oversaw and prescribed my treatment, and Dr. Grant did the surgeries. My first and almost immediate surgery with Dr. Grant was the insertion of my port, a small appliance surgically inserted right beneath the skin, used for administering massive amounts of IV drugs over a long period of time. He also removed lymph nodes during that surgery to test them for the presence of cancer.

The next two weeks consisted of a battery of tests. Due to my relatively young age of forty-one, I was referred for genetic testing, which ultimately concluded that I didn't carry the BRCA gene, so my cancer was just my random path in life. I had full-body scans to confirm the lack of cancer anywhere else in the body because my blood work indicated signs of possible metastasis. After two days of waiting, we learned the cancer had not metastasized.

The days leading up to the testing and the days spent waiting for results were difficult. There was a lot of praying and soul-searching, and the day Dan and I spent at the hospital getting scan after scan was a long, hard one, but we made the best of it. It was actually Valentine's Day—how romantic. Our date that day consisted of a brief lunch, which I went to with an IV taped to my arm. As I was lying on the exam table, having machines go over my entire body, knowing some stranger was reviewing pictures of my insides, I thought about how my whole life could be changing even more drastically than it had upon my initial diagnosis. I could be learning soon that my cancer was only treatable but not curable. I could be looking at a lifetime of fighting cancer and a possibly very shortened lifetime. My prayers during those days of testing and waiting for the results consisted of a lot of apologizing to God. I was so sorry for all the times in the last couple of years when I'd said I wanted a different life and that I didn't know if I could go on. I now wanted to live more than anything in the world. I wanted to watch my kids grow and live their lives. Even if I was in prison, I would still experience it from afar. I truly wanted to live. I needed to live, really live. I needed to pull myself out of my funk and really make my life count; regardless of what the government was trying to do to me—regardless of cancer or anything else—I was alive, and I was going to stay alive and make it count.

Chapter Eighteen

*F*ebruary 24, 2017, was the day of my first chemo treatment. I had done everything I could to prepare. I had told everyone about my diagnosis, and that would prove to be very important because of all the support I would get over the coming months. It was hard at first because I wasn't sure how to approach the conversation, and it took me several days to even be able to say the word *cancer* out loud. I learned, though, that the more I talked about it, the easier it became. I first reached out to my closest friends and family; then I sent an email to everyone at work. Gas Pipe and all our businesses were like a family, and I didn't want anyone to hear about my cancer from anyone but me. I was overwhelmed with all the responses and support I received.

I made the decision to share my diagnosis on Facebook. I debated sharing something so personal in a public forum, but after everything else that had been aired publicly about my life, why would I hide something like cancer? I believed in the power of prayer and positive thinking, and I wanted as many people as possible doing that for me. And maybe my experience could be helpful to someone else.

I attended the mandated chemo class at the cancer center. It was an hour-long meeting with a nurse who guided us through a book that explained all the potential and probable side effects of chemo, foods to eat and to avoid, hair loss, ways to stay strong and healthy during chemo such as through exercise, and even how to still feel sexual and intimate during chemo. The class was in a group setting, and the attendees on the day I went were only me and an elderly blind gentleman accompanied by his wife. I suspected our chemo experiences would be quite different due to the age difference and where we were in our lives. I was comparably young and vibrant, and I was going to conquer chemo head on, feeling confident and even sexual through the entire process. Other than the hair loss, chemo was not going to have a detrimental effect on me. I was ready for the challenge. I really had no idea what I was facing.

Dan was by my side through all the initial appointments and went to most of the chemo treatments with me except for the few he had to miss because he had to be in Alaska. He kept a calendar with all my appointments organized and included details of what each appointment was for. He did all the research he could on cancer-fighting foods, and he prepared all my favorites for me regularly so we could focus on an organic, healthy diet. He also put me on a vitamin regimen that included two thousand milligrams of vitamin C a day as well as a daily dose of B, D, E, and magnesium. I took fish oil, and I started taking probiotics daily to help with the digestive issues that would potentially accompany the chemo. Dan also made a homemade saltwater mouthwash for me to use daily to help prevent mouth sores that were a common side effect. I was ready to go and armed with everything I could possibly put in my body to achieve the most successful outcome, and all the vitamins and healthy diet did make a huge difference. There are fans of strictly homeopathic treatments that swear vitamin C alone can cure cancer. I don't think I'd go that far, but I'm confident it was and still is extremely helpful.

Two days before I had my first chemo treatment, I shaved my head and had a big party to "celebrate" with my girlfriends. There had been so little that I felt I had control over in the past couple years, and I was determined that I was going to control as much of the cancer and chemo process as I could. I was adamant that I was not going to watch my hair slowly fall out in big clumps in the shower. If I was going to have to lose my hair, I was going to do it on my terms. When I told Dr. Pippen that was my plan, he applauded the decision, although the nurse in the chemo class did not, telling me I should wait to see what my hair did on its own. I thought that was strange advice coming from someone who obviously had never gone through the experience, even though she "coached" people through it. My mind was already made up, and I told her that. I was going to do whatever I could to feel like I was conquering cancer, including shaving my own head. It gave me a sense of empowerment, and I hadn't felt empowered about anything in a while.

My best friend, Amy, came with me for the big shave. I had been referred to a place that specialized in shaving heads and using the shaved hair to make a wig, so I was going to have a wig made out of my own hair, but it unfortunately would take months to get the wig made (it turned out beautiful, though, and I hope to donate it to someone in the future who wouldn't have a wig otherwise). Amy and I went to lunch before my shaving appointment, and even though I was feeling empowered, I needed a little liquid courage to propel me forward; a quinoa salad and two Moscow mules later, I was ready to go.

Amy and I had been through so much together. We'd consoled and cheered each other through breakups, our own arguments, parenthood, divorces—all the big moments in life. And now my dearest, oldest friend—my "sister," the friend who knew absolutely everything about me and had never passed judgment—was going with me to get my head shaved because I had been diagnosed with breast cancer. She was loving, supportive, and patient, and we even had some laughs through it. She was able to see what my head looked like before I was turned around to look in the mirror. She said everything to make me feel positive about the situation and told me how fierce and powerful I looked. She was encouraging and a beacon of strength, and I am so blessed to have her in my life. Not many people have a friendship like that, and it is something I truly cherish.

My mother met us toward the end of the appointment, and then we all went back to my house, where we got ready to go to my "kick cancer's ass" party at my favorite Mexican restaurant. Dr. Pippen had told me that I could have a glass of wine from time to time during chemo, but I was sure I wouldn't feel like drinking much alcohol once the treatments began, and I didn't know how my body would process my favorite Mexican food and margaritas once I was full of all the nasty drugs. So I was going to reveal my new look without hair and enjoy my last night out with my girlfriends and margaritas.

Amy and I actually had a lot of fun getting ready for the party. There was something liberating about the day and being together. While we were in my bathroom getting ready, we laughed and had fun like we were back in high school. I tried on different outfits, pairing them with different head scarves and big earrings and necklaces. I wasn't flippant about what I was going through with cancer, but I had a new look—why not embrace it, at least for the moment? I had spent the day with my best friend, and I was about to have a wonderful evening with all my girlfriends. I was hell-bent on embracing the cancer journey because I didn't see any other choice. Also, it almost felt like the stress of the last couple of years leading up to my cancer diagnosis had prepared me for dealing with the cancer. I often wonder how I would have dealt with cancer had I not gone through the other stuff first.

The evening with my girlfriends was magical. It was filled with love, sisterhood, encouragement, laughs, and tears. By the end of the evening—and a few margaritas later—I was brave enough to take off my head scarf and reveal my bald head. There is a picture of me holding a margarita, with my newly shaved head in all its glory. I love that picture. I look happy and determined, ready to conquer the world. Over the next few months, my skin color would dull, my smile would fade at times, and I would feel drained, but I would keep moving forward. Then in the year to come, I would feel even more exhausted and challenged due to the other circumstances in my life, but that picture of me that night would always be an inspiration.

Before chemo started, I had one more meeting with Dr. Pippen's nurse Christina. She was so sweet and kind and supportive, and it was almost worth going to the cancer center just to see her. She made everything about the experience better. I had three different oral medications to take that helped either with nausea or to offset the effects of the steroids that would be given to me intravenously with the chemo, and she wanted to go over any last-minute questions or concerns. It was hard to know of any specific concerns or questions because I had never gone through chemo. Some people got really nauseated; some people didn't. Some people were really tired immediately, and others didn't feel the effects until after a couple of treatments. Everybody was different. All the doctors and nurses could really do was tell me the spectrum of what *could* happen.

Dan, my mother, and my stepdad were all there for my first treatment. My mother stayed with me the entire time, my stepdad ran errands and came and went, and Dan did the same. It was a long day, and only so many people were allowed in the chemo area, so they rotated. The experience was different than I'd expected. It was actually relaxing in a way.

The way chemo is administered now versus years ago is quite different. Patients used to have nausea and often would throw up as the drugs were being administered. Now, chemo treatments begin with an anti-nausea medicine that is administered through the IV port along with steroids to help with strength and recovery as well as Ativan to help with any nerves and to combat the aggressive effects of the steroids. During all my chemo treatments, I saw only one person get sick during the treatment.

Patients sat in leather reclining chairs that had heaters and massagers. There were rows of them in a big room. If there hadn't been IVs and nurses everywhere, it would have almost looked like a nail salon. A big cozy blanket was provided. Comfort was important because the treatment typically took about six hours, but it began with the Ativan, so there was a nice feeling of floating on a cloud. People talked and visited, and I got to know the chemo nurses and many of the patients over time since we were often there on the same days. Everybody had a story, and just like everything in life, there was always somebody that seemed to have it better than me or somebody that seemed to be doing worse, which is why we shouldn't compare ourselves to others in life. We have to honor and respect where we are, and if we compare ourselves to others, try to do it only for inspiration. We all had a story to tell, and it was nice to be able to share. There were people who were an inspiration to me, such as the lady I met who was in her late twenties and found out she had breast cancer when she was breastfeeding her newborn twins. She was joyful and so positive, and I couldn't imagine being so young with newborn twins and battling breast cancer. Then there was the lady I met who was in her sixties and was really struggling with the chemo and the side effects, and we talked about me and my twins. The next time she saw me, she said I had inspired her because every time she felt down, she thought of me and everything I was having to handle while going through treatment. It had motivated her to be more positive.

My biggest fear was being nauseous and throwing up continuously. Because of all the meds I was given for prevention and the holistic remedies such as ginger tea that I drank during the chemo, I experienced a negligible amount of nausea. But the first night that I got home from chemo, I was anxiously waiting for the sickness to hit. I could hardly sleep that night because I just knew any minute I was going to be running to the bathroom, spending the night hugging the commode. It never happened. I soon realized that the real reason I couldn't sleep was because of all the steroids that had been pumped into my system. I was wired and ready to go.

The next morning when Dan and I were lying in bed, talking, I rambled incessantly about an entire new business plan I wanted to start. I was going to open a restaurant when everything settled down—a fantasy I'd always had—and I outlined every other future plan I had ever contemplated. I couldn't turn off my brain. Dan looked at me in wonderment. I think he must have understood that it was the steroids talking. I energetically went through the day, going for a long walk, cooking, and feeling like I was on top of the world. By five o'clock that evening, it was time to remove my Neulasta mechanism, a little plastic contraption that had been attached to my stomach the previous day that injected, via a very small needle, a dose of immune-boosting drugs into my system twenty-four hours after application. Patients used to have to return to the treatment center the day following chemo to get their immune-boosting drugs via injection.

I pulled it off and then couldn't wait to get in a hot bath, since I couldn't do that with the Neulasta, and I almost always took a hot bath for relaxation.

Saturday, the day following chemo, had been great. I'd felt like I could have run a marathon. Then Sunday came, and I felt like I'd been hit by a semitruck. Just like that I went from one hundred to zero. I woke up, tried to get out of bed, and felt like my body was weighed down by bricks. I walked to the laundry room, which was right next to our bedroom, and felt like I'd walked a mile. I pulled a load of laundry out of the dryer, and by the time I finished folding it, my arms felt like I had done an intensive upper-body workout. Going up and down the stairs even one time felt like a thirty-minute StairMaster workout. If I was sitting down and realized I had to go to the bathroom, I would spend a really long time contemplating getting up because the thought of getting up was exhausting. I couldn't believe how drained I felt. Fortunately, at least for the first round of chemo, this exhaustion only lasted a few days, with each day being progressively better.

I had always been a high-energy person, so the feeling of utter exhaustion was something very foreign to me. I would learn as the treatments continued that if I could stay moderately active, even just through a walk, it helped with my overall energy level, and I did a pretty good job of doing that throughout treatment. It was tough, though, because after each treatment, the fatigue lasted longer, and by the end, I was pretty much in a constant state of fatigue.

Because I had shaved my hair before I started chemo, and it did take a few weeks for the drugs to really start affecting the body (killing off all cells—even the good ones that made hair grow), my hair had attempted to grow back in, only to start falling out immediately. It was very, very short, so it wasn't falling out in clumps, but I could pull out little pieces. I couldn't stand it and just wanted it all gone, so Dan got out his electric razor and did a close shave of my head. Now that was true love. There was nothing sexy or attractive about me being sort of bald with little patches of hair everywhere and then asking my husband to finish it off, but he did it with grace and compassion.

Shortly after my first chemo treatment, the attorneys filed my motion to ask for a continuance of the trial date. There was a lot of information that needed to accompany the motion, including letters and records from my oncologist. It was mortifying to have to explain to Dr. Pippen and Nurse Christina that I was facing a huge trial and needed them to explain my diagnosis and treatment to a federal judge as well as why I wouldn't be able to go to trial in September. I was grateful they didn't ask me too many questions, and they provided the necessary information so we could file a proper motion. I also submitted a sworn declaration to the court explaining my medical situation and the side effects I was experiencing. It didn't take long for the motion to get granted, and I suppose one reason why was because Brian Poe, the prosecutor, didn't oppose the continuance. Also, the judge who granted the continuance was very kind and sympathetic to do so because I had been told that, unfortunately, not every judge would have granted it. Mr. Poe surprisingly expressed sympathy for my situation, which yes, I did find shocking considering how unreasonable and aggressive he'd been toward us and how he had opposed every other thing we'd asked for, including a trip to Austin for a family wedding (which the court had granted anyway). He had never once treated me like a living, breathing human being. I was just a statistic to him, a notch in his belt, a stepping-stone to further his career. Cancer really does garner sympathy from everyone. We didn't have a firm new trial date, although we had asked for a one-year continuance, but I now knew that at least I didn't have to worry about going to trial in a few months. I could just focus on beating cancer.

Around the time of my initial diagnosis, I had reached out to a new attorney, a female attorney named Marlo Cadeddu. I had been referred to her by the attorneys we worked with for our Gas Pipe legal issues in New Mexico because I had thought having a female on board would be good for me. I was a mom who'd been diagnosed with breast cancer, and I think women in general process things and react to things differently than men do. Our three attorneys who had been with us on the case since 2014 were amazing attorneys, but I needed some estrogen and someone else who understood some of the desires I had for our defense. I met with Marlo prior to starting my chemo treatments, and at the time she was preparing for trial in another big, high-profile case, so she wasn't able to officially come on board and represent me until that case ended. That was fine because we were getting a continuance in our case anyway. Everything was settled—our trial was continued for at least a year, I was going to be adding an additional attorney to our team who seemed to share my ideas of what I wanted to see in our defense strategy and understood my needs as a woman, and for the next few months I could really put all the legal stuff aside and focus on my health and my family. Those two things were front and center.

I continued to take the chemo and its effects in stride. Dan went to most of the treatments with me, my mom went to a couple, and Amy went to my last one in June, which seemed appropriate since she had begun the journey with me by accompanying me to shave my head. After the completion of chemo, I would still have to go to the infusion center for nine months to get my Herceptin treatments, but mild fatigue was the only side effect from that. The chemo was the hardest, so that last treatment was a big deal. I had my picture taken with the gong that all patients got to bang after the last treatment. There was quite a contrast between that picture and the one taken of me just a few months previously, where I'd been holding my margarita and showing off my freshly shaved head. I didn't look awful, but the effects of the treatment were evident.

Everybody handles treatment differently, and everybody has a different threshold. I tried to stay reasonably active, going on walks regularly, and I even did a 5K (albeit walking very slowly) with my kids toward the very end of my treatment. What a special experience that was! I would go out with friends occasionally or have friends over, and I would try to be engaged and present but often thought the entire time, "I just can't wait to go lie down." I took lots of naps, and I was able, for the first time in my life, to comfortably say, "I'm going to rest and do nothing," because that was what people expected me to do. For someone who had always had a hard time slowing down and tended to want to cram as much into a day as possible, it was a different mind-set.

I didn't realize how truly tired I was when I was going through the chemo because I was practicing "mind over matter" and thought if I said I was doing fine, then I would convince myself of it. When I reflect back on that time, I realize I did not feel well all those months, and I certainly wasn't myself. There were some side effects I experienced besides just the fatigue that I couldn't convince myself were no big deal at the time. Chemo turned my brain to mush. I couldn't think of words midsentence, and I would lose my train of thought very easily. This continued for months after the chemo stopped. I had always been one with an outstanding memory and had been quick to think and speak, so it was frustrating. My huge physical ailment were the hemorrhoids. I'll spare the details, but it was miserable. My daily hot baths for relaxation took on a whole new meaning. Dan familiarized himself with every product at CVS that could be purchased for treatment. He really was supportive and a trooper.

I had obviously been very naive when I had gone to the chemo class and read in the book about sexuality and intimacy during chemo. I thought it wouldn't phase me a bit and that I would be as sexually vibrant as ever. Dan and I did achieve a new level of intimacy during my cancer treatment, but it wasn't of the sexual nature. There was nothing sexy about chemo, and while I wanted to feel sexy and wished I felt sexual, I didn't, and it was rather depressing. I really just felt like a sick patient, and I certainly looked like one. The one time I had a big crying breakdown after my initial diagnosis was about two months into my treatment, when I'd realized my womanhood and the things that had often made me feel womanly were going to be nonexistent for a while. I hadn't thought it would affect me the way it did, but I had been wrong. Losing my hair was difficult, but not as difficult as it could have been because I took charge of the situation. I wore my head scarves and had several in different colors, and I would use makeup to emphasize my eyes, which were already emphasized due to lack of hair. That lasted temporarily until my eyebrows and eyelashes fell out too. That was harder than losing the hair on my head. I guess I felt like it was all I had left, and then it was gone too. I contemplated getting fake eyelashes, but then when I called and inquired about them, it was pointed out to me that there have to be at least some eyelashes to use as a base for the fake eyelashes. Of course, what was I thinking? The only positive about hair loss at this point was that I lost it everywhere, so no shaving or lip waxing, but I think those would have been the last things on my mind even if I had had to do them.

Toward the end of my treatments, there wasn't a time that I wasn't tired. I think the best way to explain chemo overall is feeling like you have a constant hangover. And to think I had done that to my body on purpose at times! All in all, though, I survived the treatments and was lucky enough to have my hair start growing back within days of the last treatment. It must have been all the vitamin E I had taken. And except for an infection from the first surgery incision early on, I never got sick during chemo, which was incredible because I had kids, who, even as preteens, still brought home every germ imaginable. I firmly believe it is due to the two thousand milligrams of vitamin C I took daily and still do. I haven't been sick in two years. I thank my wonderful husband for that!

I would rely greatly on prayer and trying to find answers introspectively and through discussions with my family and friends as I continued through my cancer battle. The chemo treatment was organized for me, and there weren't many decisions for me to make in that regard. After chemo, though, I had to decide whether to have a mastectomy or not. Within that decision was the decision to have a single or double mastectomy and then reconstruction or not. I also had to decide whether I would do radiation or not. While nobody ever asked me if I wanted to do chemo—I was simply told I had to do that to get rid of the cancer—the other decisions were optional and based on statistics, probable outcomes, and a personal preference to a degree (particularly with the reconstruction).

I decided to have the mastectomy, and I would have a double mastectomy, both for health and vanity reasons. I was considered high risk because of my age, so it was best to remove all breast tissue to lessen the chance of a recurrence. I knew reconstructive surgeons were very talented, but I just couldn't imagine having one real breast and one fake one. It just seemed better to do away with them both and get two new ones. I initially had no idea what that really entailed. In my mind I thought of it as a "boob job," and cancer sucked, but I'd be getting a great new set of boobs out of the deal. Well, it wasn't like that at all, and I would soon learn what a major ordeal that process was going to be. All the tissue was removed, so it wasn't like a regular reconstruction job with implants to enhance what was already there. It was a multistep process consisting of removal, expanders—which were very painful and had to be filled with air every couple of weeks to stretch the muscle and strengthen the muscles so implants could eventually be supported—and then eventually real implants, which then had to be augmented with fat from the rest of the body. The idea of having fat taken from one part of the body and injected into another sounded appealing, but that process would be one of the most painful surgeries and longest recoveries I'd experienced. And finally, there was tattooing if one chose, because otherwise it was just a big, white, unnatural-looking mass since the nipple and areola were removed during the mastectomy as well.

I was nervous about the mastectomy and couldn't fathom saying goodbye to a part of my body, especially one that had been such a part of making me a woman, but I knew it was the right decision. I was referred to a few "friends of friends" who had gone through the experience, and that was helpful. I was able to hear different stories and perspectives. I heard everything from someone going home alone the day after surgery and fending for herself to someone who six weeks postsurgery was still having her husband help her go to the bathroom. I assumed I'd be somewhere in between, and I wasn't going to have Dan help me go to the bathroom at all. Having him shop for hemorrhoid medication had been bad enough.

The pain from the surgery wasn't as bad as I'd anticipated. I awoke from surgery with a morphine drip, so nothing really seemed wrong in the world. I threw up pretty severely for a while due to the amount of anesthesia because the surgery had been so long, and it took almost twenty-four hours for feeling to come back in my arm because it had fallen asleep when it had been dangling from the operating table. I stayed one night in the hospital, woke the next morning, and insisted I go home. I wanted to recover in the peace and comfort of my own home. I was sore—well, yeah, it actually really hurt, but every day was better, and I'd always tried to look at pain as temporary. Honor it and recognize it was there while knowing it would get better and trying to work through it. I had exercises to do so that I could start slowly getting movement and range of motion in the area again, and the more I did, the better I felt. I recovered well and was slowly doing more daily. The surgical drains (inserted to help my body release excess fluid that had built up after surgery and could cause infection) were the worst part, and I couldn't wait to get those out. There were four of them hanging from my sides, and they were cumbersome and a nuisance. I would have to have them multiple times over the next few months after each surgery, and that was truly one of the worst parts of it all. There was nothing natural about having tubes coming out of my body with little bottles hanging off the ends that had to be emptied of disgusting body fluid multiple times throughout the day.

Dan stayed in Dallas for a week after my surgery and took amazing care of me. When it was time for him to go back to Alaska, I was ready to find my independence again. Summer wasn't ideal timing for my surgery due to Dan working, but it had to take place in the summer so I could stay on schedule and be finished with all surgeries and treatments before the trial the following year. The case had been put on hold, but it was always looming in the distance.

Shortly before my surgery, we had been notified that the government was moving to sell our airplanes that they had seized. They had decided that the planes were too expensive to store and maintain, and they wanted to sell them and hold the money in escrow until the end of the trial, with the "winner" getting the money instead of the planes. This was ludicrous because we had previously filed a motion with the court to have our planes returned to us so we could use them for our business and store and maintain them ourselves. They could still be subject to seizure, but we could at least be able to use them to run our businesses while awaiting trial. The court had denied that motion, but after the government moved to sell the planes, the court suggested we get the planes back—still subject to seizure, of course—rather than the government selling them. We had to have a hearing to hash out the details, which took place about two weeks after my surgery. So much for the government having sympathy for my situation. They tried to liquidate our property right in the middle of my treatment, and I had to go in for a hearing while recovering from a double mastectomy. We did get the planes back in our possession after much unnecessary and expensive haggling due to hours of attorney bills, and one of the planes was deemed completely totaled because it had been left in a hangar with a gaping hole in the roof. The plane was completely corroded and had mold throughout. Yep, a million-dollar plane ruined, and the government had told the court in a sworn declaration that accompanied the motion to sell that the plane was somehow now valued at $1.3 million (two hundred thousand dollars more than what we had originally paid for it, which seemed odd). It had been left to sit and rot, and the government had tried to hide it by getting a court order to sell it so we would never see it. Eventually, the government would pay for that plane, but it would take a long time.

I ended the summer with a big birthday party to celebrate the end of chemo and the recovery from my big surgery. I still had more surgeries and treatment to come, but the most severe had passed. When it was all said and done, I had four surgeries over fourteen months, six rounds of chemo, and another nine months of Herceptin treatments. For fourteen months I went to the cancer center every three weeks for IV treatments. I made the decision not to have radiation because my margins came back clean after the mastectomy, and I'd had both breasts removed. What was there to get rid of with radiation at that point? The doctors were on the fence about my decision, but it was my decision to make. I compromised by starting an oral medication sooner than originally planned. Chemo was bad enough, and even though radiation didn't have as many side effects, it freaked me out more. The chemo went into the body and did its thing, and then the body expelled it over the next few days. Radiation wouldn't get expelled. And once radiation was used for treatment on one area of the body, it could never be used there again. If I were to have a recurrence, I could still have radiation as a treatment option if I forwent it now.

Throughout my cancer treatment, I said I couldn't wait for the day when I had fewer doctors and fewer attorneys in my life. They were all wonderful people, but at the peak of things, I had three doctors I was seeing regularly, and we had twelve attorneys we were working with for the legal situation and various ongoing business matters. I felt I was getting a crash course in cancer and federal law. At least it appeared my interactions with doctors would be decreasing, but the attorney interactions were about to be amplified.

Chapter Nineteen

My big goal following the completion of chemo and the big mastectomy surgery was to feel well enough to celebrate the kids' thirteenth birthday and go to Alaska with the kids, both of which I did. The birthday celebration was great, but the trip to Alaska was not the best. The kids bickered constantly—with each other, with me, and with Dan. Dan was pretty cranky, too, the entire time, partly because of the kids' behavior, but mostly because the stress of everything was wearing on him. It's not easy watching someone you love go through so much, and it seemed we were going through constant crisis.

One night I had just had it. We were all in our house, sitting in the living room. The kids were fighting, Dan was especially agitated, which really was rare for him, and I stood up and yelled, "I've had it with all of you! I don't know why any of you are so cranky. I'm the one that just went through chemo and had her breasts cut off. I'm the one that's struggling and recovering and could barely make it on this trip, and I don't understand why you all just can't be happy that I'm here and alive." I stormed into our bedroom, slammed the door, took a Valium that had been prescribed to me postmastectomy, and went to bed. I woke up the next morning to Dan and Gavin asleep on the recliner and couch. I guess Kieley had gone to her bedroom at some point. I wonder what, if anything, they talked about that night, but I decided then that it was time to go to counseling.

I'd always been a huge believer in counseling, but other than the volunteer counselor from our church whom I'd met with, I hadn't gone to counseling since the beginning of the legal mess. I think I was too embarrassed and ashamed and didn't know what I could or couldn't share with a counselor due to the privileged information about the case. But it was time to go. The kids and I were having more negative interactions than positive interactions. Gavin had seen a counselor when he was younger to deal with some issues he had been having at the time, so I reached out to her via email, explaining everything that we'd been through as a family the past few years. She responded immediately and said she was so glad I had reached out. I made an appointment for when the kids and I got back to Dallas.

I was also determined to get back in shape. Bertha had really derailed my fitness habits, and I had just started getting back into a semblance of a workout routine when I had been diagnosed. Moderate walking was the extent of my exercise during cancer, which was better than nothing but was nothing near what I had done years previously. The steroids and drugs throughout my treatment had messed with my metabolism and made me bloated. I did not lose weight during chemo. Because of all the drugs that were administered for side effects, a strong appetite—magnified even more because of the steroids—could still be present during treatment. When we got back from Alaska, I set a goal to lose weight and get back in shape. Dan had seen me at my worst and loved me anyway (he had even heard a nurse announce my weight prior to my surgery, and I couldn't believe a nurse would ever do that—I had never shared my weight), but I wanted to feel vibrant and attractive again. My hair was growing back in, so I was feeling more feminine. I followed a diet plan, and I hit the ground running—literally, by preparing to run a half marathon in February. I used to run them regularly, but this would be my first in six years, and it would take place a year and one day after I had begun chemo. It was a great goal to set for myself, and I did accomplish it. It wasn't pretty, and I huffed and puffed my way through it. I'm thankful to my cousin Amber and our friend Cynthia for doing it with me and pushing me along the way.

It would take longer to get back in shape than I'd anticipated, and I soon realized that my body had changed greatly. I would maybe never be in the shape I once had been. I was changing physically, emotionally, and mentally. I was only forty-two, but the chemo and maintenance oral medication I was now taking had catapulted me into menopause, and that affected everything. I started experiencing unbelievable hot flashes, and my body simply did not react and process things the same way it had previously. Every woman goes through menopause and has side effects from it, but it's more extreme when the body is thrust into it unnaturally and suddenly. I slowly learned to live with the changes, and part of that was accepting and honoring what I was experiencing and giving myself permission to slow down a bit but to remember that so long as I am trying, I am doing okay.

Counseling was wonderful for me and the kids. I went by myself the first session so I could bring the counselor up to speed on everything. I realized quickly that although I had reached out to friends and family for help and support during my treatment, I had still not believed it was okay to let the kids know I was struggling. I'd thought I had to put on a complete brave face for them. I hadn't understood that in vulnerability, there could be strength. I had wanted the kids to stop bickering and understand what I was going through, which could be difficult for adolescents because they were, by nature, immersed in their own worlds, but I hadn't wanted to fully expose my honest feelings to them except for when I'd had enough and was fed up and would yell, go to my room, and slam the door. I needed to learn to communicate with them in a more meaningful way and tell them what I truly needed from them rather than just expecting they should inherently know. And they needed to understand how to receive communication and communicate better with each other and with me. Dan wasn't really an issue for counseling. I asked at one point during a session if the kids thought Dan should attend when he was in Dallas, and they said no. They told the counselor that Dan was like Poseidon—calm, commanding, and steady. Although I wanted them to think of me that way as well, I knew I wasn't, but I had other attributes that could be appreciated. I was trying to grow toward more calmness and patience. I couldn't agree more, though, with their assessment of Dan.

I learned that by showing and telling my kids that I was scared and that I didn't know what was going to happen but that I was fighting to persevere, I was showing them more strength than by having the attitude of "everything is okay." We had been through a lot the past few years, and tension was to be expected, but how we dealt with it—particularly how I dealt with it since I was the adult—could make it better or worse. We continued to go to counseling and still do. I wish I had reached out for that help and support sooner, but I suppose everything happens as it's supposed to.

The trial had been rescheduled for September 2018, so it was about a year away. I had two attorneys now: David Botsford, who had been with me since the beginning, and

Marlo Cadeddu, whom I officially retained in June 2017 after her other big case had ended in an acquittal at trial in front of the same judge who would be presiding over our case, which made me feel even more confident in my choice to bring her on board. We still had our other two attorneys, George Milner and Michael Mowla. They officially represented my father and the corporations, but we were all one big team.

One of Marlo's initial suggestions was that I go in for a reverse proffer. A proffer is where a defendant goes in to talk with the government—typically the prosecutor and any other agents the government deems necessary to have at the meeting. In our case, it would be DEA agents. The purpose of a proffer is for the defendant to share (proffer) information about the case and her involvement in it, and this is all being done in furtherance of making a plea deal. A *reverse* proffer is where a defendant goes to meet with the government to *listen* and learn about what information the government has that it feels makes its case against the defendant strong. The defendant is not required to say anything or share any information. I was anxious to do this because I hadn't seen anything in the thirteen terabytes of discovery that proved anything against us except for misdemeanor misbranding.

When Marlo reached out to Brian Poe to schedule a reverse proffer, he said he'd be happy to do one, but he also told her that he was leaving the United States Attorney's Office at the end of August to go into private practice. I was elated! I was sure that another, different prosecutor would look at the case with a fresh perspective and know immediately how badly the government had overreached. I began to feel that things were turning in our favor and that we would maybe get the resolution to our case that I so desired.

We went in for the reverse proffer, and just as I expected, there was nothing damaging beyond misdemeanor misbranding. The government tried to put their own spin on some things and paint them in a negative light, even going as far as deleting parts of my emails so the meaning of them appeared differently. It boggled my mind that they didn't think I would recognize an email and know, and be able to ultimately prove, that the email they had shown me wasn't the original email in its original format. I wasn't too concerned with anything I was shown that day because I knew the truth, and I knew we could prove the truth. The hardest part of the process was having to sit quietly and not comment on their lies and fabrications.

The prosecutor who would be taking over the case was there at the reverse proffer, along with multiple DEA agents. It was designed to be intimidating, but it really wasn't. *Infuriating* is really the only word that comes to mind. I had said several times throughout the past three years that if we had to go through this battle, I at least wanted the dignity and courtesy of having an honest battle. The twisting and distorting of information so the government could portray something that really wasn't true was disgusting. We had messed up—we'd sold a product that was mislabeled. That was a crime, but it was a misdemeanor that was punishable with a fine and a maximum prison sentence of one year. But the government wouldn't be satisfied with that. They claimed what we did was dangerous, and in retrospect I agree that it was careless and irresponsible, but it wasn't anything that deserved life in prison. It was an issue of morality, not legality. There are many things in this world that aren't morally correct but are legal. I wasn't proud of my moral choice, but I also knew I wasn't guilty of what the government was accusing.

At the end of the reverse proffer, I was told of my options for pleading. I sat and listened, knowing what they were offering wasn't reasonable. They were hypothetical offers because I wasn't there to make a deal, so there was no written, formal offer. I was told by Jennifer Tourje, the new prosecutor, that she had taken the liberty to talk with the prison nearby that had a medical facility to see how my ongoing treatment would be handled there. Gee, that was nice of her. She was actually pleasant enough, though, and had a much warmer, more sincere demeanor than Brian Poe, who didn't even bother to shake my hand that day and introduce himself. Ms. Tourje and all the agents even did that. She had a few questions about my treatment, if I didn't mind answering them. So I sat there and discussed my breast cancer in front of a room of male DEA agents who had made it their life missions the past three years to destroy me and my father. I didn't know whether I should feel humiliated or validated. I didn't know whether the agents thought I deserved what I was going through—cancer and all— or if they were perhaps feeling an inkling of sympathy for me. The former wouldn't have surprised me at all because it was clear they did not see me as a human being. They had convinced themselves I was worth nothing more than garbage that deserved to rot in prison for the rest of my life.

A few weeks after my reverse proffer, and after Brian Poe was officially off the case, George and Michael went to meet with Jennifer Tourje on behalf of my father and the corporations. They impressed on her the weakness of the government's case and our desire to come to a reasonable resolution. She seemed receptive. We didn't really know *how* receptive, but it was a far more positive meeting than anything that had ever happened with Brian Poe. They agreed to keep communicating about a potential resolution.

In the meantime, Marlo suggested we add an attorney named Jim Felman to our defense team. We were hoping to work toward a resolution and avoid going to trial, but we were preparing to show a very aggressive defense to solidify a deal we could live with and be ready for trial if we had to go. Jim Felman, whom we would eventually call Mr. Analogue, would change the course of our defense and ultimately the case. He was a "hired gun," the absolute strongest tool a defendant defending an analogue case could have in his or her arsenal. I had heard of Jim Felman when I had researched analogue cases, but I hadn't known that having him on our team was an option. Marlo knew him through a mutual friend and another attorney named John Cline, and she knew of his work on analogue cases. This is one of the main reasons I say cancer saved my life. Had I not been diagnosed with cancer, the trial date wouldn't have been continued. Had the trial date not been continued, I wouldn't have had time to regroup and bring on Marlo as my attorney. Had I not brought on Marlo as my attorney, Jim Felman would have never joined our defense team. Everything happens for a reason, and the path of events in this scenario was obvious.

In October we had another team meeting in my dining room. Our team had grown, with both Marlo and Jim now joining. Jim had a wealth of information to share about the Analogue Act and his defense in cases across the country. Remarkably, he hadn't taken one analogue case to trial because once he started interfacing with the government and sharing what he knew, the government had always offered a reasonable deal. Because Jim had been working with defendants in these cases for about five years, he had discovered information and secrets within the DEA that the government didn't want exposed, and through each case he would discover a little more.

The gist of what he had learned over the years was that the DEA's own hired chemists couldn't even agree if something was an analogue or not. For a chemical to be considered an analogue, it first and foremost had to have a chemical structure *substantially similar* to a controlled (illegal) substance. Only a very experienced chemist could make this determination, and the most respected and educated chemists in this field would say that the term *substantially similar* wasn't a term of science and couldn't be defined. In other words, even highly skilled chemists couldn't agree on what made one substance substantially similar to another. Nevertheless, the DEA tried to make determinations on which substances could be considered analogues and which could not. When pressed, they wouldn't go on the record calling anything an analogue. They would say it was up to a jury at trial to determine whether something was an analogue based on testimony from different experts. All the DEA would do was have its own experts (either in-house "experts" or a chemist who received a sizable grant from the government) say they were willing to testify that they believed a substance was *substantially similar* to a banned substance and therefore could be considered an analogue. This was obviously a problem because defendants had their own non-DEA chemists saying they didn't think something could be *substantially similar,* so juries in these cases weren't just deciding if someone had committed a crime, but they were actually deciding law, deciding whether something should be considered an illegal substance (as an analogue) or not—which experienced, educated chemists couldn't even agree upon.

The DEA did keep a "running list" of what substances they had determined could be analogues, but they refused to share it publicly and, for a long time, even denied the list existed. That meant that citizens who were wanting to abide by the law had no way of knowing if the DEA had determined whether something could be an analogue. Whenever pressed about this later in our case, the DEA took the position that sharing the list would give "criminals a road map on how to break the law by providing a list of what the DEA could consider illegal." I guess the fear was that citizens could assume that if it wasn't on the list, it wasn't illegal, even though it could appear on the list later. I didn't really understand this theory—how difficult would it be to post a new, updated list every time a new substance was added? What about citizens who wanted to make sure they were following the law? Wouldn't a list be helpful in that regard? Sure it would, except the DEA didn't want to help citizens act in accordance with the law. They preferred to have a vague law that could trap as many people as possible, often people with sizable assets to forfeit. We weren't the first people they had done this to. Hopefully our defense of the case would change the course of future prosecutions. As frustrated as we were with the process, we had started believing that maybe our troubles would spur a new law that would make sense to citizens and wouldn't be so vague that even most attorneys couldn't understand it. Citizens should be able to clearly understand what is considered legal or illegal behavior.

There was a chemist named Dr. Arthur Berrier who had been employed at DEA headquarters and was considered the DEA's in-house expert on the determination of analogues. He worked in the Office of Forensic Sciences, which was the lab where new, emerging substances were analyzed after they had been discovered by the DEA's Office of Diversion Control. The Office of Diversion Control would learn of an unscheduled (not made illegal yet) substance being used in the public and would then give the Office of Forensic Sciences the task of determining if this substance could be considered an analogue. Mr. Analogue had discovered early on in his defense of analogue cases that Dr. Berrier had begun telling the Office of Diversion Control that he didn't believe certain substances to be substantially similar to banned substances (i.e., they couldn't be analogues). At first, the Office of Diversion Control had listened to Dr. Berrier reluctantly and decided they would not prosecute certain substances as analogues. Then, as Dr. Berrier started giving this opinion more frequently, they had decided to ignore his input and prosecute cases on certain substances anyway. Ultimately, they just stopped asking for his opinion because it wasn't helping them in their crusade. It was a long, complicated series of events, but through the years, Mr. Analogue had pieced all of this together, discovering more juicy tidbits of information and internal DEA emails and communications with every case he defended.

Basically, the DEA knew that their most experienced go-to chemist for the determination of analogues was telling them that he didn't believe certain substances could be considered analogues. Rather than listening to him, they just ignored him and moved forward with their prosecutions anyway and then stopped going to him for his input altogether. They hired chemists within the Office of Diversion Control who were paid to go around the country and testify that they believed substances to be *substantially similar* to banned substances. These testifying "experts" did no real analyses of the substances themselves, but they knew enough to sound somewhat educated on chemical structure and regurgitate what another chemist within the department had "determined" before them. This tactic often worked in the government's favor at trials because most people, including highly regarded defense attorneys, didn't have a higher-level understanding of chemistry. Many attorneys heard "substantially similar," and they looked only at the one-dimensional drawings of chemical structures—and if one didn't know what he or she was looking at, the drawings could have appeared to have some similarities. They didn't understand that for something to be similar (or not) there was much more that went into the analyzation than just looking at a one-dimensional drawing, and they didn't know how to properly question the DEA "experts" during trial to show the jury that these so-called experts didn't really know what they were talking about.

However, Jim Felman had become obsessed, and he had an unbelievable understanding of the chemistry involved in these cases. He was able to crucify a government expert on the stand. He knew where all the "bodies were buried" in the DEA's analogue escapades, and they didn't want those secrets going public.

I was encouraged by what we'd learned from Mr. Analogue, but I still really did not want to go to trial. Trial carried a lot of risks. Innocent people were found guilty all the time. Going to trial seemed like such a waste of time and money. We were willing to admit the one law we had broken, which was misdemeanor misbranding, and the government surely could see that we weren't guilty of anything more if they would just look at things logically, but that word *logically* continued being meaningless in our situation.

Jennifer Tourje did follow up after her meeting with George and Michael and said she wanted to meet to further discuss a resolution. We couldn't believe it. It seemed that a new prosecutor being on the case really was going to help us. George and Michael had given her loose parameters of a resolution that would be agreeable to us when they had met with her, so the fact that she was willing to follow up with another meeting meant she must be willing to work within those parameters. They set a time to meet, and all the attorneys would attend the meeting. Mr. Analogue could share his information about the DEA and analogues and really drive the point home that the government had real problems with their case. Basically, how could the government seriously prosecute defendants for violating the Analogue Act, accusing them of actually knowing what an analogue was, when the DEA's own chemists couldn't even agree on which substances were analogues? This seemed like an obvious hurdle that the government would be challenged to overcome, and we were going to use it to our advantage to get the best resolution possible.

By all accounts the meeting went well. My father and I didn't attend, so I can't speak verbatim of what took place. Plus, I don't think the details of negotiation meetings are ever meant to be public, but from what we were told after the meeting, it appeared the case was going to have a favorable resolution for us without going to trial. Ms. Tourje was given a plethora of information about the malfeasance within the DEA regarding their efforts to continue to prosecute analogue cases while concealing findings of their own chemists. Ms. Tourje did not like what she heard and asked questions about coming to a resolution and what we would be willing to do to resolve the case. I couldn't believe it when I heard from our attorneys after the meeting. It was December. Christmas was approaching. My prayers had been answered, and I was getting the best Christmas present ever.

Our Gas Pipe company holiday party that year was really special. I had completed the bulk and worst part of my cancer treatment. And it appeared we were going to come to a resolution with the government that would be something we could live with. Every year at the party I had given a speech, and we would have an award ceremony that we called the Golden Bong Awards. Employees voted for each other to win in various categories such as MVP (Most Valuable Piper), Kick-Ass Manager, and Super Service. Each winner was given a bong that was decorated with green-and-gold sparkly material. It was something we all looked forward to, and it was always emotional. My speeches in the past few years had been about how strong we were as people and as a company, how we continued to persevere during the most challenging of times, and how grateful we were to have each other, whereas before they had been about how we were the best smoke shop ever and how high our sales were. The tenor of the celebration had changed over the years. It was still a huge celebration, but it was more about *who* we were and not *what* we were. One of the most beautiful things that I witnessed from all the changes within our company was that there was now open talk about God and spirituality. For some people that was a taboo subject, and unfortunately the Gas Pipe was no different than other environments in that regard, but when I had been diagnosed, I'd talked openly about God and prayer. People at the Gas Pipe whom I'd thought had no faith or didn't talk about faith also began talking about faith and prayer. My speech that year had focused on God, faith, and hope.

We had planned a family trip to Alaska for New Year's. The kids and I had never been there during winter and had always wanted to go, so it was going to be another thing to mark off the bucket list before trial. Now we didn't think trial would happen, so it was just going to be a celebration. My father and my cousin Ben went with us too. It was a magical time because everything seemed like it was coming together and finally working out as it should. I was in my favorite place with my family. We spent countless hours playing board games— Monopoly had been a family favorite for years—and we even made a curling course on the frozen river. The whole trip was carefree, and I was so overjoyed to be with my family and simply enjoy each other's company. Alaska in the winter was calm, peaceful, tranquil, and breathtakingly beautiful. There was a constant frost on the ground that looked like someone had sprinkled diamonds across the tundra, and the stars at night made us feel as though we were in a planetarium. We rang in 2018 standing on the deck of my father's house with the stars gleaming down on us, and we had a toast at midnight to 2018 being the best year ever!

Chapter Twenty

2018 was upon us, and it was quickly apparent that our prediction of it being the best year ever wasn't coming true. January was a terrible month. We got back to Dallas after our Alaska trip to find our home infested with rats. And I don't mean just a rat here or there. They were everywhere! One time when I got home at night and walked into the dark house, one ran across my foot. Another time I opened a desk drawer that I hadn't opened in months, and a rat jumped out of it. Based on what I saw inside the drawer, the rat had made it a home. As it turned out, the bubble of Park Cities, with its lush vegetation, was a haven for the rats of the city. Yes, the irony. They were eating my houseplants and the dog food and were leaving feces throughout the house. It was absolutely disgusting, and we hired two different companies over four months, trying multiple techniques and spending thousands of dollars to get rid of them. We would ultimately prevail over the rats in the house, but the other invasion in our lives—the government—seemed to not be going away anytime soon. By the end of January, we had yet to hear from Ms. Tourje about any sort of resolution.

The month of January was also when we found out that our male boxer dog, Phin, had leukemia. Out of the blue, our healthy, vibrant six-year-old pet got sick. I was devastated and couldn't believe it. Our dogs were like our second set of children, and when I'd had Bertha, the dogs had been my only companions sometimes for days. There were treatment options, but none of them were desirable or guaranteed improvement. Within three weeks of his diagnosis, he had stopped eating and couldn't walk. The decision we had to make was clear.

Simultaneously my dear, sweet cousin and friend Jessica was having to go through a similar situation, but on a much greater and more serious level. Her husband had been diagnosed with late-stage pancreatic cancer. His condition progressed quickly, and difficult decisions—the kind nobody ever really thinks about having to make, particularly in their early forties—had to be made. January ended with his funeral, and I, like everyone else, couldn't comprehend why a husband and father of two young children had to be taken so soon. Anthony had been a good man, and he had certainly lived a far better life than I had lived. Their loss certainly wasn't about me, but it affected me deeply. I was going through my own battle with cancer, and I had kids almost the same age as his and had contemplated being taken from them for various reasons. It was gut wrenching. Now I was watching my cousin's kids go through what I had feared my kids would experience, and while I was grateful to not have died from cancer, I also couldn't understand why I was spared, with all my wrongdoings and irresponsible behavior. I had felt survivor's guilt before in my life, but not with people I actually knew and felt close to.

My cousin Jessica was and is a pillar of strength. I was in awe of how she handled everything happening in her life and still managed to be there for others. Her courage and ability to move forward inspired me. She had been a rock and source of support for me through so much—even coming to work with us after all our accounting records had been seized, using her accounting skills to get us back on track, which had been a massive undertaking. We couldn't have survived without her. She always had grace and compassion, and even when she was going through something unimaginable, she continued to stay positive and be an outstanding mother and friend to many. I hated what she and her children were going through, and I wanted to be there for her in any way I could. I realized, though, that one of the best things I could do, because I had been given a second chance (actually, a few chances) in life, was to continue moving forward, learn from my mistakes, make every day count, and live the best life I possibly could with integrity and positivity.

In February we learned there was going to be no resolution with the government. There had been a leadership change within the office. A new United States attorney had been appointed to lead the Northern District of Texas, and with that appointment came changes and people being moved into different roles. We had a new prosecutor on our case, Chad Meacham, who had previously been the criminal chief but had recently been demoted to a regular AUSA. He went from being second from the top to a regular staff attorney, and we were going to be his first case to take to trial and prove himself since his demotion. He made it clear that there would be no resolution; he had marching orders to take the case all the way to trial. He had a CCE charge in the indictment and plenty of cooperating witnesses, and he felt confident. Jim—Mr. Analogue—tried to share the information that had been shared with Jennifer Tourje about the DEA and their internal disputes about analogues, but it was to no avail.

I was devastated. I felt like every ounce of energy and will to fight had been taken out of me. I had been so sure we were going to resolve things, and after fighting cancer and then believing there was a very close light at the end of the tunnel and getting my hopes up, I just couldn't believe we were right back to square one. I felt utterly defeated. One Saturday, shortly after we'd learned there would be no resolution, I drove Gavin out to the middle of nowhere to drop him off at a Boy Scout campout. I couldn't find where I was supposed to drop him off, and my head was not clear because I was in a fog, reeling from the realization that we really were going to have to fight the government full force and go to trial. I could barely keep it together, and once Gavin got out of the car, I lost it, crying uncontrollably with big, obnoxious sobs. I was driving through some little podunk town and saw a Sonic. I pulled over and proceeded to order cheese tots and a cherry limeade, and I sat there feeding and drowning my sorrows while snot and tears ran down my face. It was a low point, and I was quite a sight, I'm sure. I got control of myself, realized what a mess I must have appeared to be, cleared my head, and once again made the decision that I had to forge ahead. There was no choice.

By the end of February, we had filed numerous motions with the court to get things moving along. The two that made the most headway were filed by Mr. Analogue, and they dealt with Brady and Daubert issues. Everybody knows what those are, right? Of course not, because if you haven't been thrust into the legal system, you wouldn't really know anything about the intricacies of criminal defense law and legal terms, which was why it was important for us to have attorneys who understood those things well. We were innocent of all the charges. The only thing we were guilty of was misdemeanor misbranding, and we weren't charged with that. The charges were defensible, and we could prevail if things were done correctly. The Analogue Act was vague and confusing, and it would be easy for a jury to get it wrong, but they could be made to understand with the right information presented.

The term *Brady* in the legal world came from *Brady v. Maryland*, a Supreme Court case that had been decided in 1962. It established that the prosecution must turn over all evidence that might exonerate the defendant. It was called *exculpatory evidence* or *Brady material*. Often the government will turn over everything they have, but they may not always do so, or there may be material that is believed to exist but hasn't been fully discovered by the defense or prosecution. This was what was happening in our case. Mr. Analogue had discovered a fair amount of internal DEA communications validating the DEA chemists' disagreements about analogues, but the communications made it evident that there was even more information out there. This information would be exculpatory because if the DEA couldn't even agree that something was an analogue or not, then how were we supposed to know it was? When it is believed that there is undiscovered information out there, the defense can file a motion to compel. The motion to compel can't be frivolous, and it has to have strong evidence to back up why the defense believes there is Brady material in existence, and we had that evidence.

In the legal world, *Daubert* refers to a standard that a trial judge will use to assess whether an expert witness's scientific testimony is based on scientifically valid reasoning that can be properly applied to the facts at issue. This was a big concern in our case because the only chemists throughout the country that would call these substances substantially similar and therefore analogues were those employed by the DEA or a chemist who received a substantial government grant and was paid an obscene amount of money to testify at trials (over double what we had to pay any of our expert witnesses). Mr. Analogue, who had been working on these cases for about five years, had yet to find one non-DEA chemist (or one not closely affiliated with the DEA) who would even agree on what it meant in the world of science to call something *substantially similar*, much less to call two substances substantially similar and therefore analogues.

When a defendant files a Brady or Daubert motion, both can lead to hearings because they deal with complex issues that need to be sorted out properly with oral argument and witnesses. The judge ordered a Daubert hearing for our case. She also told us if we believed there was Brady material within the DEA, then we should issue a subpoena to compel the DEA to turn over anything they had in this regard. This was huge for us. We had a federal judge telling us to issue a subpoena to the DEA mandating they turn over any material or communications they had regarding their internal communications about substances being analogues or not. We suspected the DEA would move to quash it, meaning they would file a motion with the court stating why they didn't think they should have to comply with the subpoena, and they did. The motion to quash and the settling of it was referred to the magistrate judge David Horan. We were thrilled! Judge Horan had presided over our detention hearing when we had been arrested and the government had tried to keep us in jail pending trial. He had already been fair with us more than once by not keeping us in jail and even by eventually ordering for Bertha to be removed.

This whole motion process with subpoenas being issued and hearings being scheduled transpired over several months. Nothing happened quickly, and every time a motion was filed, the other side had ten days to two weeks to respond (and sometimes longer), so it was a long drawn-out process. I felt as though we were getting down to the wire with a trial coming up in September, and my hope with these motions was that it would expose elements of the government's case that they wouldn't want exposed so that we could still find that resolution we wanted. Mr. Meacham, our new prosecutor, had said there would be no resolution, but certainly after it was understood that the DEA was hiding stuff, either the DEA would say, "No more; this can't go forward, or we will be exposed," or Mr. Meacham would realize that going to trial in front of a jury where the defendants were being accused of knowing something was an analogue when the DEA couldn't even agree if it was an analogue was a recipe for disaster for the government.

We were only attacking the analogue charges at this point because they were the most serious with the worst consequences. There was the charge dealing with the AB-Fubinaca snafu, but we weren't as concerned with that because it was defensible. Even the government's own cooperating witnesses had said during their proffer interviews that a legal product had been ordered, but the wrong one had been unknowingly received. It was clearly a snafu—a very serious one, but a snafu nonetheless—and a rather isolated incident over a short time period. The analogue accusations encompassed a three-year period. There was also the money-laundering charge, but that was tied to a drug charge or mail and wire fraud. No conviction on the drug charge meant no conviction on money laundering, and the mail and wire fraud charge wasn't anything our side was overly concerned with because nobody had been defrauded of money or property, and that was required for a mail and wire fraud conviction. The misbranding charge wasn't our biggest concern, either, because it was a very minimal charge compared to the rest. A conviction on that charge carried no forfeiture (versus the other charges, which could lead to forfeiture of everything). We knew we had committed misdemeanor misbranding, and we weren't going to say otherwise if we went to trial. We would defend ourselves against the accusation that we had defrauded anyone and committed felony misbranding, but we could deal with that later. Blowing a torpedo in the analogue case immediately was essential.

In May 2018 I officially finished all cancer treatment with my last infusion of Herceptin and was recovering from my final reconstruction surgery that I'd had in April. It was time to move forward from cancer, but anyone who's had cancer and survived knows it's not anything you ever fully put behind you. It's a defining life event. I'm not sure, though, whether the enormity of cancer ever fully hit me, because I had the big legal issue going on simultaneously. Yes, the legal stuff had been put on the back burner temporarily, but it was never gone. And as soon as I officially completed all cancer treatment, it was time to hunker down and prepare for trial with a firm date scheduled four months away.

Dan turned forty in June of 2018. I typically didn't go to Alaska for his birthday in early June because the kids would just be getting out of school. I was determined, though, to do something special for his big birthday and have some fun and try to put all the negativity of the case aside for at least a few days. I arranged for his best friend and I to fly to the lodge and surprise Dan. It was a quick trip—I left on a Saturday and was back home in Dallas by Wednesday morning—but it was so worth it. The best part was that I made a concentrated effort to not talk about the case and just focus on our time together. By the third day, Dan asked about the case, noticing that I hadn't brought it up once. I was glad I had made that effort and wished I had done that more over the last few years. I was going to try to make the next few months leading up to trial more focused on my family and not the case twenty-four seven. If I had limited time, I didn't want it to be negative.

I took Gavin on a trip in June to Cedar Point, an amusement park in Ohio, also known as the roller coaster capital of the world. Gavin and I had been riding roller coasters together since he was a small child. Going to Cedar Point was another bucket list item, and I got to mark another state off my list to help me reach my goal of seeing every state in the country. The trip was so much fun, and there was something gratifying about riding all the enormous roller coasters. I love the thrill of roller coasters, but it had been a few years since I'd been on one, and I had never been on any as big as the ones at Cedar Point. Life could be compared to a roller coaster with all the continuous ups and downs, but the coasters at the park symbolized something to conquer for me, and I rode each huge roller coaster with guts and glory and kept my eyes opened on every big hill, embracing the fear. There was something about the experience that gave me courage, and I felt strong.

After my two trips in early June, it was time for the Daubert hearing. Because we were challenging the government's expert witnesses, and not the other way around, the government was required to bring its witnesses to the hearing so they could testify, and the judge could make her determination. We weren't required to present our expert witnesses, but we did because they would be the best people to refute what the government witnesses had to say.

Although the case had been ongoing for years, we'd had very little interaction with Chief District Judge Barbara M. G. Lynn, the judge presiding over our case. There had been one hearing in her courtroom in the spring of 2018, but it had been brief in comparison to the Daubert hearing. I had been told repeatedly that she was the best judge in the district, which made sense considering she was the chief judge. I had no reason to believe otherwise, and I had very much looked forward to being in front of her and finally seeing this woman who was so highly regarded by all. I remember the first time I saw her come out of her chambers and sit down to preside over a hearing. It was like finally meeting the Wizard of Oz. I had known she existed, I had seen her name on various documents, and she had been making rulings in our case that affected our lives greatly, but I had never actually come face to face with her. As I heard her talk and watched how she presided over things, I could tell she was a witty, ridiculously intelligent, funny, and very interesting woman. What she thought of us and our situation, though, only time would tell.

The Dabuert hearing resulted in a favorable outcome—not as favorable as we had hoped, but it was still helpful. It was clear that the expert witnesses the government was using for the case were not well versed in the world of analogues, particularly after Mr. Analogue questioned them on the witness stand. He was able to expose holes in their theories and make it evident that their theories of certain substances being substantially similar in structure were based on nothing more than what they were required to say based on DEA protocol. We presented our own expert witnesses who were independent experts in their field—some of the best in the country—and they further exposed the weaknesses of the government's experts. It was a preview of the trial to come, even though we were still hoping to not have a trial. The ruling from the Daubert hearing was that the judge would give a jury instruction at trial that the jurors were to give no more weight to any expert (for the government or defense) than they would give a nonscience expert. There was no real science to the whole concept of *substantially similar*, which we agreed, but the confusion of that and allowing experts to testify and call something substantially similar with so much ambiguity was confusing, but it was better than not telling the jury anything at all. At least they would be told that there was no science behind this whole concept the government was trying to prove definitively, but we had hoped they wouldn't be allowed to testify at all about anything being *substantially similar*—that those words wouldn't even be permitted to be uttered.

Summer was underway, and I was trying to spend as much time with the kids as I could, but it was difficult because they were teenagers now and had very busy, independent lives. I wasn't going to have them put their lives on hold just because I was afraid of future limited time with them. I was lucky enough to squeeze in quality time with them here and there, such as my trip with Gavin to the amusement park. Kieley and I had a girls' road trip to Arkansas when I drove her to summer camp. I also got to have a very short trip with both the kids together when I flew them out to Georgia to take them to a new academic camp they had qualified to attend. I was cherishing every moment. We had a few trips to Alaska, with each of the kids going separately with me on different trips due to conflicting schedules.

That summer in Alaska was bittersweet, as so much of everything had become. I didn't know if I would be returning. I was happy to be there but sad to think of it potentially being the last time. I tried to focus on the moment, being present in the here and now. It was hard, but I kept reminding myself that nothing was definite; I could very well be back there in the future, but I was going to have to go through a really difficult process—a trial—first.

One night, when Dan and I were at our house, winding down early for the night, we got a phone call from a member of our staff telling us that the sauna was on fire. We thought she meant a little fire in the fireplace that was used to heat the sauna, so we casually started to make our way over to the lodge. As soon as we started walking down the trail, we saw huge clouds of billowing smoke in the sky. It was a huge fire. The entire wooden sauna building was on fire, and it was trying to spread to the walkways and entire lodge, which were also made of wood. Every member of the staff was standing with water hoses, trying to keep everything wet, and there was a line of people passing buckets of water from the river up to the building. Everybody from the neighboring lodges and the fire department came to help. The fire was extinguished, and all was well. The sauna was no more, but the entire lodge didn't burn down, which could have easily happened. We'd had a relatively accident-free existence at Rapids Camp Lodge for over twenty years, and then in two years we had a severe airplane crash and almost had the entire lodge burn down, on top of everything else happening in our lives. Both turned out better than they could have, but it was close, very close, to something even more catastrophic happening. It seemed as though we couldn't get off the edge of the cliff, inches from falling at any moment. There was a constant combination of feeling grateful and unsettled.

I came back to Dallas in late July so we could attend a hearing. After Magistrate Judge Horan had helped us wade through the motion process to compel the DEA to produce Brady material, he had ordered a hearing where the DEA was ordered to produce witnesses from the DEA who could testify about the internal communications and differing opinions about analogues. This was huge! There was no way the government would want to produce these people, have them testify under oath, and confirm what Mr. Analogue already knew and then some. Surely they would want to settle the case before that happened. Once again, we were wrong. Per Judge Horan's order, the DEA brought in various personnel and let them all testify. Some lied—or maybe "glossed over the truth" would be a better way to put it—but a few of them actually told everything they knew about Dr. Berrier and his opinion about certain substances not being analogues and how after a while, the DEA had stopped asking him about his opinion since they didn't like what he was saying.

Mr. Meacham, our new prosecutor, was adamant that none of this would matter come trial. His first argument was that Dr. Berrier wouldn't be testifying himself, or rather he'd be surprised if we really wanted him to testify. Dr. Berrier had found himself in some legal problems of his own, which had ultimately led to him being suspended from the DEA. This obviously cast a shadow on his credibility, but we weren't too concerned because his coworkers at the DEA vouched for his intelligence and reliability in the field of science and determining whether things were analogues. Having others speak about his knowledge and dependability in his field was even better than him saying it himself. Also, Mr. Meacham believed no matter how damning the knowledge gained during this hearing was for the government, it wouldn't matter because it wouldn't be permitted as evidence at trial. We thought otherwise, and once the hearing was over, we had the information we thought was vital to our defense. We also facilitated the judge ordering the DEA's secret list of analogues to be made public, which was huge because they never wanted people to know of that list. In the end it would be up to Judge Lynn to determine what from the Brady hearing would be allowed to come into the trial or not, but we felt we had gotten some very useful information.

I took one last trip to Alaska in early September, right before the trial began. I had set a goal for myself as a distraction leading up to trial to walk or run one hundred miles in thirty days. So Dan and I went walking daily, and I cherished every moment of those walks, fearing it could be our last time together. It was so hard to leave and go back home to Dallas. I was trying to stay positive, but it was challenging. The day my father and I left the lodge to fly home, everyone gave us prayers and good wishes. We hadn't talked explicitly about the legal proceedings with all our staff at the lodge, but they knew. It was the constant elephant in the room. I told myself over and over again that I would be back. Dan told me I would be back. We all hoped for the best and believed somewhere within us that the best would happen, but there were no guarantees in life. The concept of hoping for the best but preparing for the worst was a reality.

Chapter Twenty-One

*T*he day I'd hoped and prayed would never come was coming, and there was nothing more to stop it. My attorney would later tell me that she had never seen someone who so badly didn't want to go to trial. I knew the stakes were high, and I knew juries didn't always get it right. I had done something I wasn't proud of, but I hadn't done what the government was accusing.

We couldn't have had a better team of attorneys going into trial. A few months previously, I had decided to part ways with David Botsford because we'd had a difference of opinion, although he definitely was one of the best criminal defense attorneys in the country, and anyone would be lucky to have him in his or her corner. We still had Geroge Milner and Michael Mowla, both of whom had been with us from almost the inception of the case, and we had Marlo Caededdu and Jim Felman, a.k.a. Mr. Analogue. A few months prior to trial, John Cline had joined our team. Marlo and Jim had both known John and worked with him on cases for years. He was considered one of the top federal defense attorneys in the country, having represented some pretty high-profile people such as Oliver North. Prior to trial we'd had a unique issue in our case that was litigated "under seal," meaning not available to the public, so I won't divulge the details, but John was brought on to help with that issue and become part of the trial team. John Cline was also a master chess player, and clearly that mind-set translated well into the mind-set of a strategic trial attorney.

It was a dynamic combination. John was a strategic planner and organizer, always looking at the big picture, several moves ahead of everyone else, like a good chess player. Jim was, of course, Mr. Analogue—need I say more? Marlo was organized and very detail oriented and had a wonderful ability to look at each situation from every perspective, analyze it, and then break it down for a jury with creative visual exhibits. George was an amazing trial attorney who was brilliant, very likable, animated, captivating, and mesmerizing to listen to and watch. People naturally wanted to believe whatever he was saying. Michael could cite any statute or case law practically on demand, and he knew just about every document in all thirteen terabytes of discovery in our case and was able to write well-drafted, thorough, and thought-provoking motions throughout the trial with little time for preparation. Steve Kessler, my dear friend, only represented us in the forfeiture aspect of things, so he would not be part of the criminal trial team. We would only need him if we lost and there was forfeiture, so as much as I adored him, we were hoping he would not be making an appearance.

How we were going to pay for all these highly esteemed attorneys was the multimillion-dollar question. We had paid initial retainers in the beginning of the legal proceedings, which had been over four years ago. Those retainers had been exhausted over time with pretrial work. We had been paying as we went for a while, but as the actual trial approached, we had to pay substantial large sums of money up front so everyone could be paid prior to trial starting. The only money that had been released in the four years since everything had been seized were our company pension accounts. The government should have never seized those in the first place because they were ERISA-qualified retirement plans and protected from any seizure. I couldn't access mine because I still worked for the company, and I wasn't over seventy; however, my father was required to start taking disbursements once he was over seventy. He was able to liquidate those funds and use that for trial expenses. Some of the attorneys took credit cards, so that helped, too, but that also meant incurring more debt. We had no choice. And the final thing done to help pay for expenses was my father selling his house in Dallas—one of the only assets that was not under government seizure—and he moved in with me.

We went all in—it was like the gambler sitting at a table in Vegas and pushing his entire stack of chips into the middle of the table, going for the win of his life. Or it could be the loss of his life. Like that gambler, we were gambling with every penny we had, but we were also gambling with our actual lives, not just money. We were facing spending the rest of our lives in prison or at least, for me, a good portion of the rest of my life, if not all of it. If we lost, my father would presumably die in prison. That was something that I couldn't bear to think about. I had lived with the possibility of this for over four years, but now, within weeks of going to trial, it was becoming more and more of a reality. I couldn't deny what could happen anymore. I had to plan for it and prepare as best as I could. I had no idea how to do that, though.

One thing I knew I had to do was talk with my kids. I had spent the last four years telling them I thought we would come to a resolution. The kids had read media articles, and they had witnessed their house being raided by the DEA and lived through my time with Bertha, so they knew the seriousness of the accusations. They never believed, though, that I would really go to prison for the rest of my life. Even though the media had reported that, I had downplayed it. I had so much hope and belief that we would never go to trial and that I would never really be facing the possibility of life in prison, and I saw no need to worry the kids with that burden if I didn't have to. Well, now trial was imminent, and I had to tell them.

The kids started high school in August, which was a very exciting time. I wanted to let them get into their new routines at school and not put a damper on any of that immediately. That was naive of me, though. They weren't little kids anymore. During the four years that had passed since the beginning of our world turning upside down, they had become adolescents; they were growing up and getting smarter and more aware of everything. They knew that there had been a trial date scheduled for September, and they knew September was quickly approaching. I dreaded approaching the topic with them and played out scenarios in my mind of how I would do it, but it turned out I didn't have to. While driving home from football practice one afternoon in August, Gavin asked me about the case and if the trial was about to happen. I told him it was and that I was sorry for any negativity it would cause such as unfavorable media coverage, and I told him I was scared. I told him I didn't want to go to trial, but I didn't know what other choice I had. I couldn't plea to something I didn't do or voluntarily choose to leave my family. Trial carried huge risks, but if I had to leave my children, it wouldn't be because I had chosen to. I did believe in our innocence, but I also knew we could lose, and my smart, sensitive, loving son said, "Or you could win."

Kieley and I talked about it over the course of a few conversations, and we all talked about it as a family. Kieley seemed a little more guarded about the situation. Then one night after dinner, we were talking in the kitchen, and she asked me where I would go if I was found guilty. She knew it meant prison, but she meant more specifically geographically. I told her I wasn't sure, but I hoped it would be somewhere close so family could visit. She asked if she would be able to visit, and I told her yes, if she wanted to, but I would certainly understand if she didn't want to because of mixed emotions she could have. We cried together, and she assured me that of course she would want to visit.

That was about the extent of the conversations. I told the kids repeatedly that they could ask any questions anytime, and we could talk about things anytime they wanted. They seemed to be moving forward with their lives and assimilating to high school, not overly fixated on the upcoming trial. I was grateful for that, but of course as a mom, I was concerned whether they were truly doing okay. They were either being really strong and just accepting what was happening, or they were in complete denial, or—and this was what they kept telling me—they really didn't believe I would be found guilty.

My father moved in with us a few weeks before trial, and it really was a wonderful thing. I think we were all a little trepidatious initially. He was seventy-two and was used to having his own space and independent life. It wasn't as though he was elderly and needed care and companionship. He was hardworking and still very involved in the businesses and stayed on the go. I had my set routine and life with the kids, and Dan was of course part of that when he was in Dallas and my godmother Emma lived with us part-time. We had nightly dinner and family time, and we welcomed the idea of my father being part of it, but like everything in life, there had to be an adjustment as we figured out how to all coexist under one roof. It really took no time at all, and it quickly felt like my father had always been living with us. He was able to share stories and words of wisdom at dinnertime. There were many positives that would ultimately come out of our unfortunate legal battle, and the quality time we got to have as a family with my father was not just a positive, but a real gift.

Once the trial started, my father and I would be going to the courthouse every morning—trial would start promptly at eight thirty. Having him living at the house would make the daily routine easier and more efficient. We could get up, drive the kids to school, and head straight downtown. We had arranged for our good friend Chris to come to the house every morning and pick up our dogs and take them to our office, where they would normally go every day with us if we were going to work. My father had his own boxer dog who was a great companion to my female boxer, and earlier in the year, after our boxer Phin had passed away, we had adopted a German Shorthaired Pointer rescue named Manny. It was a decision I had made when I had thought the case was going to get resolved, but when it didn't, I had so much guilt for taking in Manny under such stressful circumstances. He fit right in, though, with our crazy, dog-loving family and became best buds with our boxer, Scarlett, and my father's boxer, Pudu. He brought some much-needed joy to our lives. So now our house had two teenagers, me, Dan when he was in Dallas, my godmother, my father, and three large dogs—with the trial of the century about to begin. There was surely never to be a dull moment, and the huge house I had felt was so unnecessary was now being put to good use.

It was time for trial—no escaping it any longer. The week before the trial, we had a pretrial conference where the judge went over the parameters of the trial such as scheduling and her rules, and each side presented any pretrial motions dealing with the dismissal of any of the charges or motions in limine. A motion in limine is a motion filed typically before trial (although they could occur during trial as well without the jury present) and argued orally, if the judge wanted oral argument, and the purpose of the motion was to limit or exclude certain evidence from trial. We had numerous motions in limine. The government filed one. They wanted to exclude the testimony and information about Dr. Berrier and the dissenting opinions among the DEA chemists. We of course wanted to have DEA personnel come and testify as our witnesses about what they knew regarding the internal DEA dispute about what substances were or were not analogues as well as Dr. Berrier's opinion on these substances. The judge decided that we could call them as witnesses. That was a big win for us—thank you, Mr. Analogue.

We asked for various things to be excluded and were granted some and not others. One of the biggest things we were granted was the exclusion of all the pleading codefendant pleas, so long as we didn't try to use the pleas against them later. Typically, the government would put each cooperating witness on the stand and begin the testimony by reading to the jury the charges the witness has pled to. This is done to show the jury that there are people who already pled to the offense that the defendants on trial are denying. Then when the defense attorneys cross-examine the cooperating witness, they will often try to point out that the witness is lying, presumably to get a better deal with their sentencing. This is known as impeaching the witness. After reading all of discovery, we felt that people were going to tell the truth, so it wasn't worth keeping the option of impeaching at the risk of multiple people going in front of the jury as guilty defendants, therefore making us look guilty.

While the codefendants' testimonies would point toward the mislabeling of products—a federal misdemeanor—nobody had been defrauded. We didn't believe that any witnesses would discuss any specific knowledge of substances being analogues or how anyone at Gas Pipe had specific knowledge of substances being analogues, because there wasn't an understanding of analogues at Gas Pipe. The AB-Fubinaca snafu was easy to explain, and we would use the government's own witnesses to do so. Without any of the drug charges sticking, there could be no CCE charge or money-laundering charge. The government had dropped the mail and wire fraud charge less than two weeks before trial (assumingly because they knew they couldn't prove it), so we just had to conquer the drug charges and explain the difference between felony misbranding and misdemeanor misbranding and show that nobody had been defrauded.

At the beginning of trial, we made a stipulation, which was a formal legal acknowledgement and agreement made between both parties that was presented to the jury. We stipulated to the effects that these herbal incense products had—making people high—and that they were intended to have that effect, and the effects were similar to a scheduled, banned substance. There were a couple of reasons for this stipulation. First, we wanted to admit the truth and be credible with the jury and the court. To say we had no idea what was really going on with these products would have been absurd, even though we had never directly sold them for that purpose. It was a disaster every time that defendants on trial in other analogue cases took the position that people didn't know these products were for human consumption. And by admitting our knowledge, we were admitting to misdemeanor misbranding, admitting that the products were not actually incense, even though they were labeled as such. So packages being labeled as herbal incense, with "Not for human consumption" written on them, was false branding. The fact that everyone knew it—retailers, customers, and law enforcement—was evidence, though, that nobody had been defrauded.

The other reason we made this stipulation was because of prong two of the Analogue Act. There were three parts (prongs) to the Analogue Act. Prong one dealt with the chemical structure of substances—they had to be structurally substantially similar to be an analogue. Prong two dealt with the effects of the substances—they had to be substantially similar in effect to a controlled substance. Prong three dealt with how the product was represented, sold, or marketed. Prongs two and three don't matter if prong one wasn't satisfied. If it couldn't be proven that the chemical in the herbal incense was substantially similar in chemical structure to an illegal substance, then it couldn't be an analogue. Even if it could be determined to be substantially similar, then it also had to be proven that the people selling it somehow knew this. We saw no need to argue prong two and have experts from both sides come and testify about the effects of these substances. The reason people were buying so many of these products was clearly because of the effects. If we didn't have to debate prong two during the trial, the jury would only have to focus on prong one, and we didn't see how a jury could determine the substantial similarity of these substances when even chemists couldn't and when there was no evidence that we ever had knowledge of it.

It was clear that the jury at our trial would be getting a crash course in chemistry, and they would have to be able to pay close attention and absorb a great deal of information. There would be many names of chemicals presented that weren't familiar to many chemists, much less a regular person from the Dallas area. The chemicals alleged to be *substantially similar* were new, emerging chemicals that had names most people had never heard of. While the herbal incense products were sometimes referred to as "synthetic marijuana," the chemicals in them were not an alleged analogue of marijuana. The effects may have been the same or similar, but the chemical structure was not even remotely similar. Nobody—not even a DEA chemist—would ever say the synthetic cannabinoids used to make herbal incense had even a remotely similar chemical structure to THC (marijuana).

The selling of herbal incense had started out as a business decision like any other product we carried—customers had wanted it and had been willing to pay a certain price for it, and all our competition had been selling it first. It had gotten way out of control, though, and it was irresponsible and not a positive thing for the community. We had always been positive members of our community even though we owned a counterculture head shop—we'd helped with community-improvement projects and contributed to numerous charities. I was and am an attentive, loving mom who was involved with my kids, their friends, other parents, and the school community. Our herbal incense business was not indicative of who I was or who I wanted to be, but I had lost my way.

The biggest question now, though, was how a jury would see it. Would they follow the law and understand that except for misdemeanor misbranding, we had not broken a law? Or would they judge us from a moral standpoint and be disgusted that we had done something that was negative and not good for people while we made millions of dollars? We were about to find out, and their judgment and opinions of us would mean more and matter more than anyone's opinion of me had ever mattered in my life.

Chapter Twenty-Two

While I was mentally and emotionally preparing for any potential outcome at trial, I was also coming to the realization that one way or another, the ordeal would soon be over. I hoped it would be in the good way, but I also was feeling some sort of relief that no matter the outcome, it would at least be over. That was becoming my new mantra: "One way or another, this will be over soon." The prospect of a negative outcome scared me more than I can put into words, and the prospect of a positive outcome excited me more than I can put into words. The reality of it simply being over made me feel calm. I would not have to deal with the unknown and what-ifs anymore. That constant uncertainty was overwhelming and exhausting.

I had mustered up every ounce of motivation, energy, hope, and faith I had to force myself through trial. I resigned myself to the fact that it was happening and that I would get through it. Win or lose, I just needed to have the emotional and mental fortitude to make it through. Once it was over, it would finally be over. The threat and fear of going to trial would no longer exist after four long years. Yes, my life could be changing dramatically for the worse, but it could also be changing dramatically for the better.

Monday, September 24, 2018, was the first day of trial, which was jury selection. I had never participated in a jury selection even as a potential juror, so I really didn't know what to expect. It was stressful because it was our lives on the line, but it was also interesting and exciting. It was fast paced with a lot of information being exchanged throughout the day. There were approximately eighty potential jurors, and they all filled out a written jury questionnaire. We had to go through the questionnaires very quickly to determine who answered questions in a way that we felt indicated they would be good jurors for us. We kept notes and rated each questionnaire according to whom we thought we would want on our jury and whom we wouldn't want on our jury. Eventually, at the end of the day, each side would get to strike so many, and some would be excused for cause by the judge, and then by the end of the day, twelve (plus four alternates) would be left.

In addition to the written questionnaires, there was the process of voir dire. This is a French term meaning "to see to speak." In the legal world, it is the process of questioning potential jurors. I'd heard the term, and I'd heard our attorneys talk about the process before trial, but I really didn't understand it. During voir dire, all eighty potential jurors sat on the benches in the gallery, and we sat at the defense table with our chairs turned toward the gallery. We were in very close proximity to the jury pool. It felt like I could reach out and touch the potential jurors sitting in the front row. I was told earlier that it would be like that, and I'd assumed it would be intimidating. Somehow it wasn't, though. There was a comfort in seeing all the prospective jurors and realizing they were people just like us. It was reassuring to hear them talk and answer questions, and I began to feel as though they maybe could understand our defense.

The voir dire was fascinating and even entertaining. George Milner, our attorney, took the lead for our side, and he had the jury pool captivated and mesmerized. The prosecution had gone first and explained the legality of the Analogue Act and presented several PowerPoint slides with pictures of chemical structures that were meaningless if one didn't have a chemistry degree. The prospective jurors looked confused and overwhelmed. Then it was George's turn. He gave them several examples that seemed hypothetical but were actually a direct application to our case, and after each example he explained why the decision would have to be "not guilty." Then he started having them reply to his hypothetical examples. By the end, he had every prospective juror saying "not guilty" in unison. One of them even said to him, "You are a really good attorney because you already have all of us saying 'not guilty.'"

It was a long day, but our jury had been chosen, and we felt like we had a good one. There were some people who were struck by the other side because they admitted to being customers of Gas Pipe or because they had very liberal views on drugs and very negative views of the government. There were some we struck because they had too conservative of views and thought way too favorably of the government. There were a couple jurors we really wanted but were sure the government would strike, but they surprisingly didn't. One of them said he knew of Gas Pipe because his wife's friend worked at Inwood Bank, where we had banked for years but had been asked to leave due to the legal proceedings. He didn't say he knew why we had been asked to leave, but he did say that his wife's friend had shared with them that she was disappointed the bank had made that decision because the Gas Pipe people were good people and had been with the bank for years. We thought for sure the government would give him the boot, but they didn't, so he made it on the jury.

There were five defendants that went to trial—well, seven if you count the two corporations, Gas Pipe Inc. and Amy Lynn Inc., that were also indicted. But there were five people: Carolyn, our office manager and close friend; Tom, a lifelong friend and our general contractor; Bridget, one of our store managers; my father; and me. Carolyn had been charged with one of the analogue-drug counts, money laundering, and misbranding. It was a stretch that she had been indicted at all because she had no real role in the buying, manufacturing, design, labeling, or marketing of the product. She had simply paid the bills. Tom managed all construction and maintenance for all our properties, and his contractor license had been used to purchase acetone, which was used in the manufacturing of the herbal incense. He wasn't charged with manufacturing, though. He was only charged with misbranding, even though he had no role in the marketing or labeling of the product. Bridget was a store manager, so she was involved in the marketing and selling of the product, and she had been charged with felony misbranding, just like all the other store managers who had pled. She, like us, was hoping to go to trial and be found guilty only of the misdemeanor misbranding—although none of us had been charged with the misdemeanor, ultimately the jury would be given the choice of misdemeanor or felony misbranding.

On Tuesday morning we were all sitting at the defense table promptly at eight thirty, ready to have our case shown to a jury. The judge had given great instructions the day prior, letting the jury know that they were there to find us guilty or not guilty based on the law, not their own personal beliefs or morals. If they couldn't do that, they should be honest and say so, and she would excuse them. Some people had said they had moral issues with the case and were excused, and I hoped those who stayed really felt they could be fair in their role as jurors. She told them if they didn't like the law, they should contact their congressman, but in their role as juror, they had to follow the law as it was explained to them. This was reassuring, and we believed that if the jurors could truly do that, we could have a shot at winning.

The trial began with opening statements. The government went first. They once again showed PowerPoint slides with pictures of different chemical structures in an effort to impress upon the jury that all the chemicals looked substantially similar, even though *substantially similar* really had nothing to do with what chemicals looked like on a one-dimensional drawing (something Mr. Analogue and our expert chemists would explain later). They also explained to the jury how when one synthetic cannabinoid chemical would be banned, we would get rid of all the product containing that chemical and then switch to a new product with a new chemical that wasn't banned, and that we did this time and time again, which was how we were staying one step ahead of the law. So according to them, staying one step ahead of the law was the same as breaking the law. If that sounds strange, it is. They also explained to the jury that we sold these products for people to get high. This wasn't something we were denying, and we admitted this to the jury in our stipulation, so the government harping on it was unnecessary. And they told the jury we were actual drug dealers.

They showed the jury pictures of the products we sold, and they showed them pictures of the "lab" where the products had been made, which was in an area in the back of our Amy Lynn Inc. warehouse. Toward the end of our herbal incense business, rather than buying premade product from vendors, we had started making the majority of the products ourselves. There were a few reasons we had made this decision. It was a decision we had contemplated off and on for a while because manufacturing ourselves would ensure quality control—we would know exactly what was going in the product. We wouldn't have to rely on the vendor to put the right chemical in there. Also, our main vendor, Lawrence Shahwan, had gone MIA in late 2013 because of some criminal activity we hadn't been aware of. We had a huge multimillion-dollar contract with Lawrence for herbal incense products, and we had paid for product that hadn't been received due to him going off the grid. One of Lawrence's employees had come to our office with synthetic cannabinoid chemical (not the ready-made herbal incense product that we had been buying from him) and showed Ro Rojas, our operation manager, how to make the finished product. Gas Pipe then began making product rather than buying it, except for a small amount we still bought from other vendors.

The pictures of the "lab" were shameful and disgusting. They were meant to look like that, and I can't say I would disagree with the jury if they had a negative impression from them. This wasn't a professional "lab"—it wasn't really a lab at all, hence putting the word in quotes. It was a room where people used mixers (like a kitchen mixer) to mix the plant material, synthetic cannabinoid, and acetone (which acted as a binding agent) together to make the herbal incense. Then the finished product was weighed into three-gram portions and packaged. Nobody kept the room very organized, and it appeared dirty. Gas Pipe did always wash the bowls and mixing equipment to avoid any cross contamination from one chemical to another, though we would later learn Lawrence Shahwan and his employees did not, which had caused problems. But overall the room looked like a makeshift science experiment gone wrong. I couldn't recall ever thinking the room looked that bad while Gas Pipe was manufacturing the product, but I hadn't personally spent much time in the "lab." Whether it looked that bad in person or not, the pictures the government showed the jury certainly made it look terrible. There was nothing we could do about those pictures—we would just have to hope the jury could distinguish between law and personal opinions.

Throughout the opening statements and the entire trial, the government continually emphasized how much money we made from selling herbal incense. There was no disputing that, and we had no intention of trying. The product had flown off the shelves. The only reason we had ever started selling the product in the first place was because of the customers' requests, and all our competition had been selling it. We hadn't sought it out nor had we needed it to make our business successful. Gas Pipe had been in business for forty years when herbal incense hit the market. It had already been a ridiculously successful company. But like any retailer would do, we had sold a new product to stay competitive and give our customers what they wanted. The total dollar amount Gas Pipe had sold in herbal incense in a three-year period was obscene—over forty million dollars—but just like everything else that could appear distasteful or offensive about herbal incense, the profit didn't make it illegal. And every penny that was made from the sale of herbal incense was done in the public retail market, in brightly lit showcases for the whole world to see, and every sale was documented and taxed. So not only did Gas Pipe make millions of dollars from the sale of herbal incense, but the government did too. Of course, the prosecution mentioned none of this nor the fact that while we sold a lot of herbal incense, during the same time frame we had also sold over sixty million dollars in other products. Yet they tried to make us look like nothing more than drug dealers who deserved to have every penny taken.

After the prosecutor finished his opening statement, it was time for our side to give ours. Each side was allotted a certain amount of time. Even though we had seven defendants (including the corporations) and therefore multiple attorneys, we were only allowed slightly more time than the prosecution. I didn't understand that, and it seemed horribly unfair, but those were the rules. I suppose it was because the burden of proof was on the government, so they should get more time to make their case. We were to be presumed innocent, and the government had to prove all accusations beyond a reasonable doubt. This had been emphasized to the jurors in voir dire and by the judge numerous times. I was glad that point had been made, but I did not feel that in the last four years, I had been treated overall like someone who was presumed innocent.

Our opening statements were fantastic! George went first, then Marlo, and then John. Jim—Mr. Analogue—opted to reserve his opening for later at the beginning of our case, after the government rested their case. That part of the trial would be mostly focused on the chemistry and chemical-structure debate, so it would be more beneficial to have him explain that to the jury later. The only one of our codefendants' attorneys who gave an opening statement was Tom's attorney. Because he had no role at Gas Pipe except as our general contractor, nobody could even really understand why he'd been indicted. His attorney wanted to make that clear up front. She gave a very short statement so that she didn't take up much of our attorneys' limited time for their statements. The other codefendants' attorneys let us take the lead on the defense, so they didn't feel compelled to speak.

George was emphatic, entertaining, and captivating in his opening statement. He began by saying in all his years as a criminal defense attorney, he had never heard the prosecutor explain to the jury how his client had actually followed the law, referring to us selling substances that were legal and then destroying them when they became illegal, and then selling a new, legal substance. He gave an easy-to-understand example of taking a long road trip and having to adjust your speed each time the speed limit changes—you may have to drive fifty at first, and then it changes to sixty, and then maybe fifty-five. Each time the speed limit changes, you change your speed in accordance. This was what Gas Pipe had done each time a chemical had been banned. This was not breaking the law; it was following the law. He told the jury that yes, we had sold something that people used to get high, but it had been a legal product, and there was no law that said people couldn't get high. He also told them that yes, it had been mislabeled. We weren't going to deny that, but nobody had been defrauded. George also tried to give the jury some insight to my father's background, talking about his tour of duty in Vietnam. Obviously this was to garner sympathy from the jury and to help them like and understand my father. He didn't get to delve too far into that before the prosecutor objected. In a criminal trial, personal things such as the background of a defendant that could help the jury have a favorable opinion of the defendant can't be used unless the defendant plans on testifying himself.

Testifying as a defendant is tricky and is always a game-time decision, most often at the end of trial. It's only done when there is confusion and incorrect information that needs to be cleared up, and that often can only be done by the defendant testifying. It's a risk, though, because once a defendant is on the stand, the prosecution can cross-examine him or her, and things can get taken out of context or misconstrued, or the defendant can have visibly negative emotions such as anger or frustration. Those emotions are due to stress, but they could easily be interpreted by a jury as guilt. We would be prepared to testify but were not planning on doing so. Along with all the other instructions the judge had given, she had also told the jury that they should not assume guilt or anything negative because a defendant chose not to testify. That was a Fifth Amendment right.

Marlo made her opening statement next, and it had a title: "Things a Drug Dealer Doesn't Do." She spent her time telling the jury all the things we did that drug dealers didn't do—we paid taxes on every penny earned, we sold our products in the public retail market in brightly lit showcases, we had a store approximately one mile from the Dallas DEA headquarters, we had a billboard on a major highway coincidentally very close to DEA headquarters, and we destroyed any products that became illegal. At the end she gave a few personal tidbits about me, but only minimal information since we didn't want to commit to me having to testify. She was able to talk briefly about me being a good mom and that I was a recent cancer survivor. Parts of her opening statement were quoted in the newspaper coverage for that day, which was a positive since the media illustrated to the public the things we wouldn't have done if we were actual drug dealers.

The local media was all over our trial. I tried not to pay too much attention to it. I didn't even notice the photographer outside the courthouse taking our picture that ended up in the newspaper. I read the articles at first and then decided to ignore them. One weekend during the trial we were on the front page of a local newspaper, according to what a friend told me, but I didn't even bother to look at it. The articles were typically negative toward us, but every once in a while, they conveyed something positive such as quoting Marlo's opening statement, and as the trial progressed, media coverage would get more positive.

John went last for our opening statements, and he did a great job of giving the jury a summary of our defense, a pre-view of what they would hear over the next few weeks, and an explanation of why we were innocent. John had a way of talking to the jury as though they were sitting down together, having a nice chat over coffee. He was calm and assured, and he made everyone in the room feel at ease.

Opening statements were complete; it was time to take a recess for lunch, and then the testimonies would begin.

I suspected I was going to hear things that were embellished or completely false that would spark a negative emotion. I had already heard some falsehoods during the government's opening statement, but some of the government witnesses were going to be former employees and people whom I had known as friends at one time. We had been told prior to trial that we could not react. We shouldn't look angry or overly happy—just calm and focused. If I had tears for any reason—such as when Marlo was talking about me as an actual person—that was okay and made me human, but there could be no visible negative reaction to anything said about us. I could look at the jury but obviously not stare at them, and when we had to rise in preparation for the jury to enter or exit the courtroom, I should look their direction with a polite acknowledgement. The first couple days were challenging, as I was constantly worrying whether I was appearing the right way, making the right or wrong face, or giving too much or too little eye contact, but then it got easier.

I was encouraged to take notes during the witnesses' testimonies and pass them to our attorneys so they could evaluate whether my input was helpful to use in their cross-examinations of the government witnesses. I took notes feverishly and was extremely focused. This helped with the nerves and angst of what I was experiencing. I became immersed in the defense and in helping the attorneys, so much so that at times it was as though I was part of a defense team of a random, interesting, complex case—except the reality was that I was one of the defendants, and our lives were on the line.

We were prepared for just about anything, but as the government witnesses took the stand one by one, it was clear that there were no hidden "smoking guns." What we had seen in discovery was all there was. The government began with putting the lead DEA task force officer on the stand and spent hours going through more pictures of the "lab," products we sold, and pictures of the Gas Pipe stores from the day of the raid in June 2014. I never knew so many pictures could be taken of the exact same thing so many times. They played a video from one of the officer's controlled buys, and there was some dialogue during the buy about him smoking the stuff, and the sales associate corrected him and said it was not supposed to be for smoking. He felt this proved that everyone knew it was really to be smoked. We had already admitted that, and his testimony that everyone knew what it was really for also substantiated that nobody was being defrauded.

During the first week of the trial, the government had Ro Rojas and Ryan Yarbro testify. Ro had been our operations manager and had been instrumental in the development of our herbal incense business and the manufacturing of it. Ryan was my good friend from high school who had worked as our corporate buyer for years, so he was instrumental in the purchasing of herbal incense products and the actual synthetic cannabinoids to make our own herbal incense products. The synthetic cannabinoid chemicals used to make the herbal incense products were either purchased from a guy in Florida or overseas from China. Ro and Ryan were both able to testify about this process. Ryan was able to confirm that although the vendors from China had shipped synthetic cannabinoids labeled as something different (mislabeled), we'd had no knowledge they were going to do that. He also confirmed that even though the vendors in China had asked for multiple shipping addresses, presumably to make the shipments clandestine and more difficult to track, we had never provided them with multiple addresses. We'd had everything shipped directly to us with nothing hidden, and we'd had no involvement or knowledge that they intended to mislabel the synthetic cannabinoids.

Ro and Ryan were also both able to testify about the AB-Fubinaca snafu and that it was a mistake. Everybody understood that Gas Pipe had ordered a chemical called THJ-2201 and that the wrong chemical had been sent, unbeknownst to Gas Pipe at the time. There was some confusion about what had happened to the AB-Fubinaca—the wrong chemical—after the snafu had been discovered. Ryan claimed to have shipped it back to the vendor in Florida, but there was zero proof of the shipment. The government alleged that returning an illegal substance to Florida, per the vendor's request, was distributing a controlled substance. Our defense team argued that we weren't even charged with that specific act of shipping it to Florida in the indictment (we were only charged with selling it out of the stores), so it wasn't relevant, and there was no proof or details of this alleged shipment. The only proof of AB-Fubinaca being "distributed" was the accidental selling of it in the store, which had been rectified as it had been pulled from the shelves as soon as we knew what had happened. There had been no illegal intent whatsoever, and Ro and Ryan both confirmed this.

At one point during Ryan's testimony, he was asked by the prosecutor if at a certain point, he had felt like what he was doing in the herbal incense business wasn't okay. He replied, "No." This was the truth, so we weren't surprised, but we were surprised the prosecutor asked him that question and then received an answer that was clearly helpful to us but not the government. Interestingly, the government never once asked Ryan about analogues—the word *analogue* didn't even come up during his testimony. He was our buyer, and he knew every chemical that was being used, and he had pled to an analogue charge before trial. Yet the government never asked him about analogues.

It was difficult to see Ryan testify. We had known each other since high school. He was the only one of all the Gas Pipe defendants who had been in jail while we had been awaiting trial. I hadn't known what emotions I would feel upon seeing him. All the defendants sitting at the defense table had tears in our eyes. We didn't understand why he'd been in custody the entire time, and it just didn't seem right. After hearing his testimony, we also didn't understand why he had pled to an analogue charge. It was heartbreaking.

Ro's testimony wasn't harmful to us either. The government pressed him about our continual cycle of using a chemical, having a mass liquidation of product when it was about to become banned, and then destroying it and replacing it with another chemical. The government tried to allege that we had mass liquidations of product so we could make as much money as possible because all we cared about was making money. Ro told them this was normal retail practice anywhere—to liquidate as much product as possible whenever a product was going to be no longer available for any reason, refuting their allegation of us being any more "money hungry" than anyone running a retail business. They did ask him about analogues, and he only gave vague answers that there had been some discussion of the Analogue Act but never a confirmation that anything was believed to be an analogue. Knowledge of something being an analogue was required for a conviction under the Analogue Act, and so far the government's top two witnesses—Ro and Ryan, who had been in charge of Gas Pipe operations right behind me and my father—had nothing incriminating to say about analogues, and they cleared up the AB-Fubinaca snafu.

In addition to the AB-Fubinaca snafu, the government had alleged the selling of a couple other controlled substances, but we had had no knowledge of those being in the products, and they weren't products that we had manufactured ourselves. The first time we learned that these products allegedly had banned substances in them was when the legal case was initiated against us. Our lab reports from those products had shown no controlled substances, and the reports had also specifically listed these other banned chemicals as not being in the products. On cross-examination, John Cline had Ryan go through every one of our lab reports and state for the record that the report specifically listed that these banned substances were not in the products. To this day I don't know why the government said their tests showed otherwise, but our tests, which we faithfully used to make sure we weren't selling anything illegal, showed nothing illegal in these products. As John went through each lab report with Ryan, and Ryan confirmed each time what the report said, I got tears in my eyes. Our story was being told— the truth was coming out.

The government also called Brody Jones as a witness during the first week of trial. He had worked for Lawrence Shahwan, making his herbal incense products. The government alleged that some of the herbal incense products we had bought from Lawrence had had an illegal substance in them. Once again, our lab results hadn't shown that, so we hadn't believed they contained anything illegal. George got his turn to question Brody, and it was phenomenal. He used an easy-to-follow example of making a chocolate cake in one mixer and a vanilla cake in another mixer; if the two mixers weren't fully cleaned and then were used to make the opposite kind of cake, the pure chocolate cake would no longer be pure, and vice versa. His presentation of this was dynamic and fascinating as he described the mixtures, the delicious cakes, and how it would be a problem if the chocolate-filled bowl wasn't cleaned properly in preparation for making a vanilla cake. This fun example of cake making and having dirty bowls was all in response to Brody testifying that they didn't wash their bowls and equipment thoroughly between productions—the cake example was used to illustrate how cross contamination could occur. That was why we had bought products that we believed contained an all-legal chemical, and later test results from the government had shown what must have been a trace amount of an illegal chemical. Once again, we'd had no knowledge or illegal intent.

The first week of trial had been a success. It almost seemed too good to be true, but we had always known the truth. I'd always wanted the truth to come out, and as much as I hadn't wanted to go to trial, I was feeling glad that we had because that was the only way to really have our story told. We still had a long way to go—the trial was projected to last up to six weeks, although it appeared it could be much shorter—but we were feeling good. The only real issue we had that was obvious was the misbranding. We would have to prove to the jury that nobody had been defrauded and that therefore we hadn't committed felony misbranding, but our biggest hurdles of the drug charges seemed to be something we could overcome.

Chapter Twenty-Three

The first week of trial was only three days—Monday, Tuesday, and Wednesday. It was going to be a long weekend, literally and figuratively. When I was in the courtroom, I didn't have time to think or get nervous. There was so much happening, and being there made me feel useful and feel that I was being proactive. During the days off, I had time to dwell on the situation, analyze every testimony, reread the transcripts that we received daily, and go through everything in detail, reassuring myself that things were going as well as I thought.

Gavin had a football game Thursday of that week. I knew the story of our trial had been all over the newspaper, and I didn't know how I felt about going to the game. I wanted to see Gavin play, and Gavin had told me he wanted me there, but the potential public humiliation was daunting. I asked two friends to go with me—strength in numbers—and put on a hat and big sunglasses, plus a big dose of courage, and made my first public appearance since trial had begun. Several people approached me, gave me hugs, and said they were praying for me. I was touched and relieved. I don't know what everyone really thought about our case, but they knew me, they knew my kids, and they knew what type of mother I was. Maybe they could accept that people mess up and make mistakes, and maybe they understood that the government also sometimes overreaches and exaggerates.

Dan wasn't back from Alaska yet. The trial started during the last week of the season at Rapids Camp Lodge. It was best for him to stay there and wrap up things, and then he could be present for the remainder of the trial. So it would just be me and the kids for the weekend. They had friends over to the house as if everything was completely normal, so I followed their lead and tried to make everything as normal as possible.

The second week of the trial was similar to the first week. It was more DEA agents testifying about the products we'd sold and more of the same pictures of the products, the "lab," our stores, and our corporate office. It was redundant and unnecessary. Nobody was disputing that we had sold the product or that it had been mislabeled. They had each agent who had been a lead for a raid at the different Gas Pipe locations testify—there were thirteen stores, so thirteen lead agents. They all pretty much said the same thing. George had the job of cross-examining the agents, and he questioned a few of them, asking questions such as, "Were there guns or hidden cash?" They all said no. He was pointing out that nothing was scandalous or like what a drug dealer would do. The agent who had been the lead for the raid of the store within a mile of DEA headquarters got a different question from George. He asked her if she believed that store was in walking distance from DEA headquarters. She confirmed it was.

The government called Lawrence Shahwan to testify the second week of trial. He was the one responsible, according to his own testimony, for introducing K2 to Dallas. He talked about how he had started in the business, and he testified that the people who he'd first bought it from in Kansas had been raided by the FDA, which was why he had started making it himself in Dallas. That was the first we had heard about anyone ever being raided by the FDA, and had we known about that early on in our herbal incense business, perhaps we would have had a different perspective on things. But nobody, especially not Lawrence, ever told us that the FDA had an issue with this product, and he didn't testify that he had ever told us that. Lawrence also testified how he had gotten Gas Pipe to start carrying his product. He said we had been reluctant to do so, so he'd had his friends and family members call Gas Pipe stores, pretending to be customers and asking about the product and then saying they refused to shop at Gas Pipe anymore and would go to the competition if Gas Pipe didn't start selling the product. We'd known about the phone calls years ago, which was why we had started doing business with Lawrence. We hadn't known that he had set up those phone calls, though, until we heard him testify.

Like Ro and Ryan, Lawrence's testimony did not reflect that any of us knew anything was an analogue, even though he had also pled to an analogue charge. There wasn't much for our attorneys to ask him on cross-examination because he hadn't said anything incriminating. Like everyone else, he said everyone smoked the stuff to get high. That wasn't big news at this point. It was an accepted fact by both sides. John did a fairly brief cross-examination of Lawrence, and during it he showed a text from 2012 where Lawrence was telling me about an issue with law enforcement in New Mexico pertaining to herbal incense. He had texted me, "Everything on my end is legal." So this was just further confirmation that none of us had believed we were doing anything illegal.

The government brought in former Gas Pipe store managers to testify, and they all said the same thing: "Everyone knew people used it go get high." No talk of analogues, and there was plenty of testimony about how much Gas Pipe did to comply with the law by taking all steps necessary to test products and never carry banned substances. The prosecutor asked one store manager if she felt like a drug dealer. He must have not known what her answer was going to be, so I wasn't sure why he asked her that, because she glared at him and said, "No, I felt like a store manager." That couldn't have gone the way he had planned.

During one of the cross-examinations, Marlo got the manager to talk about the time the police had seized the herbal incense from a Gas Pipe store and then returned it and written a check to Gas Pipe for what they couldn't return because they had opened it for testing. The manager wasn't able to go into great detail about it because she only knew of the incident via hearsay throughout the company. It wasn't permitted for the defense to introduce exhibits or illicit testimony that was based on hearsay, so once the manager started testifying about the incident with the police in response to Marlo's questioning, the prosecution objected. It didn't matter, though. We'd gotten enough of the information presented to the jury to certainly make an impact.

One store manager named Josh Campbell did testify that he was sure the reason we labeled the herbal incense with "Not for human consumption" was because of the FDA. He didn't say why he was sure of that, and he didn't reference any communication from us whatsoever that made him think that (because there was none), but he had taken a plea deal for felony misbranding (defrauding the FDA), and it could be assumed he knew that was what the government wanted him to say. Our attorneys cross-examined him only very briefly and got him off the stand because out of all the witnesses who had testified, he was the only one who had lied. It was best to get him out of there before his lies grew.

There was no evidence of the FDA being involved in our case or investigating us or of us trying to somehow defraud them. Lawrence testifying that the FDA had years previously raided his supplier of synthetic cannabinoid products (unbeknownst to us) and Josh Campbell testifying that he was sure we were selling products in a certain manner because of the FDA (even though there was not proof of that) did not prove that we had knowledge of FDA regulations or that we were trying to defraud the FDA. There was one email the government had from a store manager to me asking about an upcoming DEA ban on the product. I replied that we were "looking into the FDA ban." I was responding to an email about the DEA, so obviously FDA was a typo. There was also another email from September 2011 from me to the stores only in Texas (we had stores in New Mexico too) where I referenced an upcoming ban on a chemical and reminded everyone not to sell the products for human consumption because "they are already illegal for that purpose." It didn't look good, but it wasn't exactly what it appeared to be either. I had sent that email because of a Texas ban that was taking effect (sometimes the states banned chemicals that were still federally legal, and states had different laws than the federal laws)—hence why the email had only been sent to Texas stores. Everything I had been talking about in the email—even the illegality of human consumption—had been pertaining to a new state law and a very specific chemical.

We were on trial for violating federal law. The email was not pertinent to our current legal situation.

Those two emails, Josh Campbell's testimony, and Lawrence's testimony about the FDA were the only things I would have wanted to clarify had I testified. Everything else was so accurate and helpful to us, though, that the risk of testifying under cross-examination didn't seem worth it just to clear up those few things.

The government brought an FDA agent in to testify. He testified about labeling requirements and how something could be mislabeled, and we didn't disagree. We had mislabeled a product. However, he had never been involved in our case prior to testifying, and he never said anything about the FDA being defrauded. And we hadn't known about mislabeling laws when we had sold herbal incense, and a felony conviction required intent to defraud. After the government presented their two expert chemists, who gave their opinions about chemicals being substantially similar in structure, and Mr. Analogue got to cross-examine them and blow holes in their testimonies, the government rested their case. We then filed motions for acquittal, which was standard procedure at the end of the government's case. The judge then ruled on the motion of acquittal; if she were to grant it before the jury gave a verdict, the government couldn't appeal. The motion had to be viewed in the light most favorable to the government. There had to be zero proof presented by the government, and that was very rare.

From my perspective the government had not presented any proof—nobody had testified that any of us had known the substances at issue were analogues, and even if the jury thought somehow the substances could be analogues, they couldn't believe we had somehow known that because no evidence had been presented showing that. The controlled-substance issue had certainly been cleared up, and all the other charges such as the CCE and money laundering went away without the drug charges. No conviction on drug charges, and no other charges (except misbranding) would stick. And even the FDA's own representative hadn't said they had been defrauded. I naively thought we had a chance with this motion for acquittal.

The judge actually did grant the motion for Tom, our general contractor. We weren't surprised because nobody understood why he was ever there in the first place. He was dismissed and released. She barely even addressed our motion for acquittal, just saying very quickly that it was denied. That gave me a bad feeling. Michael Mowla had done an outstanding job of drafting a superb motion in a very quick time frame (in the middle of trial), and I thought the case was obviously clear, but the judge didn't think so. Maybe we had missed something.

It was now our turn to present our side of the case and our witnesses. Because the government witnesses had essentially been our witnesses by telling the story honestly, we didn't really need to call that many witnesses. We began presenting our side with Mr. Analogue's opening statement, which was remarkable and interesting, particularly considering how dry and boring chemistry can be for most. Jim was a very nice, likeable guy, and he connected with the jury and gave them an easy-to-follow crash course in chemistry and an education about the DEA's own internal disagreements about analogues. He then began presenting our witnesses by first calling one of our chemistry experts and then two people from the DEA who would testify about the internal disputes. Having the defense call DEA personnel as their own witnesses was pretty telling, and the week ended with the jury hearing from these witnesses that there was dissention within the DEA as to whether certain substances were analogues or not.

We had another long weekend. This time Dan was back from Alaska, so he and I went out of town to the Texas Hill Country since the kids were with their dad. It was nice to get away and clear our heads. We did some hiking and wine tasting and just enjoyed being together. I felt good, for the most part. I was discouraged that the motion for acquittal had been given no merit, but we could re-urge it at the end of the presentation, before the case went to jury deliberations, and maybe it would be granted then, after the judge had heard both sides.

There was only one day of testimonies remaining. We had two more chemistry experts we were calling. Our experts were able to clearly explain that there was no scientific standard for determining whether anything was substantially similar, and in their subjective opinions, they didn't think any of the chemicals at issue were substantially similar except for one. And that one—AM-2201—was something we sold for a very short time period, and we certainly had had no knowledge at the time of its chemical structure or it being structurally similar to anything, so we weren't too concerned. We rested our case after Mr. Analogue read a sworn affidavit from one of the DEA task force agents on our case where she had said that JWH-250 was not an analogue. Despite this statement, the government had still charged us for selling it as an analogue. It was now time for closing arguments.

The government would get two turns at the plate during closing arguments. They made an initial presentation; then all our attorneys got to make theirs, and then the government got to go again. There was no new evidence presented, as per trial rules. The defense was at a disadvantage, though, because the government got the last word. If the prosecutor said something bad or maybe not even completely true during their second presentation, the defense wouldn't have a chance to clarify it. That made me very uneasy.

The government's arguments were more of the same—that we were drug dealers and money hungry, that we had known we were breaking the law, and that we were basically terrible people. Our closing arguments were just as good, if not better, than the opening statements. Marlo had these interactive charts that illustrated things beautifully for the jury so they could have a visual imprinted on their brains of what she was saying. George was as captivating as ever, Mr. Analogue made complex chemistry easy enough for a child to understand and reiterated the disagreement within the DEA and the secrecy of their list of analogues, and John tied it all up and brought it home with his kind, calm presence. He emphasized to the jury that the prosecution wanted a law that said anything that made you high was illegal, but that was not what the law said. We never knowingly sold an illegal substance, and nobody could agree on what an analogue was, and the fact that a product made people high didn't make it an analogue. We lived in a country where citizens should clearly know if their actions were legal or not, and the Analogue Act did not provide that sort of clarification. We had clearly committed *simple* misbranding and nothing more, and we told the jury that.

We couldn't call it misdemeanor misbranding because there had been jury instructions for both types of misbranding (felony and misdemeanor) on the verdict form, but the jury wasn't permitted to know that one was a misdemeanor and one was a felony. They only knew that one involved just mislabeling, and the other involved mislabeling with defrauding someone. Federal juries weren't even allowed to know what level of punishment defendants faced if found guilty. That would maybe impact their decision-making process. If the jury felt inclined to convict us of a CCE (continuing criminal enterprise), they would not know they were sending us to prison for at least twenty years, if not life.

After closing arguments, it was now time for the case to go to the jury. A trial that was supposed to last approximately six weeks only had a little over six days of actual testimonies, spread over three weeks because of breaks. The government had made a big production for years about what a complex case it would be and how long the trial would be, and it just wasn't. The only thing now stopping the case from going to the jury would have been our motion for acquittal getting granted, and it wasn't, so our lives were officially in the hands of twelve strangers.

It's hard to describe in words the emotions and feelings during the time we waited for our verdict. It was like a roller coaster when you ride to the top of the first big hill and there is that almost unbearable pause before you go flying down the hill. Waiting for a verdict, though, is not just a brief pause. It's a pause that lasts hours, or often days, and just like the roller coaster, you know you're at the top of the hill, and there's no going back. You have to go down, and you hope it will be worth it. All that courage I had felt conquering the huge roller coasters at the amusement park with my son just months earlier felt useless and miniscule now. We had climbed the big hill of the trial. It was over. We had done all we could do, and other than the few little things I would have liked to clear up but decided weren't worth testifying to do so, we'd had an almost perfect trial. The government had done a great job of driving the point home about how much money we made by selling a drug. What they hadn't done, though, was show how we ever knowingly broke a law, and *knowingly* was a requirement for drug charges and for defrauding the government.

The jury began deliberating midmorning on Friday, October 12. The beginning of the morning was spent with the judge reading the jury instructions. Prior to my involvement with the legal system, I hadn't really understood jury instructions. I, like many people, thought the jury simply decided between guilty or not guilty. That was the ultimate result of their deliberations, but each charge in the indictment had a set of instructions that explained, in detail, what criteria must be met for the jury to arrive at guilty or not guilty and what information jurors should take into account when deciding their verdict. Jury instructions and the way they were worded could make a huge difference in the verdict. That was why it was so important when we had the Daubert hearing that we got a ruling that affected the jury instructions in a way that was positive for us. The jury was instructed that there was no real scientific basis for the term *substantially similar.* The jury was also instructed that we had to actually know a substance was an analogue. This was different from cases tried before the Supreme Court's ruling in McFadden. Before McFadden, juries were often instructed that all the government had to prove for an analogue conviction was that the defendants knew the substance made people high. That was the premise and requirement when we had been indicted in May 2015. When the ruling on McFadden had come out in June 2015, the government never adjusted their case and allegations against us, and they should have because there was clearly no evidence that we had known anything was an analogue or even that experts agreed substances were analogues.

The instructions for the misbranding—simple versus non-simple misbranding (misdemeanor or felony)—were kind of confusing, and it wasn't clear what *defraud* should mean for the nonsimple misbranding. Typically, people think of defrauding as depriving someone of money or property, but in this case it was supposed to mean more than that. It could also mean hindering a government agency from doing its job—presumably, in our case, the FDA. Well, the FDA had never been involved in our case or in investigating us, so we didn't understand how they could be hindered and therefore defrauded. We had admitted to mislabeling the products, and the FDA agent who had testified hadn't said anything about being defrauded, so we thought the jury would at least understand that.

As good as we felt about the trial, every minute that went by once deliberations started felt like eternity. There are different opinions on what a quick verdict versus a long verdict can mean. Nobody really knows for sure—talk about something that's not scientific. We could have—and we thought we did—presented the best defense in the world, but if the jury keyed on even one thing they didn't like, we could be found guilty. We tried not to overanalyze—there was no point anyway because the trial was over. Nothing more could be done, but it was hard to not focus on every little detail and play it over and over again in our minds.

The judge required that we be able to be in the courtroom within twenty minutes of the jury having a verdict. This meant we either needed to stay in the federal building or be very close, because entering the federal building required a time-consuming process of going through security. Carolyn's attorney's office was located across the street from the federal building, so his conference room became our gathering area while waiting for the verdict. Everybody was there—all the defendants, the attorneys, Dan, my mother, my stepdad, and Carolyn's parents. The only attorney who wasn't there was Michael Mowla because he was feverishly working on a motion to file to keep us from being detained while awaiting sentencing should we be convicted of the more serious drug charges, although that type of motion was rarely granted. A conviction on charges carrying a sentence of ten years or more usually led to defendants being detained immediately while waiting for the sentencing hearing (which could be several months in the future) because of the amount of time they were facing in prison. A conviction for misbranding—felony or misdemeanor—would logically not lead to us being detained while awaiting sentencing because we had already lived the last four years with the possibility of facing life in prison. Felony misbranding carried a maximum prison sentence term of five years, and misdemeanor only carried one year.

The idea of getting our verdict and being immediately taken out of the courtroom in handcuffs and into custody was my worst nightmare. There would be no goodbyes or closure with my children. There would be no tying up loose ends. Sure, I had done what I could to prepare, giving Dan, my mother, and the kids' dad all necessary information such as passwords, doctors' names, and important dates. The one thing I hadn't prepared for, and there was really no way to do so, was all our businesses shutting down immediately upon a conviction of all the counts tied to forfeiture, which was all counts but misbranding (felony or misdemeanor).

Our employees had always been like family to us. It was a mind-set that was started from the beginning of Gas Pipe's inception. It was a family business, and that translated throughout the company and throughout all our different companies. The guilt I had for putting them through so much, particularly the ones who had been indicted, was immeasurable. We had never believed we were doing anything that would cause the harm it had. So many people depended on us—they had their own families, mortgages, and bills to pay—and we had unintentionally let them down by going down the herbal incense path. Now we could let them down even more if we were found guilty of the counts with forfeiture tied to them. Everyone would be immediately without work. They had all worked so hard keeping the businesses moving forward while we had fought the battle of our lives, and they had stood by us. The idea of them being left with nothing was tormenting.

Friday came and went, and there was no verdict. It was going to be another long weekend. This time it was way more excruciating than the long weekends during the trial. There was nothing to do but wait. No more strategizing or planning our defense. It had all been presented. We were just waiting. We had friends over for dinner, and I took the kids all the places they needed to be, but no matter how hard we tried, we knew what was hanging in the shadows.

Kieley and I went to see *A Star is Born* that weekend, and I cried profusely throughout the entire movie. It was an emotional movie under normal circumstances, but I was overly emotional. The movie really spoke to me because I was struggling and fighting to change to be a better person, just like the main character in the movie; although our circumstances were different, we were both fighting to change. I had been through the battle of my life. I wasn't sure how it was going to end, but the last four years had taught me a lot about myself. I had reflected heavily on my entire life and all the bad decisions I had made and thought a lot about who I wanted to be and the life I want to live going forward. I was praying I would be given, yet again, another chance in life. God had carried us this far—we had stayed afloat financially against all odds and kept our businesses running despite not having banking at times, despite having everything taken, and despite people not wanting to do business with us. On top of everything else, I had also conquered cancer. I just couldn't believe that we could have persevered as much as we had only to lose at trial, and I knew I wanted to live my life differently. One of the songs throughout the movie, "Maybe It's Time," with its lyrics about letting old ways die and making changes spoke directly to me.

I knew I had already made many positive changes. People who knew me the best and had known me for years commented regularly on the difference they saw in my demeanor, my outlook on life, and my interactions with people. I had become more mindful, more calm, and more aware. I had never been an unkind or selfish person by nature, but I had made some selfish decisions and done things unintentionally that had hurt others because I hadn't always fully thought through my actions. A couple months before trial, Dan and I had been talking in bed one morning, and he had said, "You're just so pleasant now."

I had thanked him and then paused for a moment, processing what he had said (the old me would have reacted immediately), and then I had asked him, "If I wasn't pleasant before, then why did you marry me?"

He'd replied, "I always saw it in you, but now I see it even more." I cried. To know that someone loved me and could see past all the boisterous, loudmouthed, speak-before-she-thinks attitude and know that the real "pleasant" me was in there all along confirmed how much he loved me and confirmed the growth I felt I had experienced.

Monday, the second day of jury deliberations, began by having power of attorney forms signed for me and my father. This would allow Dan to conduct matters on our behalf should we not be present to do so. I had put off signing those forms until the very last minute. It seemed like such a negative thing to do, but it was necessary. As soon as we got the forms signed, we got a message from the court that we needed to be in the courtroom. There wasn't a verdict, but there was another matter to discuss.

There was a juror, one whom we had thought we really liked and would be good for us, who had shared personal information and beliefs with the other jurors. This was not allowed. Jurors were only permitted to base their verdict on the evidence presented at trial. The other jurors had made mention of him breaking the rules, and it had eventually made it back to the judge, so she had to address it. The final outcome was that he was dismissed from the jury. This meant there would only be eleven jurors instead of the traditional twelve. I didn't know if that affected us negatively or not, but if he had been on our side, that definitely meant there was now one less person on our side. We felt discouraged but tried to believe maybe it was a blessing in disguise. Maybe he hadn't been in our corner like we had thought.

We went back over to the conference room. I had a text message from one of our employees. She told me that a guy named Tim had called, looking for me, Carolyn, or my father. I hadn't spoken to Tim in years. He had been part of an old group of friends. My immediate thought was that something bad had happened to someone we had known years ago. I called the number that had been provided to me. Tim told me that he had a friend on our jury whom he had seen the night before, and his friend had told him that things were going really well for Gas Pipe—the jury was currently seven to five in our favor. It sounded promising, and I was intrigued, but the jury had to be unanimous, and seven to five was a close margin. I was glad it was in our favor, though. I didn't know if the recent dismissal of the juror had changed that to six to five or seven to four, and the information Tim had was based on where the jury had been at the end of the day on Friday. Things could change quickly. I asked Tim who his friend was—curiosity got the best of me—and I learned it was the juror we had really liked who had spoken in voir dire about Inwood Bank dropping us as customers.

I had to tell the attorneys about what I'd learned. We'd have to tell the judge because the juror had broken the rules by discussing the case in public. Telling the judge could lead to the juror being dismissed, which would really stink for us, but we had to notify her. We sent a message to the court saying we needed to appear before the judge. It was around lunchtime, so we had to wait. We went over to the courtroom so we could be there as soon as the judge returned. We didn't want the jury to go on deliberating any more than necessary with a juror on the panel who could be dismissed. We were trying to do the right thing as soon as possible.

We appeared in front of the judge, told her what we knew—including the seven-to-five voting in our favor—and then she asked the prosecution if they were going to seek any relief. We were sure the prosecution would ask for the juror to be dismissed, which would mean that we would either have a mistrial because a jury had to have at least eleven jurors, or one of the alternates would have to come back, and that could present other issues. The prosecution asked for no relief. We were shocked. Obviously this juror was in our corner, and he had clearly broken the rules, but I could only assume the government didn't want a mistrial or another juror. We got out of there before anyone changed their minds, and we thanked our lucky stars!

We went back across the street to continue our wait. It was a nasty day outside—unseasonably cold for October with temperatures in the forties, wind, and a constant drizzle. The multiple walks back and forth to the federal building, although short, were brutal. We got back to the warmth of inside and prepared to wait the rest of the afternoon. Within an hour we got a phone call from the judge's clerk, who said the jury had a verdict. It was October 15, 2018. It had been four years, four months, and eleven days since our world had taken an unimaginable and unexpected turn, and now it all came down to this moment and the decision of eleven people.

The clerk had instructed the attorneys to come to the judge's chambers before going to the courtroom, so they hurried ahead.

The rest of us frantically gathered ourselves together. I told Dan where I was leaving my purse and computer bag as well as the power of attorney forms, in case I wouldn't be coming back with him. I was exasperated and taking in big deep breaths. My mother looked at me and said, "It's going to be okay," and gave me a huge hug. Dan did the same. We started walking down the hall to the elevator.

I stopped my father and said, "This is it; we are going to be okay," and I gave him a big hug. We walked through the brutal weather and security and made our way up to the courtroom entrance. The hallway was packed with government personnel, DEA agents, and media. I went into the bathroom and was thankful when I realized I had it to myself. I used the restroom quickly, went out to the sink to wash my hands, and looked in the mirror. I told myself, "This is it; it has to be okay. Tim couldn't have been wrong with the information he relayed in his phone call." Still, my breathing was rapid, and my insides felt like they were being tied up in a big ball. I took a big gulp of air and walked back out to the hallway.

My father was sitting on a wooden bench. We weren't on the same floor as where we had waited three and a half years ago outside the US Marshals Office, but it was in the same building, and the bench looked the same. I sat down beside him and waited, again. Within minutes all the attorneys walked around the corner. They had just left the judge's chambers. I saw Carolyn's attorney first, and he said, "Talk to your attorneys." Our attorneys were right behind him, and they motioned for us to get up and walk over to them. John Cline, in his perfect calm, graceful, reassuring manner said, "You, Jerry, and the corporations are found guilty for felony misbranding, not guilty on everything else, and no forfeiture." I screamed and almost collapsed, and then Dan and my mother hugged me tightly.

This was a win—it wasn't a grand slam, but it was a home run. Yes, a conviction for felony misbranding still had a sentence of up to five years, and that was a far cry upward from the one-year sentence for misdemeanor misbranding, but it was even a further cry downward from the twenty years to life in prison we had been facing. And there would be no forfeiture. All our assets and money would be returned to us. I had been prepared for some sort of misbranding conviction. We hadn't committed felony misbranding, but I suspected the jury could get confused in that regard, and because they saw us as the leaders in charge, they could think we deserved more of a serious conviction than Bridget, our store manager, whom they convicted of misdemeanor misbranding. Carolyn got a full acquittal, and I was so happy for her.

The judge had implemented a new policy to start bringing attorneys into her chambers to relay the verdict, but nobody had known that at the time when we got the phone call from the clerk. It was a really nice thing for her to do because I couldn't imagine having to stand in the courtroom, listening to a verdict being read for so many different charges for multiple defendants and trying to understand who was guilty or not guilty for what. It would have been confusing and overwhelming, as if the situation wasn't already enough of that. All the traditional and usual steps of reading the verdict still occurred as they had to for the record, but all I really remember was standing there with tears streaming down my face and Marlo, my dedicated and supportive attorney, holding my hand. I knew I was still facing a potential prison sentence, but I also knew I was going home that afternoon and hugging my kids. I knew I may have to miss some special moments over the next few years, but I would still have future moments and memories to make with them. I would not be going away forever or immediately. And our businesses would continue, and all the people who depended on us greatly would still be able to stay gainfully employed.

When we left the federal building, the cold and wind and rain that had felt so brutal earlier now felt liberating and energizing. I literally danced in the rain. Dan grabbed my hand and said, "Darlin', you just dodged a huge bullet." Neither of us believed I should have been found guilty of anything but misdemeanor misbranding, but we also knew what an uphill battle it could be even for innocent defendants in the federal justice system.

I looked at him and said, "Yeah, I know, and I'm tired of dodging bullets." I was grateful to have dodged the bullets, but I also knew it was time to stop putting myself in front of the bullets. Sure, some "bullets" had just happened and weren't necessarily my fault—such as cancer, the lodge almost burning down, and the airplane crash at the lodge—but some "bullets" in my life had been brought on by my decisions. It was time to truly live my life differently. I had been working through so much positive growth and changes the last few years, and I had, once again, a new lease on life. I was determined to make the best of it.

Chapter Twenty-Four

There was a lot of celebrating the night of the verdict. First and foremost, I hugged my kids like I had never hugged them before. They had questions, and they understood that there was still a prison sentence I was facing, but they also understood that it was better than what I had been facing. Our closest friends and most of the attorneys came over to our house. Walking into my home that night—a home that had been my "jail" when I had been on house arrest with Bertha, a place where I had done so much painful soul-searching and personal growth, but also the place where I continued to make beautiful memories with my family—and knowing it was actually my home now and not an asset for the government to forfeit was such a great feeling. It was the perfect place to have a huge celebration that night.

There were so many things to plan and do. We were scheduled to be sentenced in February (it would get postponed three times), but I could spend the next few months with my family, plan a trip for the holidays, and celebrate my wedding anniversary that was just a few weeks away. Because there was no forfeiture, we would be getting all of our money and assets released and would be able to pay off the debt we had incurred. The companies had all survived the last four and a half years—albeit barely at times—so now it would be "smooth sailing." I was anxious to get our assets returned, get our heads above water, and take everything we had learned from this experience and move forward in the most positive way possible.

We didn't know exactly what to expect with the prison sentence. One of our attorneys went on the record with the media saying he didn't expect us to get the full sentence. I hoped he was right. I had no criminal record or criminal history. I'd had a hot-check incident in my late teenage years, but that shouldn't play into any sentencing over twenty years later. Also, we would be appealing the felony conviction, hoping to get it reduced to the misdemeanor. So we were hoping for the best. We had companies to run and people to keep employed, and we at least hoped that if there had to be prison time, it could be staggered for me and my father so someone could be present to run the companies at all times. Gas Pipe and Amy Lynn Inc. also had the felony misbranding conviction, which meant they would most likely be on some sort of probation, and somebody in charge would surely have to be around to make sure the corporations were acting in accordance with the probation guidelines. Regardless of whatever sentence would be imposed, from where we had started with the charges against us, this was a huge improvement.

I went to Gavin's football game the week we got the verdict. It was a completely different experience than when I had gone to the game during trial. I didn't wear a hat and big sunglasses or feel that I needed to hide. We had been vindicated of the most serious charges. I wasn't a convicted drug dealer. I had mislabeled a product, and I had admitted that. I wasn't proud of my actions, but I was glad that the jury had spoken and our story had been told. I felt like people at the game looked at me differently, in a positive way. Maybe it was just my imagination, but for over four years I'd always wondered what people were thinking when they saw me or what they said about me when I wasn't listening. Now everyone knew the truth.

I made immediate plans to go back to school. I had wanted to continue my education for quite some time, and I had thought about it often during the last few years. I didn't want to eliminate my role in the family businesses, and I couldn't. The one time I had tried in the last few years to do absolutely no work was when I'd had my double mastectomy, and I had still been answering emails and phone calls within twenty-four hours of the surgery. I didn't mind, though. I had taken true ownership of the companies, meaning I took the responsibility very seriously of making sure they continued and survived during the most challenging of times. I had been very hands on, even more so with Gas Pipe the last few years. I knew my presence was needed, but now that things could stabilize, and the companies could be completely solvent again with the release of all our money and assets, there could be a little more flexibility in management. I could continue my role managing the finances and daily big decisions, but I could also free up some time to take classes in an area of interest to me. I registered to take classes toward a degree in professional counseling at a small local university geared toward the working adult. I had benefited greatly from counseling throughout my life, and I certainly had plenty of experiences to share with others and hopefully help others, even if I did it part time or on a volunteer basis.

Everything was going to be fine. We had one more step to go through with our sentencing, but there was a light at the end of the tunnel. We had gone through the excruciating experience of the trial, we had fought our battle for over four years, and we had prevailed for the most part. We were blessed and relieved, and I was ready to focus on all the good in my life and enjoy what mattered the most—my family, friends, and health. The worst was over. I could finally breathe—or so I thought.

Because there was no forfeiture from a conviction of misbranding, the government decided to pursue the civil case, which was how the legal proceedings against us had originally started in 2014. The civil case had been administratively closed because the criminal case would have covered all the forfeiture upon a conviction (of anything but misbranding), so there had been no need to pursue the civil case while the criminal case had been pending. It would have been redundant. It hadn't been dismissed, though, just administratively closed. So even though the government had proved nothing related to forfeiture during the trial, and even though the jury had deliberated for just a little over a full day (clearly the decision for the verdict wasn't a difficult one), and even though we had been fully acquitted of any crime that had forfeiture attached to it, the government still wanted the assets and money. So they pursued reopening the civil case, and the judge reopened it, while still not releasing any of our assets. This meant that even though we had gone all in financially for the trial of the century, and we were in debt because of doing so and were barely hanging on, we still had to figure out how to now pay attorneys more money and face another trial while keeping all of our businesses operating and getting no assets released.

I felt utterly defeated. I wasn't prepared mentally, emotionally, financially, or physically for another fight. Lack of sleep, an upset stomach, and overall exhaustion would be a detriment to anyone's health. I don't think it was a coincidence I got cancer at a young age during the most stressful time of my life. Mentally and emotionally, I was spent. I had mustered up every ounce of energy and fortitude I'd had the last four and a half years, and I was done. Financially, there was no way we could go through another trial, but we maybe wouldn't have a choice. God had carried us this far, so certainly he had a plan. While I didn't believe God had given up on me, I also felt I had maybe prayed for and been granted a little too much already in my life. Maybe my good fortune was running out. Maybe we could only dodge so many bullets.

Civil cases almost always settled, and the government said from the onset that they had every intention of trying to settle the civil case. We did too. We'd been in business a long time, and like any business, we had experienced our share of lawsuits over the years. We had always settled, and we hoped this would be the same. The problem was the starting number from the government was not anywhere near what we had in mind. We had a number in mind that we felt was generous—we felt that anything we offered was generous because of the outcome of the trial—but it was nowhere even remotely close to the government's number.

I was in disbelief that we were really going to go through another battle. It was like running a marathon, finishing, and then being told, "Just kidding; you still have another fifteen miles to go." It wasn't like we were having to run another full marathon—the worst was over. We weren't going to prison for the rest of our lives, and nothing was as important as freedom. But we were still facing having everything taken from us and over a hundred people losing their jobs, and we could be broke and homeless with substantial debt and still have a short prison sentence.

Because we had only been convicted of misbranding, which had such a short prison term in comparison to what we had been facing, we were able to file a motion with the court to get our passports back temporarily and travel to our home in Baja California Sur, Mexico. It was clear at this point that we were not a flight risk or a danger to society, but the judge didn't have to allow us to get our passports back and go, and it was very kind of her to do so. We hadn't been to our home in Baja California Sur in over three years. The last time we had been there, we'd left knowing we were getting indicted.

We of course still enjoyed Baja California Sur, even though there was once again a dark cloud looming with ongoing legal matters that had an unknown outcome. But we were in Baja California Sur. I was at our home there, which was not subject to forfeiture. I had been given permission to travel out of the country; even if it was only temporary, it was something I had longed to do for years. I had to put things in perspective—we had our freedom. Yes, we were looking at having a small (relatively speaking) interruption from it, but I would get to see my kids go to college, maybe see them get married one day and have kids of their own, and I would get to grow old with my husband—God willing, if my health stayed good—and walk on that beach in Mexico when we were eighty and eighty-three. The money was just that—money. I couldn't agree to anything that would leave me homeless, and we couldn't agree to anything that would lead to several businesses closing down and therefore large numbers of people being without work, but we could offer more than what we originally had in mind.

Money and what it represented had changed for me. When I had been younger and first earning money and living on my own, I had been happy to be able to pay my bills every month and have a little left over for fun expenses. My needs had been minimal. I used to say that if I had enough money to comfortably pay my bills, maybe take a trip every once in a while, and go out to a nice dinner with a little left over, that was all I needed. Later my idea of "enough money" had changed, but the last four years had reminded me of what I really needed in life—and really what I wanted. I knew now I needed and wanted more simplicity in life. I needed to make sure that we could keep people employed and that I could keep my home and provide for my children, but beyond that my needs were slowly minimalizing.

The trial had been stressful and emotional. I hadn't cried once during it because I had been in "survivor mode." I had been too focused on all the information being exchanged, analyzing everything that happened. I had cried when the verdict was read and for days after. There had been happy tears, but the tears had also been a release of so many emotions: gratitude, shock, sadness over all that had happened even though the outcome was overall good, and fear over what had almost happened. I told my counselor I felt like I had PTSD, although I knew that sounded dramatic. She told me it wasn't dramatic at all. PTSD could come from many different experiences and many different levels of severity, and what I had been through the last four-plus years would certainly be applicable. She said she'd be shocked if I didn't have PTSD. It would take me a long time to feel like things would really be okay, and the reopening of the civil case only intensified those feelings of fear.

Part of the emotion, though, was from the disappointment I had in myself. I had realized and understood over the last few years that while we hadn't done what we had been accused of, we had done something that I wouldn't consider good or positive. The money we had made from herbal incense was not something to be proud of. Sure, it could be justified by the fact that everybody was selling the product; we weren't the only ones. Customers wanted the product and would have bought it somewhere else if we hadn't sold it—but like I told my kids constantly, just because everyone else was doing something didn't mean it was okay. Yes, we'd had every reason to believe that what we were selling was permissible on multiple levels because we had been given the green light by law enforcement on more than one occasion. But deep in my soul I had known what we were doing wasn't something good. It wasn't something that I wanted to define me, and it wasn't something indicative of who I wanted to be. I was a good, very involved mom, a very involved parent in my kids' school, and a person who cared about others and gave generously with both time and money. I liked to bring happiness to people's lives, and I think that would be how most people who knew me best would describe me. But with herbal incense it was like I had a double identity.

I've had a drug addiction. I know what addiction looks like. We most often associate addiction with things such as alcohol and drugs, but many things can be addictive. What I remember from my addiction with heroin over twenty years ago is that it became more important than anything else in my life. It dictated my life and controlled everything I did. I wanted to stop, but I couldn't until I was forced to. I am by no means comparing herbal incense itself to heroin—the possible dangers of herbal incense can be discussed and even debated among chemists and medical experts, but I don't think anyone would compare it to heroin or the opioid crisis overall, which has a staggering number of deaths. But addiction and the characteristics that accompany it are the same no matter what type of addiction it is. I had become addicted to money and power.

The selling of herbal incense had been a business decision that got out of control. Just like when an addict tries a drug for the first time or when an alcoholic takes that first drink, nobody does so with the intention of becoming addicted or hurting themselves or anyone else. When we first started selling herbal incense, nobody thought it would implode the way it did. The amount of money generated from it was staggering, and it had been enticing. I would love to say that I was strong enough to listen to my moral compass and stop and think about what it was we were selling and that it was maybe causing problems for some people, despite it being legal, but I wasn't. I stuck my head in the sand and let the money come my way. It seemed like the right thing to do for business purposes because it brought in a lot of money, and with money came power. It sounds greedy, and it was. Greed itself can be addicting. I didn't think about the consequences associated with my behavior—all the people who could have been hurt, including my family, our employees, and the community. I was addicted to the money and the power, and that had clouded my judgment, just like any addiction.

I had been in survivor mode for the last four and a half years, so I hadn't allowed myself to focus too much on the negative aspects of what we had done. I couldn't because we had been charged with a bunch of stuff we didn't do, so I could do nothing but defend myself. Now that the dust was settling, I could reflect back on everything. I sat through the trial and saw all the evidence the prosecution presented: the horrible pictures of the "lab," the emails and testimonies about customers desperately wanting our product and buying massive quantities of it, and how people continually got high from what we sold and used the product to a point of excess at times. It wasn't pleasant or positive, even if the drug itself inside the package was determined not to be illegal.

I had lost sight of my core values and started placing way too much importance on material things and my false idea of mattering in society because I had money. I had let it take priority over my family, even though I'd had more love and positivity in that area than a person could ever imagine. I'd had everything I'd ever wanted in life with my husband and children, but even so, the lure and excitement of money had taken over. I'd thought having money meant power, and power meant strength. I now know that our strength is not defined by what we have but rather by who we are—the decisions we make, how we treat others, and how we live our lives. Some people—such as my wonderful husband—just know that inherently and never waver from it, and thank God my husband never lost sight of the good in me and has been willing to stand by my side. I learned a lot of things through the legal experience, and one thing I learned was how strong I truly am, and it wasn't because I had tons of money—in fact, it was the opposite.

We didn't need to sell herbal incense. We had plenty of money before to be happy and comfortable for the rest of our lives. We had gotten sucked into it and then couldn't walk away, like an addiction. There is no excuse or justification. It happened, and there is no going back—only moving forward. But because Gas Pipe was so successful before herbal incense, there was also no excuse for the government to prosecute us as aggressively as they did and to try to forfeit absolutely everything my family had earned over forty-four years. I'm glad we stopped selling herbal incense. I was glad to stop selling it immediately, but all the government had to do was say "Stop," and we would have. Companies all over the United States get warned regularly for misbranding a product, and they get a written notice from the FDA. We never got any sort of warning from any government agency. There was no reason for them to attack us the way they did, but they did, and we survived. We found a new, better kind of strength, and I learned some very valuable lessons that will impact me forever.

Reflecting on the irresponsible decisions I have made in my life, with the most recent one being the herbal incense business, made me realize that one way to have full closure and peace was definitely to settle the civil case, even if it required forfeiting more than we'd originally thought we would. Sure, we could have gone through another trial (not sure how we would have paid for it, but we would have found a way), and we had a great shot of winning based on what we had seen in the last trial. The government had no new evidence or theories. We didn't want another trial, though, and although we greatly believed in our innocence, and settling wouldn't be an admission of guilt, it was a way to make amends for our negative (not illegal) actions. It was a way to adamantly walk away from the addiction to money. And it was a way to ensure that our businesses continued and that people stayed employed, which was most important. I had always told my kids their entire lives that if you had food in your belly, a roof over your head, and love in your life, you were more blessed, unfortunately, than many people in the world. Somewhere along the way, for no logical reason, I had forgotten that and decided I needed more. We could—and should—settle with the government, knowing we would still be very blessed and still have a very good life.

We got home from Baja California Sur and were prepared to make an offer for settlement that was much higher than what we had originally thought we would offer and closer to what the government initially said they wanted as a settlement. Rather than negotiating and making an effort to counter with something at least remotely close to our offer, the government increased how much they wanted as a settlement. We were moving in the opposite direction. It seemed clear that no matter how much they said they wanted to settle, they had no intention of doing so in good faith, despite the court issuing a scheduling order with a trial date for March 4, 2019, and encouraging both parties to work toward a settlement in the meantime. How could parties work toward a settlement when one side kept increasing the amount they wanted? That was the opposite of meeting in the middle, which was what a settlement was supposed to be.

In the midst of trying to settle the civil case, we also had to prepare for our sentencing hearing, which had been postponed to July. I had to go with my attorney to meet with the person from probation who would be writing my presentencing report so she could spend a little time getting to know me and submit a report to the judge. There was a very long written questionnaire I had to bring with me, and I had to be prepared to discuss my entire life and divulge everything about my finances, which were kind of a mess due to the seizure and potential forfeiture, so the government could determine how much I should pay in fines (on top of any civil forfeiture). Because everything was still subject to forfeiture, I was able to honestly tell her that the only thing substantial I fully owned at this point was a bunch of debt. She visited with me about my entire life, my upbringing, any drug usage, marriages, kids—everything. I had to talk in detail about my late teenage years, which was very emotional.

The thing that stood out in my mind the most about the interview, though, was when she asked me about my childhood, and before I could answer, she read from the form that I had submitted where I had written that my childhood was idyllic. She looked up at me and said, "Oh, like you had nice things and everything you wanted."

I was taken aback. I said, "No—I mean, yes, I did have nice things, but what made it idyllic was all the love and attention I had." I guess she and other people think money equals happiness and an idyllic life, even though that was not at all why I meant my childhood was great. I always knew on some level, even if I had temporarily gone off track, that happiness comes from love and other intrinsic things, not money.

I was overwhelmed and exhausted and just wanted to fulfill my punishment and put the ordeal behind us. It had consumed nearly a third of my children's entire lives and half of my marriage. We desperately wanted to settle the civil case and had no problem forfeiting a decent amount of money—way more money than we were legally required to; based on the outcome of the criminal trial, we were required to forfeit none—but we weren't going to lose our businesses if we could help it, and we weren't going to be broke. My father had exhausted all his retirement funds to pay for our defense. He had no savings left, and because of his age, he didn't have an opportunity to make a lot more money to recoup what he had spent. A sizeable settlement was fine at this point, but a settlement that left us with nothing was not a settlement.

We learned that one thing the government really wanted was for us to be deposed—testifying under oath prior to a trial and not in front of a jury. In a criminal case, defendants could plead the Fifth and not have to testify. In a civil case there was no Fifth Amendment protection because that only applied to defendants, and we were only claimants in the civil case. However, the civil case dealt with the same allegations as the criminal case, and we still had a sentencing hearing approaching and a pending appeal, so we weren't sure how that affected our Fifth Amendment rights because anything we said could potentially be used against us at the sentencing hearing. We filed a motion with the court to get clarification and see if we would be protected from testifying about at least some matters. The court had already issued a scheduling order, which outlined deadlines for parties to meet in preparation for trial. The entire discovery process (which included getting depositions) had to be completed by January 21, 2019. The government scheduled for us to be deposed on January 16, 2019. We had hoped prior to that we would get clarification on what we were required to testify about or what we could decline to testify about per our Fifth Amendment rights. We never received a ruling from the court, so we went in to be deposed.

It was actually liberating to finally speak and tell my story from my own mouth. I didn't know whether the government expected to hear some bombshell bit of information—whether they just couldn't believe that there wasn't some big secret out there that hadn't surfaced at the trial—but all they heard was the same thing that had already been told by countless others: the packages had been mislabeled, people smoked the product to get high, nobody understood analogues, we didn't ever talk about defrauding the FDA or anybody else, and we never knowingly sold a controlled substance or ever believed anything we were doing was illegal.

Maybe one reason we never got a ruling on the motion regarding our Fifth Amendment concern is because the court had ordered mediation, per our request, and that was scheduled for January 18. It would have been a logical assumption that because we were going to a mediation, that meant both sides truly intended on settling the case, so maybe there would be no depositions, and the motion regarding the Fifth Amendment protection wasn't even necessary. However, the government insisted they would only go to a mediation if we were deposed, so we complied. It seemed like we had jumped through every hoop they asked of us, including going through an enormous trial that had ended in an acquittal for the most part, but here we were still jumping through their hoops. When it was all said and done, I'm glad I was deposed. I'm glad they got to hear from me that we really were innocent. And I would be glad to settle the case and forfeit money so we could begin to move forward and keep people employed.

With the help of the mediator, we eventually agreed on a settlement amount. It was more than the highest amount we ever discussed offering, but it was a business decision and an effort to find closure. It allowed our businesses to continue and everyone to remain employed, although not as comfortably as we'd hoped. We would have to manage things very closely and operate very conservatively. It allowed us some closure, even though after a ridiculously huge forfeiture, which would be punitive by anyone's standards, we were still facing potential prison sentences.

Shortly after we agreed on the amount of the settlement, but before the settlement had been made public, an article came out in the *Dallas Morning News*. The paper had not always been kind to us, but this article had a different tenor. The author referred to us by name and as victims of government tyranny. From his perspective, we had gone through a criminal trial and pretty much won, and yet the government was still attacking us from a civil standpoint and trying to inflict punishment on us through what most people would consider "double jeopardy." He clearly was not someone who would shop in our stores, and he stated as much politely, but he also made it clear that someone's personal beliefs about Gas Pipe shouldn't lead anyone to believe that what was happening to us was acceptable. We'd had our day in court, and the government didn't like the outcome, so they were looking for another verdict from a different jury. The criminal trial should have been the end of it, but it wasn't.

I did appreciate the *Dallas Morning News* publishing that article, and it meant a lot to finally be recognized in that manner publicly. But it also meant a lot for me to recognize I had made a bad decision. I could now hold my head up high and know I was properly acquitted of just about everything, but I'd also done something I wished I hadn't, and I wanted to do what I could to move forward without negativity and to live my life with kindness and positivity and doing good for others. There is no value we can put on peace of mind and doing the right thing—those things are priceless.

Chapter Twenty-Five

So what is the moral of my story? Don't do all the stupid things I've done, but if you do—or if you do your own, different stupid things, and you feel all is lost—know and believe that things can get better if you work toward improving yourself. I wanted to give up many times in my life, and there were times that the negativity in my life was a result of my own actions. Cancer was difficult and challenging, but I knew I hadn't done something stupid to bring that on myself. I didn't want to deal with it, and it goes on the list of bullets I've dodged, but I didn't have to be angry at myself for that one. It's the anger and even self-loathing at times when the trauma being experienced is because of our own actions that make it even harder to accept what's happening to us.

My story is one of love and forgiveness. It's a story of second chances (or third or fourth or more). I've never had a shortage of love in my life, but at times I allowed other things to be more important. I had a childhood filled with love and attention. My house was the place all my friends wanted to be, and my parents were like second parents to many of my friends. But I still engaged in behavior in high school that screamed, "I want attention!" Maybe it was just my way of trying to fit in and make myself noticed among my peers. Teenagers often do negative things for several reasons, even if their homelife is great. It's part of growing up, I suppose. High school was only miserable because I was trying to find out who I wanted to be and constantly "trying on different hats," which many teenagers do, but I wish I had been more comfortable or had known who I really wanted to be.

My parents' divorce threw me into a tailspin, which I think had already started by my own set of bad decisions and feeling rejected because of normal high school insecurities that were magnified by things such as not making cheerleading my senior year—seems silly now, but it was everything to me then. I went down a dark path and forgot how much I was truly loved. I reacted poorly and selfishly, but I was young and immature. I didn't think about the long-term consequences of my actions when I drowned my sorrows in drugs, and it was a vicious cycle that I didn't know how to stop. Over twenty years later when I talk about it, I still get very emotional, and I even found myself crying while discussing it in the US Probation Office. I cry when I think or talk about it because there is shame associated with that kind of behavior, but there is also overwhelming gratitude that I survived. I thank God for that every day. Being addicted to heroin and overcoming that addiction and surviving and not having negative long-term consequences from the other drugs I did recreationally is dodging a very huge bullet.

I had to learn to start over in life in my twenties, but I was always blessed to be surrounded by love and support. Then over twenty years later, I'm having to start my life over again in some ways, or at least definitely rebuild it. I've always been shown forgiveness, but learning to forgive myself is sometimes harder. I'm continually working on that. I'm also continually working on making choices that maybe won't require me to forgive myself so much—better choices. I'm a work in progress, as we all are. I'm undoubtedly flawed, and I've made many choices and decisions that I later realized I shouldn't have made, but I have learned from those choices. The last few years, consumed with our epic legal battle, have taught me more than I could have ever imagined. It has been a profound experience. I used to feel entitled. I had everything I wanted and needed. Entitlement has now been replaced by gratitude. I will never take for granted being able to go for a walk outside and feel the sunshine or breeze on my face, or being able to get in my car and go to the grocery store whenever I want, or, most importantly, being able to hug my loved ones. I don't know if those are things that many people think about as privileges. I used to not, but I had them all taken away from me temporarily, and for over four years I lived with the prospect of losing them forever. That changes a person.

I've always said I don't believe in regrets. I do wish I hadn't done certain things, such as selling herbal incense, and I'm sorry for all the negativity it brought to so many people. I don't regret the lessons I've learned, though. I, and others, have paid a high price to learn those lessons, and I know it would have been better for a lot of people had I learned my lessons a different way, but I guess this was my path. At least I had the opportunity to learn the lessons, and I will put them to good use going forward.

Faith is also a big part of my story. With each terrible, challenging, negative experience in my life, my faith has grown stronger. I found my greatest connection to God when I was struggling. Sometimes that connection was partly because I was angry at God, but I often realized I was angry with myself. It was like a child being angry at a parent because of the consequences the child experiences because of his or her own poor behavior. Really the child should look at himself or herself as the reason for the disappointment or even anger because he or she did something wrong, but he or she instead blames the parent. Children, particularly young ones, don't have the maturity for full accountability. I do, and I will continue to look within myself to make the changes I need to make so I don't have to be angry at all. What I do know, though, is that God hasn't given up on me, so I'm not going to give up on myself. I don't know why I've been given so many chances in life, but I have, so the one thing I consistently pray about now is guidance to make good, meaningful, thoughtful decisions that will lead me down the right path.

I've learned to let go of anger and to forgive others. I used to hold one hell of a grudge with people. I don't have the energy or interest in doing that anymore. That doesn't mean I don't get angry at all. I do, but it happens less often, and I work through it much quicker. It would be easy for me to be angry forever at the government for what transpired the last few years, and I have been very angry at times. But it's not good to hold on to that anger. The fact is that we sold a product we believed to be legal, but it shouldn't have been sold. It wasn't an illegal drug, but it did not bring joy or positivity into our world or the community. The fact also is that the government didn't have to prosecute us in the manner they did, but it happened, and we survived. When I look at the last few years and all we've already been through—we were treated like a drug cartel and had everything we owned seized—it is frustrating. It wasn't right. The treatment did not fit the crime of mislabeling a product. And when I think that our punishment still isn't over— we are looking at up to five years of a prison sentence, after everything else we've already been through, including a huge forfeiture—it's discouraging. But there is no point in focusing on what we've already been through. It's done. Nothing can change it, and all we can do is learn from it. It's time to look forward, and even if the future means a little more hardship, I will have to accept that and use it as a further learning experience, but I admittedly struggle with that.

I have a different perspective in life now. I remember about eight years ago I hosted a girls' party at my house. At one point the topic of conversation was what people would be willing to do for ten thousand dollars. Someone said they would shave their head, and a few agreed. I said I would never shave my head for ten thousand dollars. I thought to myself that I had just a few months before gotten a breast lift (not implants) and some liposuction, trying to improve my appearance, which had cost just about ten thousand dollars, so why would I then turn around and shave my head for that amount of money? Six years later I would shave my head because I had cancer, and the breasts I had spent so much money on improving would be removed. I was judgmental back then about people being willing to shave their heads for money, but many people wouldn't spend ten thousand dollars to "improve" their body like I had. I was the foolish one. Those who had said they would shave their heads for money knew then it was just hair; it would grow back, and how many wonderful, worthy, and probably responsible things could they do with ten thousand dollars? I was more concerned with spending money on superficial things such as cosmetic surgery (on body parts I would later lose) and keeping my hair (that I would later lose and then grow back). Life is funny, isn't it?

We recently returned from the Bahamas, where we went to visit one of our fishing lodges. We took Gavin there for his spring break (Kieley went on a church mission trip). Because of our travel restrictions, we hadn't visited the lodge there in five years. The last time (and only time) we had gone was in

2014, when we had purchased it. All our businesses had been booming and growing, and I had taken everything for granted. I had been excited to purchase the lodge, but we had accumulated so many different things in such a short time period that I hadn't appreciated or understood how important it was. It was another business to add to our lodge portfolio, to be able to say, "Hey, look at us and how many great lodges we have now." But I hadn't fully grasped what it meant to actually run that business and be responsible for the livelihood of so many Bahamians who work there and depend on us in a remote area where jobs are scarce.

When we went this time, I saw it in a completely different way. We had fought and worked hard to keep that business, as well as all our other businesses, afloat the last few years, and it had been a real challenge at times. We were able to keep all the employees in the Bahamas employed, and they were all so appreciative. I no longer see it as just another business to boast about. It is a group of people who work hard and depend on us. It is a true investment—not just for profit, but in people and something meaningful. I did always see our businesses and employees as more than just a job and coworkers, but that viewpoint is even deeper now. When you fight with everything you have to save something, and you see how much people really need it, the feelings of responsibility, accountability, and pride really emerge.

The positivity I felt from our visit to the Bahamas was dampened slightly upon our return, when we went through customs. US citizens clear customs in the Bahamas, where the US Customs and Border Protection has an office. Because we had been found guilty and were awaiting sentencing, we'd had to get a court order from the judge to go to the Bahamas, just as we had when we had gone to Mexico. Even with a court order in hand, we were detained at customs because we were in the system as violating a law that customs enforced. I could only assume they were referring to drug laws. Carolyn, who had been acquitted of everything, was with us on the trip, and she got detained too. Luckily, after a very thorough search of our bags and some tense interactions, we were free to go. It was explained to us that once you were accused of violating a law, then you were in the system, even if a federal judge ordered us worthy of leaving the country and coming back into the country and even though we had been acquitted of the drug charges. And even though Carolyn had been fully acquitted of everything, she was still flagged. Gavin was there witnessing it all, and while we all were in a bit of disbelief and a little agitated, I also tried to use it as a teaching moment and told Gavin that this was why you never wanted to do anything that would have you embroiled with the federal government in a negative manner. It would follow you forever.

The herbal incense business and its consequences will follow me forever. As of now I have a felony on my record, and that will always be with me. We hope to get it reduced to a misdemeanor through our appeal, but even then, I don't know if we will be flagged in customs forever or in the eyes of the government or some of the general public. I know the truth, though, and I know that while I didn't do everything I was accused of doing, I did go off track in my life. I'm finding my way back, though. Not back to the same track, but to a new, better track. And once again, I thank God for giving me another chance.

My life is kind of a blank canvas right now because I'm in a state of transition. My future is kind of unknown, but I'm trying to look at that as exciting. Going to prison isn't exciting at all, but if it happens, I will have more to add to my story. I will have more experiences to share, and I will believe that God thinks that's where I need to be, even though it will be hard. Maybe I'll meet someone there who will change my life, or vice versa. But after whatever punishment I have is fulfilled, I will have a whole new lease on life, and how can that be anything but positive? I can't say my life is what I pictured it would be, but really, I'm not sure how I pictured it to be. The most important things in my life—my husband, children, family, and friends—are a million times better than I could have ever imagined or thought I deserved.

I read something on Facebook recently: "Sometimes you have to let go of the picture of what you thought it would be like and learn to find joy in the story you are actually living." I have learned to find joy in the hardest of times. In fact, when I reflect over the last few years, I realize I've had some of the best times of my life, although they were challenging at times and I often questioned how I would move forward. But when we live every moment and go through every experience wondering if that one could be our last, we view it differently. That is a gift. That's not to say I still don't have bad days, lose my temper, and get angry and frustrated, but it's not like it used to be. I'm able to see the positive in negative situations more often, and I'm able to love and forgive others and myself much more than I used to.

I have a strength now I never knew I could possess. I am a survivor mentally, emotionally, and physically. I have survived a drug addiction, an abusive relationship, cancer, and a legal battle that could have ruined me forever. I know there are people who spend their entire lives surviving and struggling because of circumstances completely out of their control, and I know that is not the case with me. The difference is not missed on me. I brought on many of my problems with my choices, but a lot of people make bad choices and don't ever face the consequences I faced. A lot of people make bad choices and face far greater consequences than I've faced. I'm lucky to be where I am, and I know that every second of every day. I've made bad choices, but I've been blessed to survive and learn many lessons, and my desire and ability to find the positive and learn from the negative is part of the surviving. I don't always excel at it—I can get negative at times and still want to have my pity party for one—but I dig deep, pray a lot, lean on my loved ones and close circle, and keep moving ahead.

One of the greatest gifts I've also been given these past few years is learning to lean on people and ask for help. I struggled with that most of my life. I thought I had to do it all on my own, all the way back to when I was six years old and couldn't sleep at night and would sit in the kitchen alone and not wake my parents. I guess I'm just wired that way. But I couldn't have survived these past few years without leaning tremendously on people. I'm blessed to have so many people, and I've been blessed to be able to fight my battles. I think of all the people I met in jail who didn't have the support of family or strong legal support. I think of all the people who lose their battles for a multitude of reasons, and I feel even more grateful. We will never know why some of us prevail and some of us don't. I'm not any better than anyone else. I've just been really blessed and really lucky.

What I leaned on the most, though, more than anything, was my faith. I do believe in God, as if that isn't obvious by now. I tell people regularly to believe in something bigger than yourself. Many people call that something *God*, but if that's uncomfortable, then give it whatever name is comfortable, but understand there is a higher power. That is the first lesson that twelve-step programs teach—that we are not in control; there is a higher power. That is the crux of the serenity prayer. There is something bigger and greater than us, and when we recognize that and understand that we aren't in control of everything, we can accept things more easily, and with acceptance comes the ability to cope. I don't think anyone lives according to that concept 100 percent of the time. It's human nature to want to control things, but when we can remember that we are not fully in charge, when we can look to our higher power for guidance and reassurance, it truly does make everything easier to handle. That's why one of my favorite sayings is, "If you want to hear God laugh, tell him your plan."

I've had plentiful love and happiness, and I've been able to find growth and gifts during horrible times. The last few years have brought me closer to extended family and friends, brought me closer to God, deepened my relationship with my children, and brought an elevated level of emotional intimacy into my marriage. So many wonderful things have come out of my turmoil, but the truth is, those things were there all along. I just had to be open to them and had to keep my priorities straight. Sometimes we forget what's right in front of us because we are worrying or consumed with what else is out there that may not even be real.

The singer Kacey Musgraves has a song called "Rainbow." The first time I heard the song, it invoked an overwhelming reaction, and I cried uncontrollably. The lyrics are about making it through the storm that never seems to pass, but there's always a rainbow, even when we can't see it. It's a beautiful song that speaks right to my soul, reminding me that the rainbow has always been there. Kieley insisted that we go together to the Kacey Musgraves concert when she came to Dallas. I stood there in the crowded concert as the song was performed, with tears streaming down my cheeks and my daughter hugging me. The nice lady standing in front of us gave me her napkin that she'd had wrapped around her beer. It was a special moment where I felt incredibly connected to Kieley. I knew in that moment that my daughter, who is much younger but also much wiser in many ways, knew what I was feeling (and perhaps the lady standing in front of me with the beer did too). I know Kieley (and my entire family) is one of the rainbows in my life; they saw me through the storm, and I am so grateful.

I've slowed down in life. I stop to smell the roses more, and I'm not on a constant quest to prove how much I can juggle or how much I can cram into a day. I enjoy silence and downtime. I'm content and even calm—or "pleasant," as Dan told me. I used to really worry about what people thought of me. I had eleven strangers say what they thought of me, and they knew nothing of me other than what they saw and heard in the courtroom. That pretty much took the cake for how important someone else's opinion of me could be. I used to worry about what people would think about Gas Pipe, where I lived, how nice of a dinner party I hosted, what I drove. The thing is, though, I've been dragged through the legal system, been publicly shamed, and had horrible things said about me in the media, and yet people still like me. When I was at my worst, my lowest of lows, I had more friends and support than I ever thought I would—lots of unconditional love. I never needed to impress anyone, but it took all this for me to really believe that. My body is a road map of scars from all the different surgeries, and it's weaker and slower than it used to be, but my soul and inner being are stronger and more intact than ever.

Many people told me I should write a book—friends, family, my counselor, and even a retired federal judge. I hope my story can help someone. Maybe someone will read this who was lost in high school, made bad decisions, was in an abusive relationship, had an addiction, went through a divorce, is going through cancer, has been indicted, or is having some other huge struggle. My first bit of advice is to have faith. There's no guarantee as to how things are going to turn out, but that's why it's called faith—it's not something we can see or know definitively. Find faith in something, take a deep breath, and hold on. Know things can get better. It may not feel like it at times. It may feel like all is lost and it's just too much to handle, but nothing lasts forever. There is a rainbow. Rainbows don't come without the rain, though, but it is worth waiting out the storm to see that rainbow. And if the hard time was brought on by your own wrongdoing, it's okay. We are allowed to mess up. Life will go on, but you have to dig deep and find a better way. Allow yourself to cry, be sad, be angry. Allow yourself to have that crying meltdown in a hotel room or in the middle of nowhere at a Sonic drive-in, and then pick yourself up, and find the courage to tackle the world.

Finally, try to not put yourself in front of bullets. I've been fortunate to dodge a few, but life is hard enough. Enough negative things happen for reasons we don't understand, so try to live positively and not add more negativity to it. We all make mistakes—it's part of our experience as human beings. Sometimes we learn from our mistakes, and they become lessons, and sometimes they have catastrophic, unrecoverable consequences, and that's the really scary part about life. Recently Kieley went to a poetry-reading competition with her school, and she didn't do as well as she had hoped. We were eating lunch with my father after, and he told her that even though she didn't win the competition, she won because she had the experience. My experiences, the good and the bad, have all been wins because I have learned from all of them. That doesn't mean I'm happy the bad ones happened, but I'm grateful I dodged the bullets, and I've seen the rainbow. And I'm thankful for what I've learned.

October 8, 2019

I gave my allocution—the speech a defendant gives to the judge at sentencing. It was heartfelt and emotional. I apologized to our customers for selling something that was not good for people, I apologized to our employees for leading them down a path that had caused so much stress and compromised their freedom, and I apologized to my family. I talked about the changes I had experienced the past five years as a result of everything that had happened and the shame I had felt. I knew I couldn't change my previous poor decisions, but it was my greatest desire to use all my lessons learned to live a positive life and help others. I worked on my speech for months, knowing I had mere minutes to express to the judge everything I wanted and needed to say to illustrate my feelings, regrets, and evolvement as a person over the last five years.

Our sentencing was supposed to take place on July 12, and at the last minute it was postponed to August 28. We appeared in front of the judge in August, with several friends and family members there for support, only to be told the sentencing couldn't be completed that day.

The government was still going for the jugular—asking for the maximum sixty-month sentence. That was no surprise, but their arguments and reasoning were flawed and faulty. We were only convicted of conspiring to defraud the FDA by misbranding a product, and the sentencing guideline range for that is zero to sixty months. However, if one has been convicted of misbranding a product in furtherance of another offense—such as distributing a controlled substance—then the guidelines can be calculated based on the drug quantities if the drug is an illegal substance. Because of the amount of the product we sold, we could have gone to prison for life if the product inside had been determined to be a controlled substance, but it wasn't, and the misbranding statute only allows for a maximum of sixty months. So because the government had charged us with distribution of a controlled substance, they believed we should be sentenced to the full sixty months and feel grateful it wasn't life. However, the judge was adamant we were acquitted of all illegal drug charges, and her philosophy as a judge was that acquitted conduct should not be used for determining sentences (although some judges will sentence on acquitted conduct—yes, one can go to trial, be acquitted of certain charges, and then be sentenced as if they hadn't been acquitted—another unbelievable concept in our criminal justice system that I learned of through this ordeal). In our case (and according to Judge Lynn) the guidelines should have been based on just misbranding a product, which came out way below sixty months considering our lack of criminal history and other factors. But in a last-ditch effort to pile it on, the government suggested at sentencing that there was another product we sold that they believed to be illegal, but they had never charged us with it, so it wasn't acquitted conduct but instead relevant conduct, which could also be used in determining sentencing guidelines. Judge Lynn said she would consider relevant conduct, but relevant conduct needed to be illegal to be relevant. Nobody, including the judge,

was fully prepared on August 28 to work through the arguments supporting or refuting the alleged relevant conduct. Both
parties were ordered to submit written briefs supporting their
position and appear on October 8 to complete the sentencing.

The alleged relevant conduct was another overreach by
the government. The allegation pertained to an herbal-incense
product that mistakenly had a substance in it called α-PVT,
which was not a synthetic cannabinoid—it was a completely
different class of chemicals. We had no idea it was in there, and
we learned about its existence after the raids, when the DEA's
test results identified the substance. We wouldn't have known
to test for it or ask the lab to test for it because we only tested
for the presence of synthetic cannabinoids. Furthermore, even
if we had known it was in there, it was not an illegal substance
(not specifically scheduled as a banned substance nor determined to be an analogue by the DEA or a jury because a jury
never got to hear the evidence since we weren't charged with it),
but the prosecutor on his own alleged it to be an analogue. So
we once again solicited the help of Mr. Analogue and prepared
to convince the judge that there was no additional illegal conduct (not a banned substance or analogue, and even if it were,
we had not knowingly sold it), and therefore no drug quantities
should be used in determining our sentence as acquitted conduct or relevant conduct.

The months leading up to the sentencing were increasingly
stressful. We were slowly rebuilding our lives financially after
the official settlement of the civil case, but it was going to take
a long time to fully get our heads above water. I kept reminding
myself that whatever sentence the judge gave was better than
life in prison, but it was hard to stay positive at times. I was
exhausted and just wanted to fulfill my sentence and have it
over. I wanted to focus on the new, improved me and the positive things I was doing. I had started an organization called

Hopeful Tuesdays that provided food, showers, and fellowship to the homeless in our community. It had all begun with me buying a cheeseburger one day for a homeless gentleman near our office and inviting him to come by the next day for lunch and a shower, and then at my suggestion he came back with friends the following day, which was a Tuesday, and it grew and expanded from there. Now Hopeful Tuesdays is an official nonprofit and serves food in the streets two days a week and lunches and showers twice a week at our Amy Lynn Inc. office, where we sit and visit with the attendees and determine how we can help them the most. Some of the attendees are no longer homeless and now work with us to run the organization. The room where the awful "lab" was for making herbal incense has been completely renovated and dedicated to Hopeful Tuesdays. We now serve approximately one hundred meals a week and have helped some get into rehabs or sober-living facilities.

Each time the sentencing was postponed, I tried to look at it as a gift because it would allow me more time with my family during the summer and time to get things more organized with the businesses. I was able to spend much of the summer in Alaska, which was wonderful and an unexpected treat because of the original sentencing date. While I appreciated getting to spend the summer with my family, I also was in agony waiting for the unknown. It was beginning to feel like my life was going to be filled with uncertainty forever.

I was also filled with angst and trepidation—a feeling of "waiting for the other shoe to drop." The first trip I made to Alaska in June of 2019 was overwhelming. I looked around and took it all in, and it was hard for me to believe that everything was really ours—it really was not subject to forfeiture anymore. I didn't trust the reality, even though I knew it was true. And I had to remind myself daily that I wasn't going to prison for the rest of my life. The last time I had left Alaska had been to go home for the trial. It was surreal returning and knowing that even if I was going to be away temporarily, it would not be forever.

The last five years had been spent in constant crisis, and it was going to take a long time for me to feel safe and calm and not feel like I was constantly waiting for the next crisis. And just as we had finally gotten the civil case officially settled, we had another crisis. My father had a stroke in late April 2019. The overall outcome was better than it could have been, and after three days in the hospital, he was released to come home with me with strict doctor's orders for a healthier, slower-paced lifestyle. He had paralysis in his face that has subsided over time, but he was seventy-three, and a stroke or any trauma to the body is not a step in the right direction. I thought surely that, if nothing else, would influence the prosecutor to be a little sympathetic, particularly after we had gone through a four-year battle culminating in a stressful trial where we had been acquitted of everything but misbranding, accompanied by a huge forfeiture that would be considered punitive by anyone's standards. I, again, was wrong.

We will never receive any sympathy or understanding from the government, even though we went to trial, and the jury clearly spoke. We went through the entire process of the justice system, and the outcome was overall favorable to us. That didn't mean I was proud of my actions—I knew we had behaved poorly from a moral standpoint, and I expressed that to all who knew me, but legally we hadn't done what we had been accused of doing. I knew I couldn't erase my past mistakes, but I had so many wonderful, new, and positive things occurring in my life, and I hated the idea of being yanked away from them, even temporarily, but more than anything I just wanted closure and to be able to finally focus on my future for the first time in five years.

Our attorneys did an excellent job of illustrating to the judge who we truly were as people and all the worthy things we were doing in life, and I had several meaningful character letters submitted by friends and family. The judge recognized at our August 28 hearing that apart from misbranding, our actions were determined not to be illegal, but she clearly was displeased with our past behavior, and she had a job to do in sentencing us.

Written briefs were submitted by both parties, and finally, almost a year after we had received the trial verdict—and over five years since the commencement of the legal proceedings—we appeared once again in front of Judge Lynn to receive our sentence. It was a long afternoon consumed with more expert witnesses to argue the issue of α-PVT. Ultimately the judge decided not to opine on whether it was an analogue, but she did say she wouldn't use it to calculate our guidelines at a higher level. She agreed that our guidelines should be an offense level of ten for just misbranding, which came out to a guideline range of six to twelve months of imprisonment—much shorter than the sixty-month maximum we had originally anticipated. She stated that she felt inclined to depart upward due to the potential risk and danger of the products we had sold (even though nobody had ever been physically harmed by anything we had sold, and we had presented evidence to substantiate that, and she had acknowledged that). Judges can depart upward or downward from the sentencing guidelines. All our codefendants who had already appeared before her for sentencing had received a substantial departure downward, with almost all of them getting probation with a substantial fine. We hoped we, too, would get a downward departure, particularly after she agreed we had an offense level of ten, and we had paid a substantial forfeiture. However, she decided we deserved a substantial upward departure. My father and I were each sentenced to thirty-six months in prison, but she did allow us to stagger the sentences so that one of us could always be present to oversee the businesses. My father insisted on going into custody first, even though he had just had a stroke six months prior.

Of course, I am grateful to still be home with my children and running our businesses, but the thought of being separated from my father and worrying about his health and well-being is painful.

For years I was facing life in prison. Then, after our conviction for felony misbranding, I was facing sixty months in prison. I know and appreciate that thirty-six months is minimal compared to where we started when we went to trial, even though I had been encouraged at the end of our lengthy sentencing hearing that our official calculated guidelines came out to twelve months. I was shocked to hear the judge impose a sentence that tripled that. However, I can work toward closure now because there is a real light at the end of the tunnel. One day this ordeal will be in the rearview mirror, but the impact it has had on me will always be present and meaningful. God does have a plan, and this is part of it. My story will continue and so will my growth.

About the Author

Amy Herrig is a mother, wife, business owner, and life-long Texan. She currently resides in Dallas with her family, but she also enjoys spending time in remote Alaska, helping run the family business there. She loves spending time in the outdoors, hiking and fishing, and she is a self-professed "foodie" who enjoys cooking with her family and hosting dinner parties for friends. Amy's family and friends are her top priority—her teenage twins are her world, and since she is an only child, many of her friends are like family. Amy is married to the love of her life, Dan, and they enjoy family time, traveling, and having date nights in their kitchen cooking together. She loves the Dallas Cowboys, dogs, movies of all genres, good conversations, exploring different views and opinions, and connecting with people on a deep level. She is almost always reading a good book, which she later discusses with her intimate book club of twelve years. Her strong faith has deepened over the years through trials and tribulations, and it is the backbone of her life. After overcoming negative circumstances in her teen years, at thirty-nine years old, Amy's world turned unexpectedly upside down. She decided to use her challenges and mistakes to connect with others and help people. She volunteers regularly and started a nonprofit called Hopeful Tuesdays to assist the homeless in her community. Her story is an example that faith and perseverance can lead to overcoming obstacles and that people can learn from their mistakes and use them to experience growth and self-improvement.

Made in the USA
Middletown, DE
12 July 2020